Sexual Dysfunction

TREATMENT MANUALS FOR PRACTITIONERS
David H. Barlow, *Editor*

SEXUAL DYSFUNCTION
A GUIDE FOR ASSESSMENT AND TREATMENT
John P. Wincze and Michael P. Carey

SEVERE BEHAVIOR PROBLEMS
A FUNCTIONAL COMMUNICATION TRAINING APPROACH
V. Mark Durand

DEPRESSION IN MARRIAGE
A MODEL FOR ETIOLOGY AND TREATMENT
Steven R. H. Beach, Evelyn E. Sandeen,
and K. Daniel O'Leary

TREATING ALCOHOL DEPENDENCE
A COPING SKILLS TRAINING GUIDE
Peter M. Monti, David B. Abrams,
Ronald M. Kadden, and Ned L. Cooney

SELF-MANAGEMENT FOR ADOLESCENTS
A SKILLS-TRAINING PROGRAM
MANAGING EVERYDAY PROBLEMS
Thomas A. Brigham

PSYCHOLOGICAL TREATMENT OF PANIC
David H. Barlow and Jerome A. Cerny

Sexual Dysfunction

A Guide for Assessment and Treatment

JOHN P. WINCZE
Brown University and
Providence Department of Veterans Affairs
Medical Center

MICHAEL P. CAREY
Syracuse University and
Syracuse Department of Veterans Affairs
Medical Center

Editor's Note by David H. Barlow
Foreword by Leslie R. Schover

THE GUILFORD PRESS
New York   London

© 1991 The Guilford Press
A Division of Guilford Publications, Inc.
72 Spring Street, New York, NY 10012

Printed in the United States of America

This book is printed on acid-free paper.

Last digit is print number: 9 8 7 6 5 4 3 2 1

Library of Congress Cataloging-in-Publication Data

Wincze, Jonn P., 1943–
    Sexual dysfunction: a guide for assessment and treatment / John
P. Wincze, Michael P. Carey; editor's note by David H. Barlow;
foreword by Leslie R. Schover.
        p.   cm.—(Treatment manuals for practitioners)
    Includes bibliographical references and index.
    ISBN 0-89862-207-7 (hard).—ISBN 0-89862-218-2 (pbk.)
    1. Sex therapy. 2. Sexual disorders—Diagnosis. 3. Sexual
disorders—Treatment. I. Carey, Michael P. II. Title III.
Series.
    [DNLM: 1. Psychosexual Dysfunction. 2. Psychosexual Dysfunction—
therapy. WM 611 W758s]
RC557.W56 1991
616.85'83—dc20
DNLM/DLC
for Library of Congress   91-16339
                                                                                            CIP

About the Authors

John P. Wincze, a licensed clinical psychologist, is currently a Professor of Psychology in the Departments of Psychiatry and Human Behavior and of Psychology at Brown University. In addition, he is the Chief of Psychology at the Providence Department of Veterans Affairs Medical Center, and a member of the Rhode Island Licensure Board. He received his BA from Wesleyan University, his MA from Boston College, and his PhD from the University of Vermont. He has served on the editoral boards of several journals, including the *Journal of Sex Research* and *Behavior Therapy*. This is his third book, and he has published over 50 articles and chapters in the areas of sexual dysfunction and deviation.

Michael P. Carey, also a licensed clinical psychologist, is an Associate Professor of Psychology at Syracuse University. In addition, he is a Clinical and Research Psychologist at the Syracuse Department of Veterans Affairs Medical Center, and a Clinical Assistant Professor of Urology at the State University of New York Health Sciences Center at Syracuse. He received his BS from St. Lawrence University, and his MA and PhD from Vanderbilt University. He has served on the editoral boards of the *Journal of Consulting and Clinical Psychology, Psychological Assessment,* and *Health Psychology,* and was recently selected to receive the President's New Researcher Award from the Association for Advancement of Behavior Therapy. This is his first book, and he has published over 40 articles and chapters in the areas of health psychology and human sexuality.

Acknowledgments

We wish to thank many individuals for their direct and indirect contributions to the writing of this book. Among our many colleagues, collaborators, and friends, we would particularly like to thank Barbara Andersen, Dennis Krauss, Larry Lantinga, Andrew Meisler, Steve Richards, Leslie Schover, and Ilana Spector. Special thanks to Sue Coleman for her invaluable work in helping us to prepare the manuscript.

The work of Michael Carey was supported, in part, by grants from National Institute on Drug Abuse (R03-DA04593) and from the American Cancer Society (PBR-38).

We would also like to extend our heartfelt appreciation to David Barlow—not only for his gracious invitation to contribute to his fine series, but also for his support throughout the writing of this book.

Finally, we would like to dedicate this book to our wives, Linnea and Kate; our children, Jeffrey, Larissa, and Brent, and Alison; and our parents, Blanche and Joseph, and Alice and Jerry, with much love.

JOHN P. WINCZE
MICHAEL P. CAREY

Editor's Note

Since the appearance of direct behavioral approaches to sexual dysfunctions made popular by Masters and Johnson, the impression has grown that there is little more to learn about treating the variety of common sexual problems that so often present to health care professionals. Nothing could be further from the truth. Early reports of success with specific sexual dysfunctions proved tantalizingly difficult to reproduce in the offices of numerous clinicians around the country. With this development, the fad of doing sex therapy passed and it is now very hard to find a competent, knowledgeable sex therapist outside of our major cities. Furthermore, there has been a veritable explosion of information in the area of sexual function and dysfunction, much of it coming from our medical colleagues. New procedures and techniques emanating from various medical specialities have resulted in advances that are being widely utilized in the care and management of sexual dysfunction.

Now, John Wincze and Michael Carey, two of the most experienced sex researchers and therapists in the United States, have produced an important guide for therapists who wish to be knowledgeable about and utilize the latest procedures for treating sexual dysfunctions. Clinicians reading this book will benefit from the authors' long years of clinical experience with a variety of sexual dysfunctions, and will also become conversant with the latest procedures from both medicine and psychology in use today. Awareness of the effects of such new approaches as vasoactive therapy and the use of vacuum devices in therapy will prove valuable to those confronting sexual problems. As the authors point out, clinicians with relatively little experience should be able to use these programs to treat the majority of sexual dysfunctions with which they are confronted and be confident that their approaches are based on the latest developments in our science.

DAVID H. BARLOW
State University of New York at Albany

Foreword

Masters and Johnson wrote the first "treatment manuals" for sex therapy in the late 1960s and early 1970s. It was the time of the sexual revolution, and every citizen was urged to attain his or her birthright and all-night ecstasy and multiple orgasms. The pendulum of social change was at the extremity of its swing toward sexual freedom and gender equality. Men and women whose road to nirvana was blocked by premature ejaculation, unreliable erections, or anorgasmia simply needed to carry out their sensate focus homework, with guidance from a sex therapist initiated into the mysteries of the curriculum.

It was easy then to set forth the principles of sex therapy, because we all believed that treatment packages worked through behavior change, with little influence of intangibles such as the therapy relationship, patient emotions and cognitions, or family-of-origin issues. Patients who did not improve with sex therapy had not worked hard enough at changing.

From the perspective of the 1990s, writing a treatment manual for sex therapy is a far more ambitious task. Our society repeated history by discovering that casual sex, with a variety of partners and positions, has limited potential to provide ecstatic fulfillment. Sex therapists discovered that structured treatment programs were no panacea.

The squeeze technique and sensate focus exercises are certainly of value, but many of the people who can benefit from these interventions learn to apply them from self-help sex books, the "marriage manuals" of our era. They do not need to seek professional help. Those who do come to our offices are not the healthy executives with excellent marriages who flocked to St. Louis to consult Masters and Johnson in the beginning. Our patients are the attorney who has good erections with his wife, but trouble performing on business trips with his female colleague from the firm; the recovering alcoholic who discovers he has premature ejaculation, now that he is trying to have a real relationship without the crutch of a six-pack before bed; the assembly line worker who was repeatedly molested as a child by her mother's boyfriends, and now is beaten by her husband if she refuses to give him oral sex; or the woman who has had a successful kidney transplant but has no desire for sex and wants to feel lusty again despite her diabetes, seven different medications, and chronic depression.

Our patients may be black, Hispanic, or Asian, bringing their own cultural values about what is normal in sex. They may be born-again Christians, Orthodox Jews, Catholics, or Hindus. They regard masturbation as anathema or as a blessing. They may be gay men bearing the burden of stigmatization and fear of human immunodeficiency virus (HIV), hoping we can help them to make safe sex erotic and teach them to resist the pull of desires that now are life-threatening. We also recognize the modest long-term success rates of sex therapy treatment packages, even under the simplest of circumstances.

A final complication is the advent of medical and surgical treatment for erectile dysfunction, and the promise (or threat, depending on one's point of view) that medications will soon be able to boost sexual desire or delay ejaculation. Many of our patients are referred by the physicians they consulted for a "medical problem," leaving the sex therapist to "sell" sex therapy as an alternative to a magic pill or bionic penis.

Given their difficult task, John Wincze and Michael Carey have succeeded in creating a succinct guide for the sex therapist. As they cover diagnostic criteria, etiological factors, assessment, treatment, and professional training, they use their extensive clinical experience to provide examples of the complex cases that make up a current sex therapy practice. Neophyte sex therapists can use this book to get the basic knowledge they need to begin assessing and treating sexual problems. Experienced sex therapists can benefit from the comprehensive, well-organized reviews presented. The information contained in this book constitutes a core of knowledge that sex therapists use. Add all your wisdom about relationships, theories of personality, and psychotherapeutic skills, and you will be prepared to treat sexual dysfunction in the 1990s.

LESLIE R. SCHOVER
Center for Sexual Function
The Cleveland Clinic Foundation

Contents

1

Overview of This Book

Sex is important to people. To find support for this statement, simply tune in to prime-time commercial television, look at an advertisement in a major magazine, or stroll in almost any major U.S. city on a warm summer evening. Sexual fantasies, role plays, seductions, innuendos, and jokes are ubiquitous. Want to get everyone's attention at a crowded and noisy cocktail party? Just say the word "sex," and notice how many heads turn your way. (We doubt you'd get the same reaction if you said "dog" or "music.") Those working on Madison Avenue have captured this phenomenon very succinctly: "Sex sells."

And when something is amiss in a person's sexual life—that is, a sexual dysfunction—there is cause for concern. Many sexually distressed individuals seek relief through various "self-help" strategies (e.g., so-called aphrodisiacs such as "Spanish fly"; extramarital affairs; use of prostitution; use of erotic toys, magazines, and videotapes; etc.), television talk shows, and advice columns in daily newspapers and monthly magazines. When these informal efforts at "treatment" fail, sexually distressed persons look to professionals for help. Pastoral counselors, nurses, social workers, family practice physicians, urologists, gynecologists, psychiatrists, psychologists, and marriage and family therapists are among those who can expect to receive requests for information and guidance. In fact, in a recent survey conducted with psychologists in the United States, "sexual difficulties" was ranked fourth (after rapid social change, child and spouse abuse, and money) among the top problems facing U.S. families; interestingly, similar findings were obtained in a survey of psychologists from the Soviet Union (Bazar, 1989).

Given the importance ascribed to, and the abundance of, sexual concerns, this area represents an opportunity to meet the needs of many people. Our goals in writing this book have been (1) to provide a state-of-the-art overview of the most common sexual dysfunctions, and (2) to present a

1

step-by-step manual for the assessment and treatment of these problems. This book is intended for accomplished sex therapists who may wish to compare their own approaches with ours, and who may find some interesting ideas described herein. This book is also intended for health care professionals who are currently in training (e.g., graduate students, medical interns, and residents), or who are currently practicing but who have little (or no) previous training in the assessment and treatment of sexual dysfunctions. It is *not* intended to replace other types of formal training, and should be used in conjunction with supervision from an experienced sex therapist, in accordance with the ethical principles of a professional discipline. The only preparation that we assume is some general experience with psychological therapies.

We begin in this chapter by overviewing our current understanding of sexual function and dysfunction, and by describing our general approach to the management of sexual difficulties. The remainder of the book is divided into three parts. In Part I (Chapters 2, 3, 4, and 5), we provide a more detailed discussion of each of the main classes of sexual dysfunctions. We focus on definitions and descriptions, prevalence, and etiology. In Part II (Chapters 6, 7, and 8), we describe our step-by-step approach to assessing and treating these problems. Finally, in Part III (Chapters 9, 10, and 11), we introduce more advanced material. Specifically, in Chapter 9, we discuss other factors that can influence sexual functioning, including chronic illnesses, substance abuse, and fear of sexually transmitted diseases such as acquired immune deficiency syndrome (AIDS). In Chapter 10, we present six detailed case histories, and discuss special issues that arise during the course of sex therapy. In Chapter 11, we provide information about how you can obtain further training and establish a successful practice in sex therapy.

Definitions of Sexual Function and Dysfunction

Controversy and Change

We are both educators. In the context of our teaching and supervision, we often wrestle with the constructs of "normality and abnormality," "health and pathology," and "function and dysfunction." We are thankful that our students and supervisees continually challenge our definitions and help us to remain open-minded and responsive to new information. This is particularly important in a socially sensitive and value-laden field such as human sexuality—a field where popular beliefs about function and dysfunction seem to be quite labile. To illustrate this point, we discuss—briefly—three areas: masturbation, sexual desire, and latency to ejaculation in males.

In previous times, masturbation received widespread condemnation. For example, in the 18th century, numerous treatises were written describing the physical and mental health consequences of masturbation (see Caird & Wincze, 1977; Gagnon, 1977). It was during this time that a particularly well-known Swiss physician, Tissot, published a volume titled *Onania, or a Treatise upon the Disorders Produced by Masturbation*. Among the many physical and mental disorders purportedly caused by masturbation were failing eyesight, consumption, gonorrhea, hemorrhoids, digestive disorders, melancholy, catalepsy, imbecility, loss of sensation, lethargy, pervasive weakness of the nervous system, impotence, and insanity! Eventually, because of the scientific work of Kinsey and others, more enlightened views about masturbation emerged. Today, in stark contrast, masturbation is prescribed as therapy (e.g., see LoPiccolo & Lobitz, 1972; Zilbergeld, 1978)! In fact, it turns out that directed masturbation (see Chapter 7) is a particularly effective treatment for lifelong inhibited female orgasm (see Heiman & LoPiccolo, 1988). (As an aside, we are reminded of the exchange between the Countess and Boris in Woody Allen's movie *Love and Death*. Countess: "You are a wonderful lover." Boris: "I practice a lot when I am alone.")

Similarly, beliefs about sexual appetite, desire, and behavior have changed 180 degrees. Beginning with the writings of the Christian theologian Paul, sexual abstinence and chastity were seen as virtuous. Indeed, those interested in maximizing their spiritual development were required to take vows of celibacy and chastity (Cole, 1956). In the first half of this century, however, scientists began to question whether sexual abstinence was contrary to human beings' basic biological nature (e.g., Parshley, 1933) and was potentially harmful. Today the absence of sexual desire is seen as a clinical disorder (e.g., Kaplan, 1979) that warrants proper diagnosis and treatment. (For an alternative view, however, see the publication *Sexual Abstinence News*, available from P.O. Box 20788, Houston, TX 77225.) Who knows what tomorrow will bring? Perhaps with the specter of AIDS, sexual abstinence will once again be regarded favorably.

At the risk of beating a dead horse, let us simply mention one more example: latency to ejaculation in men. What would now be considered "dysfunctional" was once considered normal and even advantageous (Hong, 1984; also, see Chapter 4).

We hope that these three examples (from many that we might have selected) serve to illustrate our point: Definitions of sexual function and dysfunction are inevitably influenced by current social mores, values, and knowledge. As these and other influences change, so too will our definitions of sexual function and dysfunction. Mindful of this caveat, then, we are poised to discuss current clinical definitions.

Current Definitions

Current approaches to defining sexual function and dysfunction are heavily influenced by recent biomedical research and clinical practice. This approach suggests that human sexual functioning, for most people on most occasions, proceeds sequentially. This axiom, accepted by most sexologists (i.e., experts in human sexuality), has its formal beginning with Havelock Ellis (1906), who postulated that sexual functioning has two stages: tumescence (i.e., the engorgement of the genitals with blood resulting in erection in males, and vaginal lubrication in females), and detumescence (i.e., the outflow of blood from the genitals following orgasm). Ever since, scientist–practitioners have attempted to delineate more precisely the basic biological sequencing of sexual functioning.

William Masters and Virginia Johnson, household names to most Americans, contributed immensely to our understanding of sexual functioning. During the 1950s and 1960s, they conducted a very extensive (and, indeed, highly controversial) series of scientific observations of sexual activity with human volunteers. Masters and Johnson suggested in their 1966 book *Human Sexual Response,* based upon thousands of hours of careful laboratory research, that physiological responding in healthy, well-functioning adults proceeds through four stages: (1) excitement, (2) plateau, (3) orgasm, and (4) resolution. They documented the genital and extragenital physiological changes that typically occur during each of these phases. The model they provided was instructive and elegant.

Yet something was missing. That something was most apparent to those practitioners working with not-so-well-functioning individuals and couples (e.g., Kaplan, 1979; Lief, 1977). Some of these sexually troubled persons complained of an inability to become amorous, of a lack of interest in sex, or even of an aversion to sexual activity. In the decade following the publication of *Human Sexual Response,* it became increasingly clear that there was a "stage" preliminary to the excitement phase identified and described by Masters and Johnson. This preliminary stage, subsequently labeled sexual "desire," involved a person's cognitive and affective readiness for, and interest in, sexual activity. Without sexual desire, physiological and subjective arousal, and subsequent orgasm were much less likely to occur.

Subsequent theoretical writing and empirical research have served as the basis for our current understanding of sexual function and dysfunction. Most sexologists agree that healthy sexual functioning comprises three primary stages: desire, arousal, and orgasm. (Each of these terms is defined and discussed further in the coming chapters.) Sexual dysfunction, then, consists of an impairment or disturbance in one of these stages. Although this stage model is somewhat arbitrary, in that it identifies discrete stages in what may well be a continuous process, we believe that it provides a useful heuristic from which to conceptualize and discuss sexual health. Not surprisingly, this model is compatible with current diagnostic schemes.

Recognizing Sexual Dysfunctions: The Challenge of Diagnosis

The Current Diagnostic Scheme

Although several diagnostic approaches have been proposed to classify the sexual dysfunctions (e.g., Schover, Friedman, Weiler, Heiman, & LoPiccolo, 1982), the diagnostic scheme that has been most widely adopted for sexual dysfunctions is that contained in the *Diagnostic and Statistical Manual of Mental Disorders* (hereafter abbreviated as DSM), published by the American Psychiatric Association. This series of manuals was developed to aid mental health care professionals in the diagnosis and treatment of the so-called "mental disorders." (The first edition of DSM appeared in 1952, and new editions appeared in 1968 and 1980; the third edition was revised in 1987 and is the version currently in use. The fourth edition of DSM is scheduled for publication in 1992.) Although the manual was not specifically developed for sex therapists, it contains diagnostic categories and criteria for the most commonly seen sexual difficulties.

According to the most recent edition, DSM-III-R (American Psychiatric Association, 1987), there are nine major diagnostic categories of sexual dysfunctions. These categories, which are depicted in Table 1-1, include the

TABLE 1-1. Categories of Sexual Dysfunction among Men and Women

Type of disorder	Sexual dysfunction	
	Men	Women
Desire	Hypoactive Sexual Desire Disorder	Hypoactive Sexual Desire Disorder
	Sexual Aversion Disorder	Sexual Aversion Disorder
Arousal	Male Erectile Disorder	Female Sexual Arousal Disorder
Orgasm	Inhibited Male Orgasm	Inhibited Female Orgasm
	Premature Ejaculation	
Pain	Dyspareunia	Dyspareunia
		Vaginismus

following: (1) Hypoactive Sexual Desire Disorder, (2) Sexual Aversion Disorder, (3) Female Sexual Arousal Disorder, (4) Male Erectile Disorder, (5) Inhibited Female Orgasm, (6) Inhibited Male Orgasm, (7) Premature Ejaculation, (8) Dyspareunia, and (9) Vaginismus. (These terms, and their diagnostic criteria, are described in detail in Chapters 2–5.) All nine of the dysfunctions identified in DSM-III-R should be further conceptualized along two dimensions. First, they may be characterized as "lifelong" (also known as "primary") or "acquired" (also known as "secondary"). Second, a dysfunction may be "generalized" (i.e., occurring across all sexual situations and partners), or "situational" (i.e., limited to certain situations and partners). These distinctions are believed to be important with respect to both etiology and treatment.

DSM-III-R is not perfect; for example, to our knowledge, it is not yet known how reliable the individual classifications of the sexual dysfunctions are. Because a diagnostic system cannot possibly be valid if it is not reliable, this would seem to be an important omission. Another important limitation of DSM-III-R is that it tends to simplify sexual health into a dichotomy (sexual health vs. sexual dysfunction). A more accurate approach is to view sexual health (and overall psychological health, for that matter) along a continuum, rather than to see it in such discrete, black-and-white categories (cf. Wincze, 1982).

Despite these limitations, however, this diagnostic scheme represents an advance over previous editions of DSM, where even less precise diagnostic categories were used. Moreover, because DSM-III-R classifications continue to be used in professional journal articles, by most mental health professionals (from whom referrals may originate), and by insurance companies (for third-party reimbursement), familiarity with its categories and criteria is professionally adaptive.

Sexual Deviations, Dysfunctions, and Dissatisfaction

The DSM diagnostic scheme includes the sexual deviations (i.e., paraphilias), as well as sexual dysfunctions. Paraphilias are disorders in which an individual experiences recurrent and intense sexual urges and fantasies involving either (1) nonhuman objects (i.e, a fetish), (2) suffering or humiliation of oneself or one's partner (i.e., sadomasochism), or (3) nonconsenting partners (e.g., pedophilia, exhibitionism, frotteurism). Assessment and treatment of the paraphilias is not covered in this book. (Interested readers are referred to Laws, 1989.)

As mentioned earlier, sexual dysfunctions are impairments or disturbances in sexual desire, arousal, or orgasm. One problem with the DSM-

III-R approach to diagnosis is that it tends to focus on physiological or behavioral dysfunctions, with little attention paid to self-reported dissatisfaction; this is a limitation because some clients will seek sex therapy in the absence of any real dysfunction, and many people with dysfunctions do not seek therapy. In this regard, it is interesting that Masters and Johnson (1970) reported that 50% of all American couples suffer from some type of sexual dysfunction. More recently, Levine (1989), past president of the Society for Sex Therapy and Research, provided an even bolder estimate: ". . . the lifetime prevalence of sexual dysfunctions may be so high that almost every man or woman who lives a long life can be expected to qualify for a diagnosis at some time" (pp. 215–216). Despite this apparent pandemic, not all couples are aware of, nor are they concerned about, their "dysfunction." That is, these people may be "dysfunctional," but they are not necessarily dissatisfied! A brief review of the relevant empirical research on this topic is apropos.

In a landmark study published in the *New England Journal of Medicine,* Dr. Ellen Frank and her colleagues (Frank, Anderson, & Rubinstein, 1978) at the University of Pittsburgh investigated 100 predominantly white, well-educated, and happily married couples. These researchers attempted to determine the frequency of sexual dysfunctions experienced, and the relationship of these problems to sexual satisfaction. Although over 80% of the couples reported that their marital and sexual relations were happy and satisfying, 40% of the men reported erectile and ejaculatory dysfunction, and 63% of the women reported arousal or orgasmic dysfunction! Even more surprising was the finding that the number of dysfunctions was *not* strongly associated with overall sexual satisfaction. These findings have been corroborated in a similar study conducted by Nettelbladt and Uddenberg (1979) in Europe. These authors reported that sexual dysfunction was *not* significantly related to sexual satisfaction in their sample of 58 married Swedish men.

In a recent study that is also relevant to this discussion (Bansal, Wincze, Nirenberg, Liepman, & Engle-Friedman, 1990), male alcoholics were examined as they underwent treatment for their alcohol abuse difficulties. The study found that sexual functioning, as measured by degree of erectile impairment in nocturnal penile tumescence monitoring, did not correlate with sexual complaints. In other words, not all men with impaired erectile capacity complained of sexual problems; some even reported no problems!

These empirical findings remind us that sexual health involves more than just intact physiology and typical "functioning" (i.e., progression through desire, arousal, and orgasm phases). In our culture, and in many others as well, sexual health is enhanced to the extent that it occurs in a rich interpersonal context that involves respect and trust, open lines of communication, and mutual commitment to all aspects of the relationship. (This is not to say that other approaches to sexual behavior are wrong, but rather to describe the conditions under which sexual satisfaction is maximized.) Sexual health is most likely to occur in individuals who are psychologically as well as neurologically, hormonally, and vascularly intact. Because existing diagnostic schemas, which focus exclusively on sexual "functioning," cannot encompass the richness of sexual health, such schemas (and diagnosis in general) have been criticized (e.g., Schover et al., 1982; Szasz, 1980; Wincze, 1982). This limitation notwithstanding, most scientist–practitioners find the DSM classification schema useful for communicating among themselves, for presenting information about subclasses of problems, and for treatment planning. Indeed, the existence of the diagnostic system allows researchers to conduct epidemiological studies in order to determine the frequency with which disorders occur.

How Often Do the Sexual Dysfunctions Occur?: Prevalence and Incidence

Do sexual problems occur frequently enough that all health professionals should take the time to be adequately informed? As mentioned earlier, Masters and Johnson (1970) estimated that 50% of all couples in the United States have a sexual dysfunction. This prevalence[1] estimate was not based upon a representative sample, and therefore might not be reliable. A more recent study estimated that 24% of the U.S. population will experience a sexual dysfunction at some time in their lives (Robins et al., 1984, p. 952). Moreover, a comprehensive review of the sexuality, psychopathology, and epidemiology literatures (Spector & Carey, 1990) suggests that sexual problems may be very common. Finally, the anecdotal evidence obtained from practicing social workers, psychologists, psychiatrists, and physicians involved in primary care indicates that sexual dysfunctions occur frequently and are distressing to many people. In later chapters, we present prevalence data separately for each dysfunction.

Although sexual problems do appear to be quite prevalent, they are understudied. Perhaps this is because, as a society, we consider sexual adjustment and health to be a luxury: If people are lucky enough to stumble into good adjustment, then great; otherwise, tough luck. Perhaps sexual health and adjustment receives less study because this domain encroaches too close to moral and religious values, making sexuality a taboo topic. There are certainly other factors that have stifled the scientific study of sexuality. Regardless of these factors, however, given the prevalence of the sexual dysfunctions, it is noteworthy that they are less well understood than other, less prevalent clinical problems. This is especially true when it comes to research on the etiology of the sexual dysfunctions.

What Causes the Sexual Dysfunctions?: Etiology

To treat sexual dysfunction or dissatisfaction effectively, it is helpful (but probably not necessary) to understand how that dysfunction or dissatisfaction developed. Unfortunately, our understanding of the etiology—that is, the cause(s)—of the sexual dysfunctions is preliminary and incomplete. Moreover, much of our understanding comes from clinical observation rather than from well-controlled research. In the study of psychopathology, this is not unusual; however, we do need to be mindful of the methodological limitations of such quasi-experimental research, cautious about our judgments, and continually open to new clinical and research data.

With these caveats in mind, we are nonetheless confident about the following general statements regarding the etiology of the sexual dysfunctions:

1. In most cases, sexual difficulties are multiply determined. That is, there is usually not just a single cause for a problem; rather, one can expect to find an array of factors which contribute to the development of a sexual difficulty. Appreciation of this principle can help to explain why treatments need to be customized to the individual, as well as why treatments need to be empirically eclectic, multimodal (Lazarus, 1988), or broad-spectrum (LoPiccolo & Friedman, 1988) rather than dogmatically designed and narrowly focused.

2. Within such a multicausal context, causes can be organized for communication purposes into three temporal categories (Hawton, 1985). First, "predisposing" factors are those prior life experiences (e.g., childhood sexual trauma) and inherited characteristics (e.g., diabetes) that make a person vulnerable to certain types of dysfunction. These predisposing factors serve as diatheses that place an individual at risk; predisposing factors may be necessary, but they are rarely sufficient to produce a dysfunction. Second, "precipitating" (or triggering) factors (e.g., stress associated with job difficulties) are those life events and experiences associated with the initial onset of a symptom or dysfunction. A precipitating factor serves as the proverbial "straw that broke the camel's back." Third, "maintaining" factors (e.g., lack of privacy) are those ongoing life circumstances or physical conditions that help to explain why a dysfunction persists.

3. Causes can also be classified, again for heuristic purposes, into three human systems or frames of reference. First, causes may be inherently biological or medical. Thus, for example, the presence of penile microangiopathy (i.e., small-vessel disease) in a middle-aged male diabetic can cause erectile difficulties. Similarly, the hormonal changes that can accompany menopause in women can produce vaginal dryness and dyspareunia. Second, causes can be psychological in nature. Gross disturbances in reality testing

(e.g., paranoid delusions), major depression, and serious anxiety disorders have all been implicated in the pathogenesis of sexual dysfunction. Less obvious psychological contributions to dysfunction include negative body image and fear of negative evaluation or rejection. Finally, causes can arise from a person's social context. At the dyadic level, factors such as poor communication and relationship inequalities can foster sexual dysfunction. Larger sociocultural influences, such as sex-role prescriptions or religious proscriptions, may also have an impact upon sexual functioning.

In summary, we propose that the etiology of most sexual dysfunctions will be multiply determined, involving the transaction of biological, psychological, and social factors over a period of time. Thus, a major challenge for us as sex therapists will be to recognize these multiple sources of influence, and to appreciate that sexual dysfunction represents but one manifestation of a complex process. As our knowledge of etiology increases, it is likely that we will also develop more reliable and valid assessments, as well as more efficacious treatments.

What to Do?: Assessment and Treatment

After introducing the dysfunctions, this book devotes most of its pages to the assessment and treatment of sexual dysfunction and dissatisfaction. This material commences in Chapter 6. Before then, however, we wish to make clear the beliefs that influence our approach to assessment and treatment.

First, we are strong advocates of the biopsychosocial approach to health care, which is now receiving increased attention in the training of many health care professionals (see Engel, 1977). This model has important implications for both assessment and treatment, which will become manifest throughout this book. Clearly, this model requires continuing efforts to stay abreast of developments—not only in one's own discipline, but also in related disciplines.

Second, we are equally committed to the scientist–practitioner model of health care training and delivery. This model, espoused by the American Psychological Association as its primary training approach, has been much misunderstood, misapplied, and subsequently criticized. However, as we understand it, this model requires practicing clinicians (1) to stay abreast of recent scientific developments and, more importantly, (2) to adopt an empirical approach to their work. We discuss each of these "requirements" in turn.

The rationale for the need to stay current is nicely captured in Bob Dylan's famous line, "The times, they are a'changin'." This observation is particularly true for the field of human sexuality. With the media explosion, in-depth coverage of sexuality-related topics has occurred in both print journalism (e.g., *Cosmopolitan, Playboy, Vogue, Redbook,* and even *Reader's Digest!*) and television (e.g., the talk shows of Dr. Ruth Westheimer, Phil

Donahue, Sally Jessy Raphael, Oprah Winfrey, etc.). As a result, clients are more sophisticated and knowledgeable. Professionals, especially those who promote themselves as "experts" in an area such as sexuality, must remain informed of recent advances, controversies, and other developments. This is much more true today than was the case in the recent past.

The recommendation that one adopt a scientific approach to one's work requires careful, ongoing assessment and critical self-evaluation (see Barlow, Hayes, & Nelson, 1984; Carey, Flasher, Maisto, & Turkat, 1984). We believe that a scientific approach is especially necessary in a controversial and understudied area such as human sexuality, because there is an increased probability of conjecture and subjective (or even distorted) information. Thus, the scientist–practitioner approach, which sensitizes one to the need to be critical of current "knowledge," is especially valuable in a field that is susceptible to potentially harmful information.

Third, we believe that a wide variety of sexual practices and orientations have been prematurely labeled as psychopathological, deviant, or abnormal. Therefore, with some obvious exceptions (e.g., coercive sexual practices with a nonconsenting partner), we try not to make value judgments regarding the "rightness" or "wrongness" of practices that are not universally approved in our culture (e.g., homosexuality). Instead, we call for continued research and study of these practices to increase our understanding of the richness and diversity of human sexual expression.

We have attempted to prepare a book that is equally applicable to male and female, as well as to homosexual and heterosexual, concerns. At points where our coverage seems biased or one-sided, please understand that this was not our intention; such instances may reflect the state of current knowledge, or our inability to express ourselves as well as we would have liked.

Finally, we would like to encourage all professionals to adhere closely to the ethical principles of their disciplines. Because our own professional training is in psychology, we follow the guidelines proffered by the American Psychological Association. Further information is available from the *Casebook on Ethical Principles of Psychologists* (American Psychological Association, 1987), or from the state licensure boards of the various professions.

Note

[1] To discuss this question, we must introduce two terms from epidemiology: "incidence" and "prevalence." "Incidence" refers to the number of new cases of a dysfunction that occur during a discrete time period (e.g., the year 1991). "Prevalence" refers to the number of people who have a disorder at a specific time. Prevalance rates, the more commonly reported of the two, are influenced by how often a dysfunction occurs (i.e., its incidence) as well as by how long it lasts (i.e., its duration).

I

THE SEXUAL DYSFUNCTIONS

Sexual difficulties can be broken down into three broad categories: the sexual dysfunctions, the paraphilias, and the gender dysphoria conditions. As we have indicated in Chapter 1, the purpose of this book is to provide a guide to the assessment and treatment of the sexual *dysfunctions*. Therefore, in the first part of this book, we provide an introduction to the most common sexual dysfunctions. Specifically, in Chapter 2, we discuss sexual desire disorders; in Chapter 3, we overview the sexual arousal disorders; in Chapter 4, we introduce the orgasm disorders; and, finally, in Chapter 5, we discuss the sexual pain disorders. In each chapter we provide basic descriptions and definitions for each class of disorders, as well as providing information (where available) on the prevalence and etiology of specific dysfunctions within that class. This introductory material sets the stage for our discussion of the assessment and treatment of such dysfunctions in Part II of the book.

2

Sexual Desire Disorders

Sexual desire is a nebulous construct. To nonprofessionals, desire is synonymous with "horniness" or "lust" or "passion"; to many mental health professionals, desire represents the most recent translation of the Freudian notion of "libido." Freud (1905/1962) considered libido to be an erotic "instinct" or "drive" that was endogenous and required release. According to Freud, failure to experience this endogenous force or high desire was indicative of psychopathology. Thus, in traditional Freudian thought, desire was seen as a natural biological drive to behave sexually, which was thwarted only by intrapsychic conflict. In contrast, recent theory (e.g., Bancroft, 1988; Levine, 1984, 1987) and empirical findings (reviewed below) suggest that desire is more multifaceted. Rather than being a biological drive, it is seen as the endpoint of a complex interaction of biological (e.g., neuroendocrine), psychological (e.g., cognitive and affective), social (e.g., relationship), and cultural (e.g., religious upbringing) forces.

Low Sexual Desire

Although great variability within and across individuals is recognized (e.g., Denney, Field, & Quadagno, 1984), mainstream thinking currently holds that "healthy" individuals will experience sexual desire regularly, and, moreover, that they will take advantage of appropriate opportunities for sexual expression when they arise.[1] In contrast, individuals who are persistently and recurrently uninterested in sexual expression, and who report the absence of sexual fantasies, are said to be experiencing what DSM-III-R terms Hypoactive Sexual Desire Disorder (see Table 2-1).

A number of terms have been used to describe this phenomenon, including "Inhibited Sexual Desire" (American Psychiatric Association, 1980),

TABLE 2-1. Diagnostic Criteria for Hypoactive Sexual Desire Disorder (302.71)

A. Persistently or recurrently deficient or absent sexual fantasies and desire for sexual activity. The judgment of deficiency or absence is made by the clinician, taking into account factors that affect sexual functioning, such as age, sex, and the context of the person's life.
B. Occurrence not exclusively during the course of another Axis I disorder (other than a Sexual Dysfunction), such as Major Depression.

Note. From the *Diagnostic and Statistical Manual of Mental Disorders* (3rd ed., rev., p. 293) by the American Psychiatric Association, 1987, Washington, DC: Author. Copyright 1987 by the American Psychiatric Association. Reprinted by permission.

"frigidity," and "impotence." These other terms are less precise and have been used for almost all of the other dysfunctions; thus, we advise against using them. In addition, the label "Hypoactive Sexual Desire Disorder" is currently preferred because it is not seen as pejorative, and it does not connote a particular theoretical point of view with regard to etiology.

As noted in Chapter 1, all sexual disorders are usually further classified as "lifelong" (existing for the entirety of the person's adult life; also referred to as "primary") versus "acquired" (developing after a period of normal functioning; sometimes referred to as "secondary"), and as "generalized" (i.e., occurring across all partners, sexual activities, and situations) versus "situational" (i.e., limited to certain partners, sexual practices, or situations).

How should we define (and structure our assessment of) Hypoactive Sexual Desire Disorder? That is, should we focus on behavior, cognition, or affect? Sexual *behavior* among individuals typically diagnosed with this disorder is somewhat variable, making diagnosis quite difficult on the basis of behavior alone.

An important question arises in the context of using behavior to define "normality": How often should a person be sexually desirous? The third edition of DSM (American Psychiatric Association, 1980) suggested diagnosis of Inhibited Sexual Desire if the reported frequency of all sexual behavior was twice per month or less over the previous 6 months. In the revised third edition (American Psychiatric Association, 1987), however, no attempt to specify a minimum frequency of sexual activity was made. Instead, DSM-III-R encourages the use of clinical judgment. This judgment must take "into account various factors such as frequency and chronicity of the symptom, subjective distress, and effect on other areas of functioning" (p. 291). The advantage of the more flexible DSM-III-R criteria is that they allow a clinician to diagnose Hypoactive Sexual Desire Disorder in an individual who may be sexually active (i.e., coitus once per week) in response to a partner's demands, but who lacks any real interest in sexual activities. The disadvantage consists of an increased likelihood of low interdiagnostician reliability.

In a recent study, Schreiner-Engel and Schiavi (1986) reported that the majority of Hypoactive Sexual Desire Disorder patients they studied had attempted intercourse only once per month or even less during the previous 6 months; this does seem unusually infrequent. The confusing part, however, is that other subjects reported much higher levels of coital activity; as it turned out, this greater frequency was usually in response to their partners' pressure for more frequent intercourse. In any event, our point is this: We should not rely exclusively on the frequency of intercourse to diagnose low desire, because some people will have intercourse out of obligation (or even coercion) rather than out of interest or desire.

So, what about masturbation as a behavioral "marker," or indicator? In the Schreiner-Engel and Schiavi (1988) study cited above, the frequency of masturbation was similarly heterogeneous. That is, 35% of the women and 52% of the men did not masturbate at all; 45% and 39%, respectively, reported that they masturbated once per month or less; the remaining subjects reported more frequent masturbation. Thus, sexual behavior (i.e., intercourse or masturbation) does not appear to be an ideal indicator of desire.

Cognitive correlates (i.e., fantasies and urges) of sexual desire might also be used to define Hypoactive Sexual Desire Disorder; at first glance, these correlates would seem to be less variable. For example, using frequency data, Schreiner-Engel and Schiavi (1988) indicated that the vast majority of their patients rarely had sexual fantasies. Nutter and Condron (1983, 1985) also documented that both men and women with Hypoactive Sexual Desire Disorder fantasized less than normal controls during foreplay, intercourse, masturbation, and general daydreaming. Interestingly, when fantasy did occur, there were no differences in the *content* of the sexual fantasy between patients and "normal" controls.

The use of cognitive correlates to define and diagnose Hypoactive Sexual Desire Disorder is plagued by a major confound—namely, the likelihood of gender differences in fantasy frequency and content. For example, Person, Terestman, Myers, Goldberg, and Salvadori (1989) reported that, nomothetically (i.e., as a group), men fantasize more often; men also exhibit greater interest in sexual variation than do women. Specifically, compared to women, men prefer fantasies involving partner variation (e.g., "involvement in orgies," "sex with a famous person," "sex with two or more lovers"), domination (e.g., "forcing partners to submit"), and active, initiatory behavior (e.g., "masturbating your partner," "seducing partner"). Men also show more interest in oral–genital sex and sex in unusual positions. Similar findings have been reported by others (Denney et al., 1984; Jones & Barlow, 1987; McCauley & Swann, 1978, 1980). Thus, cognitive descriptors of desire need to take nomothetic gender differences into account.

If affect were seen as the primary characteristic of Hypoactive Sexual Desire Disorder, then three subtypes might be discerned. First, Hypoactive Sexual Desire Disorder may be accompanied by an equanimity—a kind of affective neutrality. In this subtype, a person's attitude regarding sex is that he or she can "take it or leave it." Such persons do not have positive or negative feelings about sexual expression. It is unlikely that such a person would seek professional assistance, and it is questionable whether such a person should be diagnosed at all (see Tobias, 1975).

A second, and probably more common, subtype of Hypoactive Sexual Desire Disorder occurs in the person with low sexual desire who is also experiencing negative affective states, perhaps as a result of the low desire.[2] Such persons, who may seek out (or be forced to enter) treatment, may feel guilty and depressed because of their absence of sexual interest and urges. This negative affect may be the result of a discrepancy between a person and his or her partner, or between the person's behavior and socially transmitted expectations about what is "normal." (In this regard, we are reminded of the scene from the Woody Allen movie *Annie Hall,* in which Annie [Diane Keaton] and Alvy Singer [Allen] are pictured separately in simultaneous conversations with their therapists. Although Annie and Alvy agree on the absolute frequency of their sexual activity, Alvy summarizes this by saying, "We never have sex." In contrast, Annie states, "We have sex all the time.")

A third subtype of Hypoactive Sexual Desire Disorder can be seen in the person with low sexual desire who is fearful of, and wishes to avoid, sexual activity. When avoidance of sex is accompanied by an extreme aversion to genital sexual contact, Sexual Aversion Disorder is the more accurate diagnosis (see Table 2-2). Although we believe that Hypoactive Sexual Desire Disorder and Sexual Aversion Disorder are more accurately viewed as points along the same continuum, in DSM-III-R they have been conceptualized as qualitatively distinct diagnostic entities. In this view, Sexual Aversion Disorder is characterized by fear and avoidance, whereas Hypoactive Sexual Desire Disorder is typified by depression and a lack of response initiative.

TABLE 2-2. Diagnostic Criteria for Sexual Aversion Disorder (302.79)

A. Persistent or recurrent extreme aversion to, and avoidance of, all or almost all, genital sexual contact with a sexual partner.
B. Occurrence not exclusively during the course of another Axis I disorder (other than a Sexual Dysfunction), such as Obsessive Compulsive Disorder or Major Depression.

Note. From the *Diagnostic and Statistical Manual of Mental Disorders* (3rd ed., rev., p. 293) by the American Psychiatric Association, 1987, Washington, DC: Author. Copyright 1987 by the American Psychiatric Association. Reprinted by permission.

This distinction is similar to the one that is sometimes made between anxiety and depression (see, e.g., Barlow, 1988). Indeed, Kaplan (1987) has directly linked Sexual Aversion Disorder with Panic Disorder. For both Hypoactive Sexual Desire Disorder and Sexual Aversion Disorder, there may or may not be other obvious signs of current psychological disturbance (American Psychiatric Association, 1987).

In summary, then, one needs to attend to behavior, affect, and cognition when attempting to diagnose the desire disorders. We believe that reliance on one source of information may be misleading.

The Clinical Presentation of Hypoactive Sexual Desire Disorder

Perhaps some mention of how desire disorders may be presented by patients is appropriate at this point (also, see Cases 2 and 4 in Chapter 10). In this regard, it is not uncommon for a man to say, "I have no interest in sex." From such a statement, it is difficult to determine whether he is referring to his low sexual desire, or whether he may really be talking about his lack of erection. Thus, as a clinician, it is crucial for you to separate an arousal disorder (see Chapter 3) from a desire disorder. There are several ways this might be done. For example, you might ask the man, "Despite your lack of interest, can you still get an erection?" Obviously, if he can still get an erection, you have ruled out an arousal disorder. Alternatively, you might ask, "Compared to your past, how would you rate your interest in sex?" (If appropriate, you may want to use the word "horniness.") Or you might ask, "Compared to other guys, how horny do you get?" You might also ask, "If you could get an erection, do you think that you would be interested in having sex?" On the basis of the man's answers, you will have to make a judgment regarding whether the disorder involves a desire deficiency or an arousal problem.

When evaluating a woman's low sexual arousal, we find it easier (usually!) to make the distinction between low desire and arousal difficulties because women tend, nomothetically, to be more in touch with their feelings than are men. With women, you may have to be particularly careful to assess whether the low desire is partner-specific, because this is a common presentation. (We expand upon this in Chapter 6.)

Before concluding this section, we want to mention a clinical phenomenon that arises occasionally—namely, the "madonna–whore syndrome." A number of men present with low sexual desire with their usual partners (most often, their wives). Even though they report that this primary relationship is fulfilling in many ways (e.g., it is characterized by a good family life), one or both partners report low sexual desire. Typically, sex is limited to "making babies" or to perfunctory satisfaction of "marital duties." Men with this syndrome, however, report that they are sexually desirous and can function sexually with "slutty" partners, but not with "good" partners. For a case illustration of this syndrome, see Case 4 in Chapter 10.

Excessive Sexual Desire

Thus far, we have limited our discussion of desire disorders to instances of low or absent desire. However, brief mention should be made of a related phenomenon involving "abnormally" high sexual desire; this phenomemon can be found at the other end of the aforementioned continuum (i.e., the *hyper*active end). Disorders involving excessive sexual desire have been referred to as "sexual addiction," "sexual compulsion," "nymphomania," "satyriasis," or "Don Juanism." Unfortuantely, there is little agreement on the usage of these terms. The term "sexual addiction," in particular, has been used recently to explain such varied practices as frequent masturbation, impersonal sex, emotional dependency, and extramarital affairs. In extreme cases, sexual addiction has been called a "progressive form of insanity" (Carnes, 1983, cited in Levine & Troiden, 1988)! However, this term has not been the focus of much (if any) empirical work and remains more of a popular press curiosity than a common clinical problem. "Sexual addiction" has also been evoked as a convenient excuse for irresponsible sexual behavior (e.g., extramarital affairs) as well. (Please note: Instances of excessive desire are not uncommon in the paraphilias, but, as mentioned earlier, these disorders are not the focus of this book. Interested readers are referred to Coleman, 1987, 1990, and Laws, 1989.)

Prevalence

The frequency with which difficulties involving low sexual desire appear, both in clinical practice and in the general population, seems to be increasing (Spector & Carey, 1990). In the early 1970s, Inhibited Sexual Desire (as it was then called) represented approximately 37% of the presenting problems in sex clinics (LoPiccolo & Friedman, 1988). According to a study by Frank, Anderson, and Kupfer (1976), males seeking marital therapy were more likely to experience desire disorders than were those seeking sex therapy, while the opposite pattern was true for females. By the mid-1970s, females accounted for 70% of those individuals presenting for treatment with desire disorders (LoPiccolo & Friedman, 1988). By the end of the 1970s, 46% of the couples presenting for sex therapy reported that low sexual desire was their chief complaint (LoPiccolo & Friedman, 1988); interestingly, in only 60% of these couples was the female identified as the "patient." During the 1970s, community studies (which attempt to determine prevalence data for the general population) indicated a rate of approximately 34% (Frank et al., 1978; Hite, 1976) among females and 16% among males (Frank et al., 1978), paralleling the gender differences observed in clinical samples.

During the early 1980s, the number of couples presenting with desire disorders continued to increase, reaching 55% in clinical samples; however, at this time, almost 60% of presenting partners were *male*. So, two changes appear to have occurred during the 1970–1990 interval: (1) The prevalence of Hypoactive Sexual Desire Disorder appears to have increased in clinical samples; and (2) the gender proportion changed so that by the late 1980s, males outnumbered females. Unfortunately, there are no data from community studies to help indicate whether these changes reflect a trend in (1) the prevalence of the dysfunction, (2) reduced prevalence or improved treatment for the other sexual dysfunctions, or (3) help-seeking behavior. Also, the current state of knowledge does not allow fine discriminations regarding the differential prevalence rates of Hypoactive Sexual Desire Disorder and Sexual Aversion Disorder.

Etiology

What causes "abnormally" low sexual desire? Answering this seemingly simple question remains a challenging problem for scientist–practitioners, who have only recently begun to study this issue. Most of the research on sexual desire has focused on biological influences in *nonclinical* samples. Typically, the results of such studies for both sexes have been inconsistent and confusing (see Bancroft, 1988, for a review).

Research with clinical samples (i.e., persons seeking treatment) is only beginning. Virtually no systematic, well-controlled work with persons seeking treatment for Sexual Aversion Disorder is available; however, clinical experience suggests that such persons have almost always been the victims of a sexual trauma (e.g., child sexual abuse, rape). Some research has been conducted on patients presenting with Hypoactive Sexual Desire Disorder. To overview the kind of research that is being done, we provide a sampling of three recent studies below.

In a biologically oriented investigation, Schiavi, Schreiner-Engel, White, and Mandeli (1988) compared pituitary and gonadal hormones and nocturnal penile tumescence in 17 physically healthy men with Hypoactive Sexual Desire Disorder and 17 age-matched physically healthy, nondysfunctional volunteers. The men with the disorder had significantly lower plasma testosterone than controls, and there was a positive relation between testosterone and frequency of sexual behavior. However, the differences between the low- and normal-desire men were modest; that is, these differences were of doubtful clinical significance. Moreover, there were no group differences on a number of theoretically relevant variables, including free testosterone, prolactin, luteinizing hormone, and estradiol.

At the psychological level of analysis, Schreiner-Engel and Schiavi (1986) studied 46 married patients who were currently complaining of Hypoactive Sexual Desire Disorder. These patients were matched (on age, relationship status, and relationship duration) with 36 control subjects, and subsequently compared with regard to lifetime psychopathology, current psychological adjustment, and (for female subjects) premenstrual syndrome. The results indicated that the Hypoactive Sexual Desire Disorder subjects were twice as likely as control subjects to have had a prior episode of affective disturbance; interestingly, there were no differences between the low-desire and control subjects with respect to *current* psychological symptoms, except, of course, for the presenting problem of low desire. Although obtained retrospectively, there was some evidence to suggest that the depressive episodes had *predated* the first onset of desire difficulties, leading the authors to speculate that there might be a common etiology or that affective disturbances might contribute to the development of Hypoactive Sexual Desire Disorder.

Finally, at the interpersonal/social level of analysis, Stuart, Hammond, and Pett (1987) studied 59 women seeking treatment for Hypoactive Sexual Desire Disorder and 31 control subjects (i.e., women who were satisfied with their level of sexual desire). These two groups were compared on a large number of demographic, religious, hormonal, psychological, marital adjustment, sexual history, and current sexual functioning variables. Compared to control subjects, women with low desire (1) had more negative perceptions of their parents' attitudes toward sex and toward the demonstration of affection; (2) reported that they had engaged in premarital sex more frequently; (3) had poorer marital adjustment; and (4) evidenced lower levels of emotional closeness, romantic feelings, and attraction toward their partners. Overall, these findings led the authors to conclude that the *quality of the marital relationship,* rather than physiological or psychological factors, was most important in the development of Hypoactive Sexual Desire Disorder in women.

Thus, in these three investigations, we have seen associations between biological, psychological, and social factors on the one hand, and Hypoactive Sexual Desire Disorder on the other. Of course, the correlational nature of these studies does not permit firm conclusions about cause and effect. Nevertheless, these studies have identified several factors that may be important in understanding the etiology of Hypoactive Sexual Desire Disorder, and should be assessed carefully in clinical practice (see Chapter 6). A number of other possible causal agents have been identified on the basis of careful clinical observation, and are reported next.

LoPiccolo and Friedman (1988) have provided a long list of individual and relationship causes of low sexual desire. Among the individual causes are religious orthodoxy; anhedonic or obsessive–compulsive personality; gender identity (i.e., transsexualism) or object choice (i.e., heterosexual, homosexual, or bisexual) conflicts; special sexual phobias; fear of loss of control over sexual urges; masked sexual deviation (e.g., transvestism); fear of pregnancy; "widower's syndrome" (i.e., inadequate grieving following the death of a spouse); depression; hormone deficiencies; medication side effects; and aging-related concerns (e.g., changes in physical appearance). To this list we might add fear of sexually transmitted diseases, especially acquired immune deficiency syndrome (AIDS) (cf. Katz, Gipson, Kearl, & Kriskovich, 1989). We discuss this further in Chapter 9.

Clinical experience suggests that victims of sexual traumas such as rape are particularly vulnerable to desire disorders, especially Sexual Aversion Disorder (also, see Stuart & Greer, 1984). As LoPiccolo and Friedman (1988) point out, for some victims each sexual experience can reactivate the memory of the rape, and may be accompanied by flashbacks (as in combat-related Post-traumatic Stress Disorder). Thus, victims are motivated to avoid sexual intimacy and may present with desire difficulties after they have become involved in a relationship. Consider the following case example from our files.

Mrs. Dent entered therapy with her husband complaining of lack of sexual interest. The couple had been married for 12 years and had two children (6 and 11 years old). Both had advanced graduate education, and Mr. Dent was a successful medical professional. The couple had met in college, and both described their early relationship as very rewarding and sexually active.

Immediately after college, Mrs. Dent went to graduate school in social work; in her second year of training, she counseled victims of rape and violence, as well as families of murder victims. She also had to appear in court to testify in support of the victims. On numerous occasions she was threatened with rape and murder; on one occasion, a killer–rapist stalked her. In addition, a close working colleague was raped and another was murdered.

Following this work experience, Mr. and Mrs. Dent were married. Within the first year of marriage, the couple had a child who was very sickly. Mrs. Dent quit her job to care for their child full-time. In addition to this stressor, the couple had financial problems; as a result, both partners felt that the first 7 years of their marriage were quite stressful. After this time, their financial situation improved, but Mrs. Dent lacked self-confidence and began to feel distant from her husband. The couple communicated well, but Mr. Dent would often burden Mrs. Dent with his problems, and would speak to her in a belittling way. Sexual activity waned, and Mrs. Dent's lack of sexual interest became a focal point of many heated discussions.

When Mrs. Dent was initially seen alone in assessment, she denied any upsetting past sexual experiences (i.e., any history of rape or other sexual abuse as a child). She made no connection between her vicarious sexual trauma that she had experienced as a young social worker and her current lack of desire, so she failed to mention this work-related experience to the therapist.

Therapy was undertaken with the couple with an initial focus on marital conflict (e.g., Mr. Dent's belittling style). At the second session, Mrs. Dent appeared alone because her husband had to respond to a medical emergency. The session was spent focusing further on Mrs. Dent's sexual development. In passing, she mentioned that she had worked with rapists. The therapist picked up on this, and questioned her in detail about her experiences. During that session, she became very upset as she recounted numerous upsetting episodes. Because of her reaction, the therapist suggested that she attend the next session alone.

At the beginning of the next session, Mrs. Dent reported she was having flashbacks and nightmares associated with fears of rape. She had remembered many more incidents since the prior session, and had been teary, agitated, and depressed since the last meeting. She wanted to focus more on her past upsetting experiences in therapy, a goal that was appropriate and supported by the therapist. During this session, the client and therapist processed her reactions to the experiences. Afterwards, Mrs. Dent was less agitated, and by the end of the week she reported that she felt much better. Her nightmares stopped, and she reported that she felt more self-confident. Progress in therapy continued, and her sexual desire increased.

This case is a good example of how past negative experiences can influence a person's sexual expression. As this case illustrates, it is not necessary for a person to experience the trauma directly as a victim; vicariously experiencing a sexual trauma, especially at a vulnerable stage in one's life, can be just as damaging. McCarthy (1990) points out that five dimensions should be considered in assessing the impact of sexual trauma: (1) violent versus gentle; (2) perpetrated by a family member versus a stranger; (3) kept secret versus acknowledged and resolved; (4) involving genital focus with oral, anal, or vaginal penetration versus involving exhibition only; and (5) occurring intermittently versus occurring once only. McCarthy (1990) suggests that "the greater the violence; the more trust is broken by a family member or adult authority figure; the longer the secret is kept (increasing the sense of stigma and cognitive distortion); the more physically invasive and orgasm-oriented the incidents; and the longer the period of time the incidents occurred, and on an intermittent basis, the greater the trauma" (p. 144).

A number of the key elements for increasing the impact of the trauma were present in Mrs. Dent's experiences. Although Mr. Dent was aware that

Mrs. Dent had worked with rapists and rape victims, the couple had never discussed these experiences, and he was unaware of the impact that they had had on her. Once these experiences were discussed in therapy, he had a greater understanding of her negative emotions associated with sex, and he no longer "blamed" her for the sexual problem.

The relationship causes identified by LoPiccolo and Friedman (1988) include lack of attraction to one's partner, poor sexual skills in the partner, marital conflict, fear of closeness, couple differences regarding optimal closeness, passive–aggressive solutions to relationship power imbalance, and inability to coordinate love and sexual desire (e.g., the "madonna–whore syndrome" mentioned earlier in this chapter, and discussed in Case 4 of Chapter 10).

Noteworthy here is the notion of differential levels of sexual desire in a couple. That is, some couples will identify one partner as having "low desire." Although the "identified patient" is occasionally desirous, he or she experiences desire less often (and/or less intensely) than his or her partner. Some couples construe this as a "disorder" in the identified partner, rather than framing it as one of the many natural differences that arise in a relationship. Of course, these kinds of differences require negotiation and compromise, and many couples resolve differences in other domains (e.g., amount of sleep, choice of vacations) quite easily; however, when the differences occur in the sexual domain, they can be very threatening, and spouses can question their "rightness" for each other. Perhaps this happens because, in our culture, the terms "love" and "sex" are often used interchangeably. A corollary then becomes this: If one partner is sexually desirous more often, that partner may love the other more. Of course, this is a fallacy that is easily resolved with straightforward education (see Chapter 7).

Segraves (1988) has provided a list of pharmacological agents that are believed (and, in some cases, have been demonstrated through empirical research) to cause Hypoactive Sexual Desire Disorder. Potential culprits among the prescription drugs include the antihypertensive (e.g., diuretics, adrenergic-inhibiting agents, beta-blockers), psychiatric (e.g., neuroleptics, antidepressants, monoamine oxidase [MAO] inhibitors, lithium), and anticonvulsant medications. In addition, cancer chemotherapy protocols are known to impair sexual desire (Chapman, 1982; Chapman, Rees, Sutcliffe, Edwards, & Malpas, 1979). Among the so-called "recreational drugs," alcohol and cocaine have been associated with impaired desire, especially after chronic use (Schuckit, 1989). Unfortunately, in many cases this research has not advanced to the stage where it is possible to talk about the mechanisms by which drugs exert their effect (Segraves, Madsen, Carter, & Davis, 1985). That is, drugs may impair desire through several means, including neurotransmitter or hormonal changes, decreased overall well-being, and the like. (Interestingly, despite late-night television advertisements to the contrary, there are no medications that have been demonstrated to enhance sexual desire reliably—even though numerous major pharmaceutical companies employ neuropharmacological scientists who are working to develop such a product. In Chapter 8, we discuss yohimbine and other drug therapies that have been tried to enhance desire.)

In summary, there are many potential "causes" of Hypoactive Sexual Desire Disorder. As LoPiccolo and Friedman (1988) emphasize, there is probably no single cause for this disorder; rather, it may be a final common pathway for a heterogeneous array of etiological agents. Nevertheless, we recommend strongly that you follow the professional literature to stay abreast of new developments in clinical research (see Chapter 11 for a list of relevant journals). Those interested in an excellent and current comprehensive overview of desire disorders are referred to Leiblum and Rosen (1988).

Notes

[1] Alternative views, both religious and secular, propose that sexual abstinence should not be labeled and pathologized (see Chapter 1). Readers interested in studying these viewpoints might consult Tobias (1975).

[2] Alternatively, depression can also cause low desire; see the Schreiner-Engel and Schiavi (1986) study discussed later in this chapter.

3

Sexual Arousal Disorders

"Sexual arousal" refers to the physiological, cognitive, and affective changes that serve to prepare men and women for sexual activity.

In men, the most conspicuous physiological changes seen during sexual arousal are penile tumescence and elevation of the testes. In our clients' parlance, we are referring to getting an erection or having a "hard-on." In women, a more extensive and complex pattern of physiological changes occurs; this pattern includes vasocongestion in the pelvis, vaginal lubrication, swelling of the external genitalia, narrowing of the outer third of the vaginal barrel, lengthening and widening of the inner two-thirds of the vaginal barrel, and breast tumescence. Clients tend to simplify and summarize these changes to "getting wet." Although these physiological changes occur both within the genital region and outside it, typically it is reduced arousal in the genital region that brings people to seek professional assistance.

The cognitive and affective components of sexual arousal are more subtle than the physiological one. The cognitive component involves the focusing and narrowing of attention to erotic stimuli (e.g., one's partner), fantasies, and sexual cues (e.g., music, perfume, lingerie, etc.). The affective component involves the subjective sense of sexual excitement, romance, and pleasure that a person experiences concurrently with the aforementioned physiological changes and cognitive focus. In some persons, there can also be an "anxious" or excited tinge to the affective experience of sexual arousal. In our clinical experience, women tend to be more aware than are men of the cognitive–affective changes associated with sexual arousal.

Although the physiological changes associated with arousal are relatively clear, it can be very challenging to distinguish diminished subjective arousal (i.e., the cognitive and affective components) from low sexual desire (see Chapter 2). DSM-III-R offers no information to aid differential diagnosis in this instance. In our experience, difficulties in sexual arousal can involve the complete absence of these physiological, cognitive, and affective changes. Most commonly, however, arousal disorders can be differentiated from desire disorders by the premature termination or incomplete nature of physiological arousal. That is, individuals may approach the sexual situation eagerly (i.e., they are desirous), but find that they cannot sustain their arousal level to the degree that they would like (e.g., to adequate lubrication or to full erection).

In DSM-III-R, sexual arousal difficulties in men are referred to as Male Erectile Disorder, whereas in women they are called Female Sexual Arousal Disorder.

Male Erectile Disorder

Description

In men, inadequate arousal is typically experienced as the partial or complete inability to attain, or to maintain, an erection that is sufficient for intromission and subsequent sexual activity. Male Erectile Disorder may also involve a lessened or absent sense of excitement and pleasure. This difficulty has also been referred to as "erectile dysfunction," "erectile incompetence," and "impotence." The term "impotence" is no longer preferred because it suggests a global "lack of power" and is thus both imprecise and pejorative.[1] Similarly, "erectile incompetence" is not used for its obvious negative connotations.

Like other sexual dysfunctions, Male Erectile Disorder can be further classified as "lifelong" or "primary" versus "acquired" or "secondary," and as "generalized" versus "situational." When erectile dysfunction is characterized as lifelong and/or global, the problem is typically seen as more serious and difficult to treat. The DSM-III-R criteria for Male Erectile Disorder are presented in Table 3-1.

TABLE 3-1. Diagnostic Criteria for Male Erectile Disorder (302.72)

A. Either (1) or (2):
   (1) persistent or recurrent partial or complete failure in a male to attain or maintain erection until completion of the sexual activity
   (2) persistent or recurrent lack of a subjective sense of sexual excitement and pleasure in a male during sexual activity

B. Occurrence not exclusively during the course of another Axis I disorder (other than a Sexual Dysfunction), such as Major Depression.

Note. From the *Diagnostic and Statistical Manual of Mental Disorders* (3rd ed., rev., p. 294) by the American Psychiatric Association, 1987, Washington, DC: Author. Copyright 1987 by the American Psychiatric Association. Reprinted by permission.

Some men with Male Erectile Disorder may report that they are completely unable to obtain an erection; however, such complete dysfunction is, in our experience, rare. It is more common for men to report that they are able to obtain a partial erection, but that this erection is too soft to achieve penetration; alternatively, they may report that they can achieve a full erection, but that they are unable to maintain their erection long enough to permit penetration and intravaginal ejaculation. Some men will report that full erections are possible during noncoital stimulation—for example, during masturbation or nocturnally during rapid eye movement (REM) sleep. The amount of tumescence and rigidity that a man achieves may depend upon the extent of physiological involvement (discussed further in the "Etiology" section; also, see Case 1 in Chapter 10).

As a result of their erectile difficulties, men often report that they are embarrassed, discouraged, depressed, and even suicidal. Many will have tried several "home remedies" such as self-medication with alcohol or other drugs, viewing erotica, or becoming involved in an affair. These remedies often fail. Part of the reason why such self-help strategies fail is that men often approach affairs or masturbation under less than ideal conditions; that is, masturbation is often approached with the same attitude as with a partner—namely, with a demand to "perform." Thus, the man may masturbate to "see if it works," and he may not approach masturbation in a relaxed, erotic way.

An example of such an approach was seen in one of our clients, who reported that he tried to have sex with another woman to see whether his erectile dysfunction was "just a problem with his wife." The man was unable to achieve an erection with the other woman as well. When asked about the conditions under which sex was attempted, the man reported that they tried to have sex in the back seat of a Volkswagen in a church parking lot during the daytime! Not exactly a relaxed, erotic environment, to say the least.

When such self-help approaches do not work, they can have their own negative sequelae: additional frustration and dysphoria, as well as marital or relationship discord. Thus, by the time the client and his partner reach your office, it is likely that a great deal of negative affect surrounds sexual activity.

Prevalence

Erectile difficulties seem to be ubiquitous. For some men, they will represent a transitory problem, whereas others will experience erectile difficulties that are more persistent and troublesome. In either case, it has been estimated that as many as 50% of all men will experience erectile difficulties at some point in their lives (Kaplan, 1974). The commonness of this problem is suggested by several indirect indicators; for example, (1) the number of self-help organizations for men with erectile problems (e.g., Impotents Anonymous, Maryville, TN; Recovery of Male Impotence, Southfield, MI); (2) the numerous advertisements that appear in the so-called "men's magazines" offering magical "cures" of one type or another; and (3) an active and flourishing commercial interest in medical treatments (see Chapter 8).

More precise estimates of the prevalence of Male Erectile Disorder, however, can be culled from the professional literature. A recent review of this literature (i.e., Spector & Carey, 1990) indicated that erectile dysfunction may be the most common complaint for males who present to sex therapy clinics. For example, Frank et al. (1976) and Bancroft and Coles (1976) found that between 36% and 40% of males presenting for sex therapy had erectile dysfunction as their primary complaint. In Hawton's (1982) replication of the Bancroft and Coles (1976) study, the rate of this dysfunction increased to 53%. Masters and Johnson (1970) reported that 50% of men requesting treatment at their Institute in St. Louis experienced secondary (i.e., acquired) erectile dysfunction, and 8% experienced primary (i.e., lifelong) erectile dysfunction. More recently, Renshaw (1988) found a similar discrepancy at her clinic in Chicago between primary and secondary erectile dysfunction, with primary dysfunction measured at 3.5% and secondary dysfunction measured at 48%.

The figures cited above are from psychosocially oriented sex therapy clinics. An even larger number of men may initially present to erectile dysfunction clinics located in departments of urology. Unfortunately, data are not available from these settings but it can be assumed that the figures cited above are underestimates of the true prevalence of erectile dysfunction.

In community-based studies, erectile difficulty rates are estimated to be between 4% and 9% (Ard, 1977; Frank et al., 1978; Nettelbladt & Uddenberg, 1979). Interestingly, Kinsey, Pomeroy, and Martin (1948) found that erectile dysfunction occurred in less than 1% of the male population before age 19, increasing to 25% by age 75. In DSM-III-R, it is estimated that approximately 8% of the young adult male population has Male Erectile Disorder.

Etiology

Without a doubt, erectile difficulties have been studied more than any other sexual disorder; as a result, our understanding of the causes of such problems is more advanced than is the case for most of the other sexual dysfunctions. The current conceptualization of erectile disorder has advanced well beyond the "organic" versus "functional" dichotomy that once plagued the field. Well-trained professionals now recognize that the etiology of acquired Male

Erectile Disorder, in most cases, will involve a complex interplay of biological, psychological, and social influences. (Lifelong erectile dysfunction is usually caused by psychological factors.) Although an exhaustive review of the literature is beyond the scope of this book (indeed, at least four entire books have been written on erectile dysfunction; see Bennett, 1982; Krane, Siroky, & Goldstein, 1983; Segraves & Schoenberg, 1985; Wagner & Green, 1981), below we list and discuss briefly the many possible causal agents.

ENDOCRINE DEFICIENCIES

Endocrine deficiencies have long been suspected by both professionals and nonprofessionals as a leading cause of erectile difficulties. This notion resulted from early research that established a relationship between low levels of plasma testosterone and erectile capacity. More recent work, which is methodologically superior, has provided only mixed support for the hypothesis that reduced testosterone levels are responsible for Male Erectile Disorder (Jones, 1985). For example, numerous reports document that fact that men with prepubertal levels of serum testosterone can continue to obtain adequate erections (e.g., Davidson, Camargo, Smith, & Kwan, 1983; Heim, 1981). In apparent contrast, other investigators of hypogonadal men have reported increases in the frequency of spontaneous erections following testosterone replacement (e.g., Salmimies, Kockott, Pirke, Vogt, & Schill, 1982). Subsequent, more fine-grained analysis suggests that testosterone may be more important to fantasy-based arousal (and sexual desire) than it is to externally stimulated erections (Bancroft & Wu, 1983).

A recent study (Bansal et al., 1990) muddies the waters even further. These authors reported a positive correlation between testosterone levels and penile tumescence changes during both sleep and during exposure to erotic stimulation in chronic alcoholic men. Although the testosterone levels in the men in their sample were all within normal limits, it appears that overall arousal may be associated with testosterone level. This association may be very individualistic, so that for a given person, a decrease in testosterone may translate into lowered responsivity to erotic cues.

Similarly, research investigating the relationship between serum prolactin and erectile difficulties has been equivocal. Although severe hyperprolactinemia (which is rare) is probably associated with erectile dysfunction, mild hyperprolactinemia probably does not cause erectile difficulties (Buvat et al., 1985).

Despite these mixed findings, most experts agree that hormonal factors are rarely the sole or primary cause of most cases of erectile dysfunction (e.g., Bancroft, 1984; Jones, 1985; Schover & Jensen, 1988).

VASCULAR PROBLEMS

Vascular diseases and difficulties, on the other hand, represent a much more serious threat to erectile functioning (Papadopoulos, 1989). Because erection is primarily a vascular phenomenon (i.e., erection is achieved by a threefold increase in penile blood flow), malfunctions in either the arterial (i.e., inflow) or venous (i.e., outflow) systems are likely to result in erectile difficulties.

Arterial inflow may be insufficient as a result of any pathological condition that limits the amount of blood reaching the penis; diseases affecting the central pelvic arteries (supplying the legs) and/or the finer arteries (supplying the penis directly) may be implicated. Arteriosclerosis (i.e., thickening, hardening, and loss of elasticity of the walls of the arteries) may be the most common cause of arterial insufficiency (Wagner & Metz, 1981; see Chapter 9 as well). Ruzbarsky and Michal (1977) completed postmortem investigations of 30 men aged 19 to 85, and reported that all men over 38 years of age began to show signs of vascular disease in the penile arteries. The adequacy of the arterial inflow can be assessed with Doppler studies (Jetvich, 1980; also, see Chapter 6 for further details), and surgical revascularization interventions are available (see Chapter 8). At the time of this writing, however, revascularization cannot be considered a perfected option, as the results tend to be quite mixed.

The role of the venous system in erectile dysfunction was first recognized by Lowsley and Bray (1936), and has subsequently received considerable research attention (e.g., Ebbehoj & Wagner, 1979; Lue, Hricak, Schmidt, & Tanagho, 1986). The basic problem here is "venous leakage"; that is, arterial inflow of blood is adequate to produce an erection, but the venous outflow occurs so rapidly that the erection cannot be maintained. Assessment of venous leakage problems is possible by inducing an artificial erection with papaverine and studying the escape pattern of the blood from the penis (i.e., cavernosography; see Chapter 6 for further explanation of this procedure). Moreover, treatment by surgical revascularization can successfully treat some cases, providing indirect support for this etiological mechanism (e.g., Lewis & Puyau, 1986; Williams, Mulcahy, Hartnell, & Kiely, 1988). It should be noted, however, that venous leakage problems probably account for only a small percentage of erectile dysfunction cases, and they may be the most difficult to repair surgically (see Chapter 8).

NEUROLOGICAL DISEASE

Neurological disease can also contribute to erectile difficulties. Potential etiological contributors include diseases of the cerebral hemispheres (e.g., epilepsy), diseases of the spinal cord (e.g., multiple sclerosis), diseases of the peripheral nervous system (e.g., diabetes, renal disease), and trauma (e.g., damage from pelvic cancer surgery or spinal cord injury).The most common neurologically based cause may be diabetes, which places men at high risk for neuropathy and subsequent erectile dysfunction. Several studies have addressed this issue; although comprehensive reviews are available (e.g., Meisler, Carey, Lantinga, & Krauss, 1989), we describe three sample studies below (also, see Chapter 9).

Ellenberg (1971) compared 45 diabetics with erectile dysfunction to 30 diabetic controls. Eighty-four percent of the dysfunctional patients evidenced some symptoms of peripheral neuropathy (e.g., pain, paresthesia, absent deep reflexes), as compared to only 20% of the nondysfunctional patients. Ellenberg concluded that "in most instances the cause [of erectile dysfunction in diabetics] is neurogenic" (p. 217). In a subsequent study of 175 diabetic men, Kolodny, Kahn, Goldstein, and Barnett (1974) found that neuropathy was the only factor to discriminate significantly between dysfunctional and nondysfunctional groups. Recently, Sarica and Karacan (1987) used stimulation of the bulbocavernosus reflex to test neurological function in 24 diabetic men and 14 normal controls complaining of erectile dysfunction. The results indicated that 66% of the diabetic patients exhibited significantly slowed (or, in some cases, absent) bulbocavernosus reflexes, supporting further the importance of the neuropathic factor. Thus, the available evidence suggests that neurological factors are often implicated in diabetic erectile dysfunction.

With regard to diabetes, it is important to mention, as Schover and Jensen (1988) point out, that different mechanisms may be operative for Type I (i.e., juvenile-onset) versus Type II (i.e., adult-onset) diabetes. Erectile dysfunction in the former is more likely to be a consequence of neurological factors, whereas erectile dysfunction in the latter is more likely to be a consequence of vascular disease (Schover & Jensen, 1988).

ALCOHOL AND OTHER DRUGS OF ABUSE

Alcohol and other drugs have been implicated in the etiology of Male Erectile Disorder. Research on the acute effects of alcohol on arousal indicate a negative linear relationship (Wilson, 1977); that is, the more a man drinks, the less physiologically aroused (as measured by penile tumescence) he becomes in response to erotic stimulation. (It should be noted that *subjective* arousal appears to be enhanced, at least to a point, by alcohol consumption.) Chronic alcohol consumption is also associated with increased risk for erectile dysfunction, perhaps by instigating premature neuropathy (Schover & Jensen, 1988). Fahrner (1987) recently reported the results of a study of 116 patients in an alcohol treatment program in Germany. Twenty-three patients (20%)

reported frequent episodes of erectile dysfunction, and 26 patients (22%) reported very frequent or continuous episodes of erectile dysfunction. Fahrner also cited numerous other studies documenting the higher prevalence of erectile dysfunction among chronic alcoholics. Although the association between alcohol and erectile dysfunction is well established, two important questions remain unanswered: (1) What is the exact mechanism by which alcohol causes erectile difficulties? and (2) Is alcohol-initiated erectile dysfunction reversible?

The effects of other substances of abuse on erectile functioning are less well studied (Buffum, 1982, 1986). It has been suggested that the frequency of erectile dysfunction among heroin users is 28–43% and among methadone users is 40–50% (Segraves et al., 1985); both estimates are considerably higher than the frequency found in the general population. Reliable estimates are not available for other commonly abused substances (e.g., amphetamines, marijuana, cocaine). The illicit status of these drugs makes well-controlled studies in humans very challenging. Thus, we recommend strongly that your assessment include careful attention to substance use for all clients.

PRESCRIBED MEDICATIONS

It is widely believed that antihypertensive medications impair erectile functioning (Bansal, 1988; Moss & Procci, 1982; Papadopoulos, 1989; Segraves et al., 1985). Critical examination of the research on this topic, however, finds few studies that provide support for this belief. In one of the methodologically strongest studies, Rosen, Kostis, and Jekelis (1988) investigated, prospectively, the effects of four beta-blockers (atenolol, metoprolol, pindolol, and propranolol) on sexual functioning in 30 healthy men. Over a 70-day period, the subjects received each of the four drugs and a placebo, and assessment of erectile functioning was obtained with measures of nocturnal penile tumescence (see Chapter 6). The results indicated that only minor, and clinically insignificant, decrements in tumescence were observed.

In a recent review of the literature, Bansal (1988) points out that, even where erectile difficulties do occur in connection with the use of antihypertensives, the mechanism is not clear. That is, erectile difficulties reported during antihypertensive therapy may be the result of the disease (i.e., hypertension), its treatment (i.e., the medications), and/or the patient's reaction to the disease or treatment. More fine-grained study is necessary before we can understand the impact of antihypertensives.

Segraves and his colleagues (Segraves, 1989; Segraves et al., 1985) have reviewed the literature to determine the effects of psychiatric medications (including the antipsychotics, MAO inhibitors, tricyclic antidepressants, lithium, and minor tranquilizers) on erectile functioning. Most of these medications have been reported to have sexual side effects, but few if any studies have successfully disentangled the effects of the drugs from the psychopathology itself.

PSYCHOLOGICAL FACTORS

Indeed, numerous psychological factors have been linked with erection problems. Negative affect, particularly anxiety, has been suggested as an etiological factor by several theorists. For example, Kaplan (1974) has stated that performance anxiety "almost invariably contributes to impotence" (p. 129). Similarly, Masters and Johnson (1970) highlighted the "profound role played by fears of performance" (p. 84). Meisler and Carey (1991) recently found that acute depressed affect (not to be confused with the clinical syndrome of Major Depression) could also reduce subjective arousal—in nondysfunctional men. Interestingly, penile tumescence was unaltered by this affective state.

The work of Barlow and his colleagues (e.g., Barlow, Sakheim, & Beck, 1983; Beck, Barlow, & Sakheim, 1983; Sakheim, Barlow, Beck, & Abrahamson, 1984) has been especially instrumental in delineating important psychological factors related to erectile failure. In an ingenious series of studies, they have compared men experiencing erectile failure to men not experiencing any erectile problems. Several interesting findings have emerged:

- Men who experience erectile failure tend to underestimate the amount of erection response they are actually achieving, whereas functional men are more accurate in their estimation of arousal.
- Men who experience erectile failure tend to increase their erection response when they focus on nonerotic stimuli, whereas men who experience no erectile failure tend to decrease their erection response when they focus on nonerotic stimuli following arousal.
- Men who experience erectile failure tend to decrease their erection response when demands to get aroused are made, whereas functional men experience the opposite.
- Men who experience erectile failure display negative affect in the presence of erotic stimulation.

In a recent review of the empirical research, Barlow (1986) concluded that cognitive interference and negative affect specific to sexual stimuli are central to Male Erectile Disorder.

PSYCHOSOCIAL STRESS AND RELATIONSHIP FACTORS

Psychosocial stress may also play an important role in the erectile difficulties of some men. In a recent study, Morokoff, Baum, McKinnon, and Gillilland (1987) evaluated the interactive effects of chronic (i.e., actual or threatened unemployment) and acute (i.e., giving a speech about their sexual behaviors) stress. Their results suggested that erection impairment occurs as a result of a combination of chronic and acute stress.

Relationship factors have implicated by many writers (e.g., Kaplan, 1974), and their importance may seem obvious. Certainly one would expect that a man must be attracted to his partner if he is to become aroused. Clinical experience suggests that anger toward one's partner, or being in a relationship that is not characterized by trust, is a risk factor for Male Erectile Disorder. Relationships characterized by critical interactions are also believed to place a man at greater risk for erectile difficulties. To our knowledge, however, little research has been completed on the relationship between dyadic adjustment and Male Erectile Disorder.

Female Sexual Arousal Disorder

Description

Female Sexual Arousal Disorder refers to a lack of responsiveness to sexual stimulation in women. Previously, disorders of female sexual functioning (including desire, arousal, and orgasm disorders) were grouped into the global category of "frigidity." The term "frigidity" is imprecise, in that it does not distinguish among the three stages of sexual functioning. Furthermore, like its male counterpart "impotence," it is pejorative; consequently, it is no longer preferred by most sex therapists.[2]

Physiologically, Female Sexual Arousal Disorder is characterized by the absence of vaginal lubrication and expansion. In contrast to Male Erectile Disorder, these signs may go undetected or unreported by a woman, and certainly by her partner. Subjectively, this disorder is accompanied by a failure to find pleasure in sexual activities and by a lack of erotic feelings. (Here the distinction between Female Sexual Arousal Disorder and Hypoactive Sexual Desire Disorder [see Chapter 2] can become blurred.) Like other sexual dysfunctions, Female Sexual Arousal Disorder can be classified as "lifelong" or "acquired," and as "generalized" or "situational." The DSM-III-R criteria for Female Sexual Arousal Disorder are presented in Table 3-2.

According to Tollison and Adams (1979), a woman is not as likely as a man is to show an extremely negative response to an arousal disorder. These

TABLE 3-2. Diagnostic Criteria for Female Sexual Arousal Disorder (302.72)

A. Either (1) or (2):
   (1) persistent or recurrent partial or complete failure to attain or maintain the lubrication–swelling response of the sexual excitement until completion of the sexual activity
   (2) persistent or recurrent lack of a subjective sense of sexual excitement and pleasure in a female during sexual activity

B. Occurrence not exclusively during the course of another Axis I disorder (other than a Sexual Dysfunction), such as Major Depression.

Note. From the *Diagnostic and Statistical Manual of Mental Disorders* (3rd ed., rev., p. 294) by the American Psychiatric Association, 1987, Washington, DC: Author. Copyright 1987 by the American Psychiatric Association. Reprinted by permission.

authors suggest that women may respond with an array of feelings, ranging from casual acceptance to mild anxiety or depression. Compared to the more extreme reaction of men to erectile dysfunction, this lessened emotional response may reflect a kind of sexual "learned helplessness" (see Seligman, 1975); that is, women have traditionally been discouraged from seeking pleasure from sex, and thus are less likely to complain when their pleasure is compromised. Alternatively, because women can "solve" their arousal problem (i.e., by using a vaginal lubricant) much more easily than men can solve their problem, it may be that women's arousal problems have received less attention (Schover & Jensen, 1988).

Prevalence

Owing to the definitional and reporting problems noted above, it is difficult to meaningfully review the epidemiological literature regarding the prevalence of Female Sexual Arousal Disorder. Bancroft and Coles (1976) reported that 62% of females seeking sex therapy were diagnosed as experiencing "general unresponsiveness"; of course, it is not entirely clear whether this term referred to desire, arousal, or orgasm difficulties. In Hawton's (1982) replication, using the same assessment procedures and clinical site, this rate decreased to 51%. Frank et al. (1976) reported that 57% of females seeking sex therapy experienced arousal-phase disorders, whereas 80% of those seeking marital therapy experienced this difficulty.

Community studies suggest that arousal-phase disorders occur in 11% (Levine & Yost, 1976) to 48% (Frank et al., 1978) of the general population. According to Levine and Yost (1976), only 14% of the arousal disorders reported in their sample could be categorized as lifelong. No data are presented in DSM-III-R regarding the prevalence of this disorder.

Etiology

Little research has been conducted on the etiology of Female Sexual Arousal Disorder. Nevertheless, given that physiological arousal relies on vascular and neurological integrity, we can speculate that impairments to either system are likely to cause difficulties. Thus, pelvic vascular disease can result in lowered vaginal lubrication (Schover & Jensen, 1988); similarly, neurological impairment secondary to diabetes or multiple sclerosis may also impair arousal (e.g., Schreiner-Engel, Schiavi, Vietorisz, Eichel, & Smith, 1985). Hormonal changes, especially decreases in estrogen, can also increase vaginal dryness and may lead to dyspareunia (see Chapter 5). Such changes are likely following menopause or oophorectomy (see Chapter 9) or during lactation. It is not clear whether oral contraceptives interfere with normal vaginal lubrication (Bancroft, 1989). Virtually no evidence is available regarding the effects of medicinal and recreational drugs on female sexual arousal.

As with Male Erectile Disorder, numerous psychological factors have been identified as possible impediments to female arousal. Tollison and Adams (1979) list the following candidates: doubt, guilt, fear, anxiety, shame, conflict, embarrassment, tension, disgust, irritation, resentment, grief, hostility toward partner, and puritanical/moralistic upbringing.

The research on psychological factors has focused on emotional and cognitive factors. For example, in a clinical study, Morokoff and Heiman (1980) compared 11 women seeking treatment for Female Sexual Arousal Disorder to 11 normal control subjects. Both groups viewed an erotic film, listened to an erotic audiotape, and engaged in sexual fantasy while physiological and subjective arousal were monitored. Contrary to expectation, the two groups did not differ in their physiological response to erotic stimuli; however, dysfunctional subjects did rate their subjective arousal as less than that of the adequate-arousal group. As a result, the authors cautiously suggested that cognitive and affective factors are important to understanding Female Sexual Arousal Disorder.

Beggs, Calhoun, and Wolchik (1987) isolated the effects of a particular affective state (namely, anxiety); to do this, they compared sexual arousal occurring during sexual anxiety stimuli to sexual arousal occurring during sexual pleasure stimuli in 19 sexually functional women. Although both sets of stimuli enhanced arousal, increases in the pleasure condition were greater than those during the anxiety condition. Although intuitively appealing, these results are inconsistent with those obtained in previous research (e.g., Hoon, Wincze, & Hoon, 1977); thus, further research is clearly necessary.

Cognitive factors have also been studied. Adams, Haynes, and Brayer (1985) exposed 24 female subjects to baseline, erotic stimulus, and erotic stimulus plus distraction conditions. What they found was that erotic stimulation led to the expected increases in both subjective and physiological arousal, and that distraction attenuated both forms of arousal.

Clinical experience suggests that history of sexual abuse may be an important etiological factor (Becker, 1989). In our experience, the arousal dysfunction may be specific to the type of abuse that occurred. For example, a woman who was abused by her father by fondling may be responsive to kissing and intercourse, but nonresponsive to petting and foreplay. In other instances, the arousal dysfunction may be more global. Thus, careful and sensitive assessment of prior sexual experiences is warranted.

Relationship factors, including lack of adequate stimulation, poor communication, or timing, have been suggested by many writers, and their importance may seem obvious. Nevertheless, little research has been completed on the relationship between dyadic adjustment and Female Sexual Arousal Disorder.

Notes

[1] You should be aware, however, that "impotence" is universally used by urologists, and is the official search term used by both *Psychological Abstracts* and *Index Medicus*. When working with urologists and other physicians, you should try to get a more precise description of the problem, if possible.

[2] It is noteworthy that "frigidity" rarely appears in the current medical literature, whereas "impotence" appears regularly. As noted earlier, "impotence" is the official search word in two major data bases.

4

Orgasm Disorders

A good orgasm is, as one of our patients subjectively described it, "the fourth of July . . . fireworks and music and excitement . . . ecstasy." Hite (1976) asked women to describe their experiences of orgasm. One woman responded: "There are a few faint sparks, coming up to orgasm, and then I suddenly realize that it is going to catch fire and then I concentrate all my energies, both physical and mental, to quickly bring on the climax—which turns out to be a moment suspended in time, a hot rush—a sudden breathtaking dousing of all the nerves of my body in pleasure . . ." (p. 149).

More prosaic descriptions of orgasm mention the peaking of sexual pleasure, with the release of sexual tension and rhythmic contractions of the perineal muscles, anal sphincter, and pelvic reproductive organs (Masters & Johnson, 1966). Orgasm in men is accompanied by the emission of semen. In women, there are contractions of the wall of the outer third of the vagina.

Although we do not consider orgasm to be the *raison d'être,* the be-all-and-end-all of sexual functioning, many people do. Often clients will present with concerns about the absence of coital, multiple, or simultaneous orgasms; they feel disappointed that they cannot achieve what "everyone else" enjoys, and they seek a cure of their "deficits." As is discussed in the treatment chapters, such clients often benefit from some gently delivered education regarding normative data, and reassurance regarding their sexual health.

In this regard, it is important to know that many women do not regularly experience coital orgasms (Kaplan, 1989); that is, such women do not reach orgasm *solely* through intercourse, because the stimulation obtained by penile thrusting is not intense and direct enough to produce an orgasm. This is not a "dysfunction"—it is natural and normal. To repeat: The absence of orgasm during intercourse is not a sexual dysfunction! Even for the women who do experience orgasm during intercourse, these women may not have an orgasm during every "coital connection" (to borrow from Master and Johnson's terminology). Similarly, simultaneous orgasms make for excellent drama on the silver screen (or on the home-based VCR), but such sexual synchrony rarely occurs for most couples. Finally, multiple orgasms occur infrequently, in a very small percentage of women and men. For example, Kinsey, Pomeroy, Martin, and Gebhard (1953) reported that 14% of their female sample were capable of multiple orgasms on some occasions. Recent evidence presented by Dunn and Trost (1989) suggests that some men do not always experience detumescence following an orgasm, and that they have been able to experience a series of orgasms.

For many people, however, orgasm never occurs, it occurs only after prolonged stimulation, or it occurs with such rapidity that it causes concern for both partners. Thus, in this chapter we discuss the one female and the two male complaints about the orgasm phase—namely, Inhibited Female Orgasm, Inhibited Male Orgasm, and Premature Ejaculation.

Inhibited Female Orgasm

Definition

Among the disorders seen in women, Inhibited Female Orgasm is believed to be the most common. Part of this perception may result from the large variety of terms that have been used for this dysfunction. For example, Masters and Johnson (1970) described three types of orgasmic dysfunction: "masturbatory dysfunction," "coital dysfunction," and "random dysfunction." They also further specified "primary" and "secondary" orgasmic dysfunction. Kaplan (1974) described "absolute" and "situational" orgasmic dysfunction. Other terms that have been used include "anorgasmia" and "frigidity." Unfortunately, the variety of terms used has only served to increase confusion about the nature of the disorder.

In DSM-III-R, Inhibited Female Orgasm refers to the persistent or recurrent delay in, or absence of, orgasm in a female despite normal sexual arousal (see Table 4-1). Inhibited Female Orgasm may be acquired or lifelong, and it may be generalized or situational. Lifelong (which is typically also generalized) Inhibited Female Orgasm is equivalent to Masters and Johnson's primary orgasmic dysfunction and Kaplan's absolute dysfunction, and refers to women who have never experienced orgasm, alone or with a partner, through masturbation or through intercourse; lifelong Inhibited Female Orgasm is believed to be the most severe type, but, paradoxically, may be the most treatable (Wakefield, 1987). In contrast, acquired Inhibited Female Orgasm may be either situational (e.g., a woman may be orgasmic during masturbation but not during manual stimulation by, or intercourse with, her partner) or generalized (i.e., occurring across all sexual situations, partners, etc.).

TABLE 4-1. Diagnostic Criteria for Inhibited Female Orgasm (302.73)

A. Persistent or recurrent delay in, or absence of, orgasm in a female following a normal sexual excitement phase during sexual activity that the clinician judges to be adequate in focus, intensity, and duration. Some females are able to experience orgasm during noncoital clitoral stimulation, but are unable to experience it during coitus in the absence of manual clitoral stimulation. In most of these females, this represents a normal variation of the female sexual response and does not justify the diagnosis of Inhibited Female Orgasm. However, in some of these females, this does represent a psychological inhibition that justifies the diagnosis. This difficult judgment is assisted by a thorough sexual evaluation, which may even require a trial of treatment.

B. Occurrence not exclusively during the course of another Axis I disorder (other than a Sexual Dysfunction), such as Major Depression.

Note. From the *Diagnostic and Statistical Manual of Mental Disorders* (3rd ed., rev., p. 294) by the American Psychiatric Association, 1987, Washington, DC: Author. Copyright 1987 by the American Psychiatric Association. Reprinted by permission.

The DSM-III-R guidelines require considerable judgment on the part of the clinician to determine that adequate stimulation has occurred. This reliance upon clinical judgment has led some to argue that this diagnosis is particularly susceptible to gender-related biases (M. Kaplan, 1983; Wakefield, 1987).

Prevalence

As mentioned above, Inhibited Female Orgasm is typically cited as the most common sexual difficulty presented to practitioners (e.g., Burnap & Golden, 1967; Derogatis, Fagan, Schmidt, Wise, & Gilden, 1986; Kaplan, 1974). In sex therapy clinics, the frequency of Inhibited Female Orgasm as the presenting problem ranges from 18% (Bancroft & Coles, 1976) to 76% (Frank et al., 1976). The Bancroft and Coles (1976) study was replicated subsequently by Hawton (1982) in the same clinic using the same assessment procedures. Hawton found an orgasmic dysfunction rate of 24%, suggesting a slight increase in this dysfunction over the 6 years. However, the differential prevalence rates of Bancroft and Coles (1976) and Hawton (1982) compared to those of Frank et al. (1976) are puzzling. Since both the Frank et al. (1976) and the Bancroft and Coles (1976) studies were carried out in the same year, it is unlikely that the different rates reflect a change over time. One difference between the Bancroft and Coles (1976)/Hawton (1982) studies and the Frank et al. (1976) study was the method of assessment—namely, interview versus self-report questionnaire. A second difference among these studies involves the samples; Frank et al. (1976) conducted their study in the United States, whereas Bancroft and Coles/Hawton completed their evaluation in the United Kingdom. Perhaps cultural differences may be important in interpreting the differential prevalence rates. A fourth study of a sex clinic sample, conducted by Renshaw (1988) in the United States between 1972 and 1987, revealed a primary orgasmic dysfunction rate of 32% and a secondary orgasmic dysfunction rate of 37%. These rates are also slightly higher than those of Hawton (1982) and Bancroft and Coles (1976).

In community studies, the rate of Inhibited Female Orgasm has also varied. Kinsey et al. (1953) found that 10% of all women reported that they had never experienced orgasm (i.e., lifelong orgasmic dysfunction). Later, Levine and Yost (1976) found that 5% of their subjects were anorgasmic, perhaps indicating a decrease over time in the number of women who had never experienced orgasm. In studies conducted in the 1970s, which focused on women who never or infrequently experienced orgasm, the rates ranged from 15% to 20% (Ard, 1977; Athanasiou, Shaver, & Tavris, 1970; Hunt, 1974). Related findings indicated that unmarried women were more likely to experience dysfunction (Kinsey et al., 1953), as were women with a lesser socioeconomic status (SES; Levine & Yost, 1976). Hite (1976) reports that 4% of women are anorgasmic during masturbation, whereas as many as 70% are during coitus.

Etiology

Morokoff (1978) has provided an excellent overview of the determinants of female orgasm. Among the biological variables she identified in 1978, the condition of the pubococcygeus muscle seemed to be the one most likely to be associated with Inhibited Female Orgasm. Subsequent research, however, has challenged her conclusion. Chambless et al. (1982) investigated the relationship of pubococcygeus condition to orgasmic responsiveness in 102 nonclinical subjects. Contrary to expectation, pubococcygeus strength was not associated with frequency or self-reported intensity of orgasm. Moreover, women with greater pubococcygeus strength did not report that vaginal stimulation contributed more to the attainment of orgasm; nor did these subjects rate vaginal sensations during intercourse as more pleasurable. A follow-up intervention study (Chambless et al., 1984) supported these earlier findings. In the 1984 study, females with a low frequency of coital orgasm were taught to use Kegel exercises to improve their pubococcygeus strength. Despite a significant increase in pubococcygeus strength, no improvement in coital orgasm frequency was observed.

The effects of hormonal variation on orgasm are also unclear, especially in older women. Sherwin (1985) studied eight women who had been maintained on a combined estrogen–androgen drug since undergoing hysterectomy (i.e., removal of the uterus) and bilateral oophorectomy (i.e., removal of the ovaries) 2 years previously. Although hormone replacement did influence sexual desire and arousal, rates of orgasm were unchanged. Similar findings were reported by Sherwin, Gelfand, and Brender (1985). However, in a third study, Sherwin and Gelfand (1987) found that orgasm rates were enhanced following the administration of the estrogen–androgen preparation.

There is evidence that the use of alcohol and other drugs may interfere with orgasmic functioning. Wilsnack (1984) reviewed the literature to determine the relationship between alcohol consumption and sexual dysfunction. On the basis of numerous clinical reports and laboratory research, she concluded that rates of inhibited female orgasm are higher in alcoholic women, relative to rates found among normative samples (i.e., Kinsey et al., 1953). Among the better studies she reviewed was one conducted by Malatesta, Pollack, Crotty, and Peacock (1982). These authors investigated the effect of acute intoxication on female orgasmic response. The results indicated that higher blood alcohol concentrations were associated with longer orgasmic latencies and decreased subjective intensity of orgasm.

In her 1978 review, Morokoff also examined the evidence for numerous social and cultural determinants of orgasmic capacity. Considered in this category were factors such as length of marriage, decade of birth, educational level, SES, and religious affiliation. Of these variables, the most significant relationship was that between decade of birth and orgasmic experience; that is, being born later in the century was related to higher frequency of orgasm.

Morokoff's (1978) review also considered psychological and interpersonal factors. However, factors as diverse as early childhood experience, global personality structure, and sexual techniques of the woman's partner did not appear to be strongly related to orgasmic functioning. Subsequent research has also addressed some of these factors.

McGovern, Stewart, and LoPiccolo (1975) compared six cases of lifelong Inhibited Female Orgasm with six cases of acquired Inhibited Female Orgasm. These two groups did not differ with regard to age, overall physical health, length of married life, or most aspects of sexual behavior. Two important differences did emerge. First, women with the acquired disorder were much more dissatisfied with their marital relationships than were women with the lifelong disorder. Second, women with acquired Inhibited Female Orgasm had an established and constrained pattern of orgasmic release; that is, most of these women could reach orgasm through one rigid and narrowly constrained method of masturbation. The authors suggested that this pattern may have been maladaptive, especially with regard to treatment-assisted change.

Kilmann et al. (1984) compared 48 couples in which the woman had acquired Inhibited Female Orgasm to 63 "sexually satisfied" couples. Compared to satisfied couples, Inhibited Female Orgasm couples reported greater dissastisfaction with the frequency and range of their sexual activities. Within the Inhibited Female Orgasm group, males reported low self-acceptance as well as low mate acceptance; females reported lower self-acceptance. Males in the Inhibited Female Orgasm couples also exhibited less accurate knowledge of their partners' sexual preferences.

Derogatis and his colleagues have investigated the relationship between orgasmic functioning and psychopathology. In two early studies, women with Inhibited Female Orgasm were found to have a psychological profile characterized by high levels of distress (Derogatis & Meyer, 1979; Derogatis, Meyer, & King, 1981); however, great heterogeneity in symptom distress was evident. Therefore, in a more recent study (Derogatis et al., 1986), two subtypes of Inhibited Female Orgasm were identified. One subtype included women who were relatively well informed about sexuality, possessed more liberal sexual attitudes, had higher levels of desire, and reported a richer fantasy life. Derogatis et al. (1986) speculated that the etiology of Inhibited Female Orgasm in these women was more likely to involve either biological or interpersonal factors. In contrast, the second subtype included women who possessed feelings of inferiority, negative body images, and higher levels of psychological symptoms. The authors speculated that the principal etiology for this subtype was psychogenic.

Inhibited Male Orgasm

Definition

What do the terms "blue balls," "dry runs," "aspermatism," "ejaculatory incompetence," "retarded ejaculation," "absence of ejaculation," "ejaculatory impotence," "ejaculatory inhibition," and "Inhibited Male Orgasm" have in common? All of these phrases have all been used to describe the problem some men have in reaching orgasm. Rather than refer to such clients' difficulty as "retarded," "incompetent," "impotent," or "inhibited," all of which have either a pejorative or a theoretical slant, we would prefer simply to describe the problem directly and without inference, thus: "delayed or absent male orgasm." Despite our preference, however, the most common phrase you will encounter in clinical settings is that provided in DSM-III-R—namely, "Inhibited Male Orgasm."

Inhibited Male Orgasm refers to the persistent difficulty or inability to achieve orgasm despite the presence of adequate desire, arousal, and stimulation (see Table 4-2). Most commonly, however, the term refers to a condition in which a man is not able to ejaculate with his partner, even though he is able to obtain an erection, and may be able to ejaculate during masturbation or sleep. (Nocturnal emissions, or "wet dreams" as they are commonly called,

TABLE 4-2. Diagnostic Criteria for Inhibited Male Orgasm (302.74)

A. Persistent or recurrent delay in, or absence of, orgasm in a male following a normal sexual excitement phase during sexual activity that the clinician, taking into account the person's age, judges to be adequate in focus, intensity, and duration. This failure to achieve orgasm is usually restricted to an inability to reach orgasm in the vagina, with orgasm possible with other types of stimulation, such as masturbation.

B. Occurrence not exclusively during the course of another Axis I disorder (other than a Sexual Dysfunction), such as Major Depression.

Note. From the *Diagnostic and Statistical Manual of Mental Disorders* (3rd ed., rev., p. 295) by the American Psychiatric Association, 1987, Washington, DC: Author. Copyright 1987 by the American Psychiatric Association. Reprinted by permission.

occur commonly in men. By the age of 40, about 80% of all men have experienced an orgasm during their sleep; see Kinsey et al., 1948.) Like other sexual dysfunctions, Inhibited Male Orgasm can be lifelong or acquired, generalized or specific.

It is important to distinguish between Inhibited Male Orgasm and "retrograde ejaculation." The latter difficulty occurs as a result of some medications (e.g., anticholinergic drugs), after some (but not all) prostate surgeries, and occasionally as a consequence of diabetic neuropathy. With retrograde ejaculation, a man does ejaculate and experiences orgasm, but the ejaculatory fluid travels backward (into the bladder) rather than forward and out the urethra. The sensation of orgasm is perserved for most men who experience retrograde ejaculation, although some do report a slight diminution in pleasurable sensation.

It is also important to distinguish between emission and ejaculation. Ejaculation has three stages: (1) emission, (2) bladder neck closure, and (3) ejaculation proper (Segraves et al., 1985). Emission refers to the release of the ejaculate into the pelvic urethra; this release is caused by the contraction of the vas deferens, seminal vesicles, and smooth muscle of the prostate. Bladder neck closure prevents retrograde ejaculation. Finally, ejaculation proper results from contractions of the bulbocavernosus, ischiocavernosus, and urethral muscles (Segraves et al., 1985).

Prevalence

Inhibited Male Orgasm is believed to be relatively rare, and may be the dysfunction least often encountered in clinical practice. Masters and Johnson (1970) reported only 17 cases of Inhibited Male Orgasm out of 448 male sexual dysfunction cases they assessed and treated in an 11-year period. Other clinical studies reveal that the dysfunction accounts for 3–8% of the cases presenting for treatment (Bancroft & Coles, 1976; Frank et al., 1976; Hawton, 1982; Renshaw, 1988). A higher estimate was reported by Frank et al. (1976), who found that 17% of males seeking marital therapy were diagnosed as experiencing Inhibited Male Orgasm. (This higher prevalence in couples with marital difficulties may signal an etiological risk factor.)

Community prevalence studies report dysfunction rates as ranging from 4% to 10% (Frank et al., 1978; Nettelbladt & Uddenberg, 1979).

As we indicate below for premature ejaculation, the definition that is used to describe Inhibited Male Orgasm may help to account for the different rates that have been observed. To date, for example, there is no consensus as to whether it should be defined in terms of the amount of time required, or the man's subjective feeling of not controlling the orgasmic event.

Overall, however, it is apparent that Inhibited Male Orgasm is one of the least common dysfunctions among males, both in clinical and in community samples.

Etiology

Due in part to its infrequent occurrence, very little systematic research has been reported on the cause(s) of Inhibited Male Orgasm. Instead, the literature contains numerous case studies, each of which seems to put forth its own etiological formulation. At the psychological level of analysis, the possible etiologies that have been identified include fear (of castration, pregnancy, or commitment); performance anxiety and "spectatoring"; strict religious proscriptions; previous sexual traumas; and hostility (toward one's partner or oneself). We, too, can contribute an interesting case example to the literature.

Together, we treated a middle-aged man who complained of Inhibited Male Orgasm. This patient was an articulate, highly intelligent Viet Nam war veteran who was very passionate about his partner; both were very commited to the relationship, and engaged in a wide variety of stimulating and creative sexual activities. Nevertheless, the man was unable to ejaculate. Related to this difficulty, in our judgment, was the man's Post-traumatic Stress Disorder. He reported numerous difficulties with "giving up control" (e.g., falling asleep). He was hypervigilant and found it difficult to relax under any circumstances, even during coitus.

Relationship factors have also been implicated in Inhibited Male Orgasm. A man may be ambivalent about his commitment to the relationship, or he may be anorgasmic as a way of assuming power in a troubled relationship. Shull and Sprenkle (1980) suggest that a simpler relationship problem may also be common—namely, inadequate stimulation. They suggest that the partners may not have created the proper ambience, are using inadequate stimulation techniques, or are engaged in a sexual ritual that has lost it romance.

Thus, it appears that there many be many pathways to Inhibited Male Orgasm. Indeed, after reviewing the psychosocial literature, Shull and Sprenkle (1980) concluded: "If the literature is searched long enough, almost any and every psychological problem can be associated with [Inhibited Male Orgasm]" (p. 239). Despite the richness of these clinical hypotheses, virtually no systematic research has been conducted on the individual or relationship factors described above.

Similarly, at the biological level of analysis, Munjack and Kanno (1979) reviewed the medical literature for possible drug-related etiologies, and identified over 20 different drugs that have been associated with this disorder. Primary culprits include the anticholinergic, antiadrenergic, antihypertensive, and psychoactive drugs. These findings make it abundantly clear that our knowledge about the etiology of Inhibited Male Orgasm is incomplete.

Premature Ejaculation

Definition

Some men complain that they arrive at orgasm too rapidly. What is "too rapidly"? In some cases, ejaculation occurs before the man has entered his partner. Obviously, this would be a serious problem if conception was the goal. In other cases, the man ejaculates "shortly after" intromission. Because the latter phrasing is still imprecise, several theorists have attempted to develop a more precise definition. For example, Masters and Johnson (1970) suggested that premature ejaculation be diagnosed when a man "cannot control his ejaculatory process for a sufficient length of time during intravaginal containment to satisfy his partner in at least 50 percent of their coital connections" (p. 92). The problem with this definition is that the majority of women, perhaps as many as 75%, cannot reach orgasm through intercourse regardless of how long it lasts!

In 1987, the American Psychiatric Association suggested in DSM-III-R that Premature Ejaculation be defined as shown in Table 4-3. Kaplan (1989) has expanded upon one phrase in the DSM-III-R definition, "before the person wishes it," by emphasing the notion of voluntary control over ejaculation. According to her, "the essential feature of [premature ejaculation] is that the man lacks adequate voluntary ejaculatory control with the result that he climaxes involuntarily before he wishes to" (p. 8). She also emphasizes that ejaculatory control should be "natural, easy, and voluntary," and that a man should be able to stay at the plateau level of sexual arousal (in Masters and

TABLE 4-3. Diagnostic Criteria for Premature Ejaculation (302.75)

Persistent or recurrent ejaculation with minimal sexual stimulation or before, upon, or shortly after penetration and before the person wishes it. The clinician must take into account factors that affect duration of the excitement phase, such as age, novelty of the sexual partner or situation, and frequency of sexual activity.

Note. From the *Diagnostic and Statistical Manual of Mental Disorders* (3rd ed., rev., p. 295) by the American Psychiatric Association, 1987, Washington, DC: Author. Copyright 1987 by the American Psychiatric Association. Reprinted by permission.

Johnson's stage model) to allow him to savor the pleasure of his impending orgasm.

In addition to the differences of opinion regarding definition, another debate involves consideration of whether premature ejaculation should even be considered a dysfunction. As noted by Kinsey et al. (1948), the majority of mammals ejaculate at intromission or shortly thereafter. Interviews conducted by Kinsey's group indicated that 75% of their sample of over 6,000 men ejaculated within 2 minutes of vaginal containment. On the basis of these two sources of information, Kinsey and his colleagues went on to suggest that from an evolutionary perspective, such a quick and intense ejaculatory response was probably adaptive and, in this sense, "superior." More recently, a similiar position has been argued by Hong (1984); after reviewing the literature, Hong concluded that "premature ejaculation by itself should not be of clinical concern unless it is extreme, such as occurring before intromission" (p. 120). To those who might ask about the partner's pleasure, Hong went on to say that "sexual fulfillment in women can be achieved by other and perhaps better means."

These debates notwithstanding, many men are troubled by premature ejaculation, and this difficulty can have a destructive effect on a man, his partner, and their relationship (see Case 6 in Chapter 10). Kaplan (1989) suggests that premature ejaculators are at risk for developing a general sense of inadequacy and failure, depression, and other sexual dysfunctions (notably, erectile dysfunction and Hypoactive Sexual Desire Disorder). Some men may not understand why they have premature ejaculation and make inappropriate inferences about their difficulty, such as "I must really be selfish." One of our patients construed his premature ejaculation as a sign that he was a latent homosexual. Moreover, because the thought of being homosexual was morally repulsive to him, he coped with this information by excessive drinking, which eventually cost him his job and his family.

Although most women enjoy foreplay and direct clitoral stimulation, others believe that coital stimulation is "better," or that intercourse is the only acceptable form of sexual activity. Such women will inevitably be disappointed by, and may lose interest in, sexual intercourse. Partners, too, can make inappropriate inferences (e.g., "I must not be very attractive if he wants to get it over so quick," or "He does not love me"). It is not difficult to see how such outcomes, especially if combined with other concerns, can have undesirable effects on a relationship.

Yet another side effect of premature ejaculation is that a man may try to prolong his "staying power" by any of several home remedies. Some may try to postpone orgasm by holding back, physically or emotionally. Others will try to distract themselves from their pleasurable sensations by thinking of financial concerns or other difficulties. A few may apply anesthetic creams, multiple condoms, or mechanical devices to their penises in an effort to deaden their physiological sensitivity. These "solutions" may have iatrogenic effects, and may also lead to erectile problems.

Overall, despite its relatively minor nature, Premature Ejaculation can have far-reaching and negative consequences for many people.

Prevalence

As with all of the other sexual dysfunctions we have discussed, the prevalence of premature ejaculation is difficult to determine. Nevertheless, it is typically cited as being the most common sexual dysfunction (e.g., Kaplan, 1974, p. 289). Consistent with this view, Malatesta and Adams (1984) indicated that 60% of the men entering sex therapy did so with the presenting problem of being premature ejaculation.

Research estimates of the frequency of premature ejaculation in the general population suggest that 36% (Frank et al., 1978) to 38% (Nettelbladt & Uddenberg, 1979) report difficulty controlling ejaculation and reaching orgasm too fast on a regular basis. Other estimates have been more conservative; for example, Catalan, Bradley, Gallwey, and Hawton (1981) found that 13% of their subjects were premature ejaculators. From a reanalysis of the Kinsey data, Gebhard and Johnson (1979) determined that nearly 4% of the men interviewed reported ejaculating within 1 minute of intromission. However, it is not known what percentage of these men believed that they were unable to control their ejaculations, or what percentage felt that they experienced orgasm too quickly.

Two interesting asides occur to us at this point. The first is based upon an empirical finding; that is, Frank et al. (1978) found that 11% of the women in their sample reported that they reached orgasm "too quickly." However, we have no "Premature Female Orgasm" in DSM-III-R or other diagnostic schemes. Perhaps this is because women can continue coitus after orgasm; if fact, they may even experience additional orgasms. In contrast, men are less

likely to be able to continue intercourse once they have ejaculated, as detumescence is likely.

The second involves one unanticipated benefit of aging. That is, there is
a tendency for young men to ejaculate quickly, and the prevalence of premature ejaculation is believed to decrease with advancing age (Masters &
Johnson, 1970, p. 318).

Etiology

Several hypotheses have been proffered to explain how premature ejaculation
may develop. As already mentioned, premature ejaculation may reflect a
physiological characteristic that is adaptive, and therefore has been preserved
through evolution. This characteristic might be expressed as a kind of
"hypersensitivity" to penile stimulation (e.g., Assalian, 1988; Damrav,
1963). Alternatively, premature ejaculation may reflect a man's poorly developed sensory awareness; that is, regardless of what his genital sensitivity
might be, the man with premature ejaculation may fail to develop an appreciation of when he is close to the point of ejaculatory inevitablity (Kaplan,
1989). Yet a third view is that premature ejaculation develops as a result of
numerous adolescent/young adult practices (e.g., visiting a prostitute who
encourages ejaculatory rapidity, having sex in the back seat of a car or other
setting not conducive to relaxed lovemaking) that condition a rapid ejaculatory response (Masters & Johnson, 1970).

Fortunately, there are some data that bear on these hypotheses. For
example, Spiess, Geer, and O'Donohue (1984) compared 10 premature ejaculators with 14 control subjects. Subjects were interviewed regarding their
sexual experiences, and then participated in a laboratory assessment in which
they were exposed to tape-recorded stories, erotic slides, and sexual fantasy;
their physiological responses and self-reported arousal were assessed. The
premature ejaculators were compared to the controls in order to evaluate the
following hypotheses:

- Men with premature ejaculation become aroused faster.
- Men with premature ejaculation show more sexual arousal to the same
  stimuli/situations.
- Men with premature ejaculation get sexually aroused in more potential
  sexual situations.
- Men with premature ejaculation make less accurate judgments about
  their sexual arousal.
- Men with premature ejaculation ejaculate at a lower level of arousal.
- The latency of ejaculation is inversely related to the period of absti-
  nence from intercourse/ejaculation.

• Men with premature ejaculation have longer periods of abstinence from intercourse/ejaculation than do men without premature ejaculation.

Of these hypotheses, only the last three were supported; that is, the results obtained suggested that the premature ejaculators did ejaculate at lower levels of sexual arousal, and did have longer periods of abstinence from intercourse and ejaculation, than did the controls. Also, there was an inverse relationship between period of abstinence from intercourse/ejaculation and ejaculatory latency. Interestingly, the latter two findings have been challenged by more recent research conducted by Strassberg, Kelly, Carroll, and Kircher (1987).

Strassberg et al. (1987) studied 13 men with premature ejaculation and 13 control subjects. All subjects were shown videotaped erotica in the laboratory while subjective arousal and penile tumescence measures were collected continuously. Contrary to expectation, premature ejaculators and control subjects did not differ on latency, amplitude, rise time, and rise rate of either subjective or physiological arousal. Also contrary to expectation, both groups showed significant positive correlations between the physiological and subjective measures of arousal. Interestingly, these data refute previous notions that men with premature ejaculation are simply unable to assess their level of sexual arousal correctly (cf. Kaplan, 1989). Comparison of premature ejaculators with controls on items from the Sexual Response Inventory revealed that, as expected, the premature ejaculators required less time to, and had less control over, orgasm—both during masturbation and during intercourse (see Table 4-4). Contrary to the data presented by Spiess et al. (1984), the rates of sexual activity did not differ between premature ejaculators and controls. The authors argue for a diathesis–stress model, in which pre-existing somatic vulnerability or hypersensitivity to physical stimulation interacts with anxiety and fear of evaluation.

In our experience, premature ejaculation can also be a problem of sexual misunderstanding (see Case 6 in Chapter 10). That is, very often, either partner may identify the rate of ejaculation as premature almost without reference to the actual time from intromission. Subsequently, there is an intense focus on the rate of ejaculation; if it occurs before they expect, then the partners throw up their hands in disgust and stop what they are doing. Of course, this kind of reaction exacerbates the "problem" because orgasm is no longer enjoyed, but looked upon as something to fear and avoid.

A case example will serve to illustrate this point. We treated a couple in which the male was a handsome 26-year-old owner of a body-building studio, and the female was a 24-year-old model and former beauty queen. She told him that her former lover always lasted between 30 and 60 minutes after intromission before ejaculation. The male in this couple was dejected and felt inadequate because he lasted "only" 15 or 20 minutes! By providing

TABLE 4-4. Means and Standard Deviations in Premature Ejaculators versus Normal Controls

Variable	Premature ejaculators	Controls
Time to orgasm during intercourse (in minutes)	1.94 (0.88)***	11.85 (9.92)
Control of orgasm during intercourse (higher = more)	2.33 (1.07)***	3.77 (0.72)
Time to orgasm during masturbation (in minutes)	3.42 (2.54)**	8.84 (6.12)
Control of orgasm during masturbation (higher = more)	3.50 (1.38)*	4.46 (0.66)
Frequency of intercourse (per week)	3.98 (3.15)	2.29 (1.48)
Frequency of masturbation (per month)	7.25 (7.85)	6.96 (6.71)

Note. The data are from Strassberg, Kelly, Carroll, and Kircher (1987).
*$p < .05$.
** $p < .01$.
*** $p < .005$.

this couple with normative information about length of time to ejaculation, we were able to reduce both partners' concerns. The point we wish to make, however, is that misinformation, myths, and "tall tales" persist and can lead to considerable distress. Fortuntately, these problems can easily be solved with accurate information from a respected authority.

5

Sexual Pain Disorders

Many jokes are made about sex and pain. These jokes typically evoke notions of sadomasochism, and intimate that the association between sex and pain brings pleasure. However, in the sexual pain disorders, nothing could be further from the truth. In this chapter, two related disorders are considered: dyspareunia and vaginismus. Both include a component of genital pain, represent common clinical complaints (especially among women), and present unique diagnostic challenges. We wish to emphasize that these dysfunctions have *nothing* in common with sexual sadism or masochism—two paraphilias that involve pain and suffering to enhance sexual pleasure.

Dyspareunia

Definition

"Dyspareunia" is derived from the Greek word, *dyspareunos,* which means "unhappily mated as bedfellows." This euphemism is currently used, however, to refer specifically to a recurrent pattern of genital pain that occurs before, during, or after coitus. The criteria for a DSM-III-R diagnosis of Dyspareunia are presented in Table 5-1. Most commonly, the pain is experienced during intercourse. Like other dysfunctions, dyspareunia may be characterized as lifelong or acquired, and as generalized or situational. It is believed to be more common in women (Masters & Johnson, 1970), although few data bear directly on this issue (see the "Prevalence" section). Because of the sparse literature on dyspareunia in men, most of our discussion focuses on dyspareunia in women.

Pain, a subjective experience, eludes careful measurement and description. Thus, many different accounts of the phenomenology of dyspareunia are

TABLE 5-1. Diagnostic Criteria for Dyspareunia (302.76)

A. Recurrent or persistent genital pain in either a male or a female before, during, or after sexual intercourse.

B. The disturbance is not caused exclusively by lack of lubrication or by Vaginismus.

Note. From the *Diagnostic and Statistical Manual of Mental Disorders* (3rd ed., rev., p. 295) by the American Psychiatric Association, 1987, Washington, DC: Author. Copyright 1987 by the American Psychiatric Association. Reprinted by permission.

available. Abarbanel (1978) suggests that these accounts may be summarized into four categories: (1) the perception of a momentary sharp pain of varying intensity, (2) intermittent painful twinges, (3) repeated intense discomfort, and/or (4) an aching sensation. The pain may also be described as superficial or deep. In addition to the immediate discomfort and the accompanying distress this causes, dyspareunia places a woman at risk for the development of vaginismus (see below), as well as secondary desire, arousal, and orgasm dysfunctions.

Complaints of sexual pain during intercourse present what may be the most challenging diagnosis for health care professionals. Clearly, differential diagnosis must begin with a thorough physical examination by a competent physician. A large number of physical factors (see "Etiology") must be assessed and ruled out prior to embarking upon a psychosocially oriented intervention. However, as Masters and Johnson (1970) eloquently point out, "even after an adequate pelvic examination, the therapist frequently cannot be sure whether the patient is complaining of definitive but undiagnosed pelvic pathology or whether, as has been true countless thousands of times, a sexually dysfunctional woman is using the symptomatology of pain as a means of escaping completely or at least reducing markedly the number of unwelcome sexual encounters in her marriage" (pp. 266–267). In some cases it will be possible to identify a clear precipitant, but in most it will have to be assumed that a combined etiology is operative.

Prevalence

The incidence and prevalence of dyspareunia are difficult to determine. Community prevalence studies of women have provided estimates ranging from 8% (Schover, 1981; Osborn, Hawton, & Gath, 1988) to 33.5% (Glatt, Zinner, & McCormack, 1990). Glatt and his colleagues (1990) surveyed 313 women, most of whom were reported to be in their early 30s. Thirty-nine percent of their sample reported that they had never had dyspareunia. More surprising, however, was the finding that 27.5% of the women had had dyspareunia at some point in their lives but that it had resolved; and the finding that 33.5% still had dyspareunia. Of these, nearly half reported that they had had dyspareunia for their entire active sex lives! Many of the women with dyspareunia had not discussed this problem with a professional, and most were unaware of the cause of their difficulty.

Reports from sex therapy settings have provided prevalence estimates in women ranging from 3% (Hawton, 1982) to 5% (Renshaw, 1988). Compared to the community estimates cited above, this lower clinical rate suggests that women may be somewhat disinclined to seek treatment for sexually related pain; alternatively, women may be more likely to interpret pain as a "medical" symptom, and to report it to a physician rather than to a sex therapist. Indeed, this latter hypothesis was supported by Burnap and Golden (1967) who found that dyspareunia was commonly reported to general practitioners, and by Steege (1984), who suggests that painful intercourse is the most common sexual complaint received by obstetricians/gynecologists.

To our knowledge, few data are available on the frequency of dyspareunia in men. Bancroft (1989) reports that only 1% of the men seen in his clinic in Edinburgh had dyspareunia as their primary complaint, whereas Diokno, Brown, and Herzog (1990) found that 1.4% of men aged 60 years and older reported pain during intercourse. In our clinical experience, pain in men is often associated with a urinary tract infection. The pain may occur during urination as well as during ejaculation. Men who are uncircumcised may also describe pain during intercourse. Finally, Peyronie's disease is sometimes associated with pain during erection. In all cases of reported pain in men, the client should be referred to a urologist for further evaluation.

Etiology

As suggested above, a large number of physical factors must be considered when assessing dyspareunia. Bancroft (1989) suggests that an important and often overlooked cause of dyspareunia is tender scarring following either episiotomy or vaginal repair operations. Among the many other candidates are hymeneal remnants, the presence of a pelvic tumor, prolapsed ovaries, endometriosis, and pelvic inflammatory diseases. (For a more comprehensive list of potential causes, see Sandberg & Quevillion, 1987.)

Recently, increased attention has been paid to vulvar vestibulitis, a condition that involves multiple tiny erythematous sores in the vulvar vestibule (Friedrich, 1987; Woodruff & Parmley, 1983). Women with this condition report intense superficial pain. The etiology of vulvar vestibulitis itself remains unknown; however, surgery combined with sex therapy has been successful in selected cases (D. D. Youngs, personal communication, October 9, 1990).

In women using oral contraceptives, or in pregnant and postmenopausal women (see Reamy & White, 1985; Wallis, 1987), hormonal changes (i.e., decreased estrogen) may lead to reduced vaginal lubrication and resultant soreness and irritation during penetration. Cancer treatments that involve radiation to the pelvis and/or removal of the ovaries (see Chapter 9) also reduce estrogen production and increase the risk of dyspareunia. Obviously, mental health professionals are not qualified to evaluate such conditions, but such assessments should constitute part of a comprehensive biopsychosocial intake.

Psychosocial problems may lead to a complaint of coital pain or may exacerbate pre-existing discomfort. Individual risk factors such as anxiety, fear, and depression, as well as religious orthodoxy, decreased self-esteem, and poor body image, have all been suggested (Reamy & White, 1985). Interpersonal factors, including anger at one's partner, inadequate communication, and distrust, should also be considered. Moreover, dyspareunia may be most likely to occur in couples where the male partner is overly unassertive and accommodating. Thus, such couples' transactional style may place them at risk. (We do not mean to imply that women with dyspareunia should be treated more forcefully by their partners; we do wish to suggest that the overly sensitive nature of the partners in these cases may be worth noticing.)

Finally, whenever there is a complaint of genital pain, especially in the absence of confirmed organic pathology, you need to determine whether your client might be a survivor of sexual abuse or trauma. Complaints of pain during intercourse or other sexual activity can be an important sign of such a history.

Vaginismus

Definition

"Vaginismus" is usually defined as the involuntary spasm of the pelvic muscles located in the outer third of the vaginal barrel; the muscle groups affected include the perineal muscles and the levator ani muscles, although in severe cases the adductors of the thighs, the rectus abdominis, and the gluteus muscles may also be involved (Lamont, 1978). In the DSM-III-R criteria for a diagnosis of Vaginismus, it is further stipulated that the spasms be recurrent or persistent, and that they interfere with intercourse (see Table 5-2).

TABLE 5-2. Diagnostic Criteria for Vaginismus (306.51)

A. Recurrent or persistent involuntary spasm of the musculature of the outer third of the vagina that interferes with coitus.

B. The disturbance is not caused exclusively by a physical disorder, and is not due to another Axis I disorder.

Note. From the *Diagnostic and Statistical Manual of Mental Disorders* (3rd ed., rev., p. 295) by the American Psychiatric Association, 1987, Washington, DC: Author. Copyright 1987 by the American Psychiatric Association. Reprinted by permission.

Typically, the muscle spasms occur in anticipation of intercourse or during intromission. Thus, when penile penetration is attempted, couples report that the sensation is as if "the penis hits a 'brick wall' about one inch inside the vagina" (Lamont, 1978, p. 633). However, spasms may also occur during pelvic or self-examination; in extreme cases, this reflex contraction may follow attempts to insert anything into the vagina, including tampons, finger(s), or a speculum.

Differential diagnosis of vaginismus (i.e., distinguishing it from dyspareunia, Sexual Aversion Disorder, and even Hypoactive Sexual Desire Disorder) can be extremely difficult. Thus, we do *not* recommend that diagnosis be made solely on the basis of patient or partner self-report. Instead, we encourage confirmation of this dysfunction by pelvic examination, performed by a physician (preferably an experienced and sensitive female gynecologist). The primary purpose of this examination is to rule out organic pathology. However, it can also be useful to demonstrate the global nature of the response. As Bancroft (1989) noted, the partner should be present for educational purposes—that is, to correct misinformation and to alleviate fears and other negative emotions. It should be noted, however, that a danger of this approach is that occasionally a woman will be able to tolerate a gynecological exam, but will still exhibit vaginismus during intercourse (Tollison & Adams, 1979). If this possibility is not anticipated and addressed immediately, the presence of the partner could backfire.

A woman with vaginismus will usually be quite distressed about these involunatry spasms, over which she perceives that she has no control. The sense of embarrassment and frustration may be enhanced if the woman remains sexually responsive, which is likely. For example, Duddle (1977) reported on 30 women seeking treatment for vaginismus. Of these, 56% were orgasmic during petting, 41% in dreams, and 28% through masturbation. Simply providing information of this nature can be therapeutic. Remember: There are many myths regarding sexuality. In the absence of opportunities to talk openly with an expert, many people will develop self-critical beliefs about their experience.

Prevalence

Estimates of the prevalence of vaginismus in sexual dysfunction clinics have ranged from 5% to 42% of the patients presenting for sex therapy (Bancroft & Coles, 1976; Hawton, 1982; Masters & Johnson, 1970; O'Sullivan, 1979; Renshaw, 1988). The lowest estimate (i.e., 5%) comes from Renshaw (1988), but her criteria were the most stringent; that is, she counted only women who complained solely of vaginismus in her estimate. Women with other concurrent (i.e., comorbid) disorders (e.g., orgasmic dysfunction) were counted separately. Thus, Renshaw's estimate may be artificially low. The highest estimate (i.e., 42%) comes from O'Sullivan (1979) in Ireland, and may be the product of factors unique to the Irish culture (see below). Finally, data from these reports probably underestimate the prevalence of vaginismus; many women with vaginismus initially seek help through fertility clinics because vaginismus is believed to be a leading cause of the nonconsummation of marriage (see Barnes, 1981; Hawton, 1985). Thus, on the basis of data from clinic samples, it would appear that vaginismus is not an uncommon disorder.

To our knowledge, no broad-based epidemiological surveys have provided data on the prevalence of vaginismus in the general population. However, clinic samples indicate that there may be important differences in the prevalence of vaginismus across cultures. J. Barnes (personal communication, April 11, 1988) believes that lifelong vaginismus is an extremely rare clinical entity in North America and in most of Western Europe, but that it is not uncommon in Ireland, Eastern Europe, and Latin America. Barnes (1981, 1986a, 1986b) has conducted research with Irish women, and suggests that vaginismus is the most common cause of unconsummated marriages. On the basis of data obtained from infertility studies, Barnes (1981) suggests that vaginismus occurs in 5 out of every 1,000 women, a rate of 0.5%. The unusually high prevalence of vaginismus among Irish women has also been reported by O'Sullivan (1979).

Etiology

A variety of hypotheses have been put forward to explain the development of vaginismus. A number of physical processes have been associated with vaginismus, and these need to be carefully evaluated in every case. In a study of 76 patients seen for vaginismus, Lamont (1978) found evidence for contributing physical factors in 24 patients. These factors included previous surgery (e.g., vaginal hysterectomies), episiotomy, atrophic vaginitis, *Monilia* vaginitis, *Trichomonas* vaginitis, constipation, retroversion, and pelvic congestion. Tollison and Adams (1979) have suggested that the following physical factors must be ruled out: endometriosis, relaxation of the supporting uterine ligaments, rigid hymen, hemorrhoids, painful hymenal tags, stenosis of the vagina, pelvic tumors, pelvic inflammatory disease, senile atrophy of the vagina, childbirth pathologies, and urethral caruncle. As both Lamont (1978) and Tollison and Adams (1978) point out, most of these conditions may not be directly responsible for the vaginismus, but may be associated with vaginismus indirectly through a classical conditioning process.

The classical conditioning formulation of vaginismus suggests that a woman may experience significant pain (i.e., dyspareunia) upon her initial attempts at intercourse. This pain, which functions as an unconditioned stimulus, leads to a natural, self-protective tightening of the vaginal muscles (the unconditioned response). Over time, stimuli associated with vaginal penetration (e.g., the presence of one's partner without clothes) or even the thought of intercourse can become conditioned stimuli and lead to reflexive muscle spasms (the conditioned response). This classical conditioning mechanism, depicted in Figure 5-1, is strengthened by basic operant conditioning. That is, in order to prevent these spasms, a woman tries to avoid coitus; this avoidance behavior relieves her anticipatory anxiety and serves to reinforce her avoidance.

As with dyspareunia, avoidance behavior may be more likely in couples where the male partner is particularly unassertive and overly accommodating. This is *not* to say that women with vaginismus should be treated more forcefully. Rather, the point we wish to make is that couples in which the male is more traditionally gender-typed are less likely to present for the treatment of vaginismus (see Case 3 in Chapter 10).

Not all instances of vaginismus, however, are classically conditioned, and a plethora of other psychosocial causes have been suggested. For example, on the basis of their experience with 29 cases of vaginismus, Masters and Johnson (1970) suggested that all of the following might be implicated:

Before association has occurred		
Conditioned stimulus (thought of intercourse)	→	No response or irrelevant response
Unconditioned stimulus (pain)	→	Unconditioned response (muscle spasm)
After association has occurred		
Conditioned stimulus (thought of intercourse)	→	Conditioned response (muscle spasm)

FIGURE 5-1. Classical conditioning model of vaginismus.

the inhibiting influence of religious orthodoxy, response to a partner's sexual dysfunction, a prior sexual trauma, and a response to sexual orientation concern. Poinsard (1968) suggests that other factors—such as an unwillingness to assume the adult role, as well as fears of pregnancy, sexually transmitted disease, or injury—may be implicated.

Unfortunately, there is little research to inform our discussion of etiology. In a rare empirical study with a comparison group, Barnes (1986b) interviewed 53 women who presented for treatment of lifelong vaginismus. All were seen at a psychosexual clinic in Dublin, Ireland. These women were compared to 66 women treated at the same clinic for a variety of other sexual difficulties and dysfunctions (e.g., orgasmic dysfunction). The primary focus of the interview was on the patient's prior relationship with her parents. As can be seen in Table 5-3, subjects with vaginismus were more likely than were comparison subjects to have a tyrannical father. (Interestingly, O'Sullivan, 1979, also reported that 70% of the 23 vaginismic women he treated remembered their father as a threatening, fearful, and often violent figure.) In addition, negative sexual conditioning involving religious themes was more common in the vaginismic women, as was the presence of additional psychopathology. Surprisingly, the lifetime prevalence of sexual trauma in subjects in this study was low. These findings, although interesting, should be considered preliminary; additional research is clearly necessary.

TABLE 5-3. Comparison of Subjects with Vaginismus to Subjects with Other Sexual Dysfunctions on Factors Believed to Be Associated with Vaginismus

Factor	Vaginismus subjects ($n = 53$)	Comparison subjects ($n = 66$)
Tyrannical father	12 (23%)	6 (9%)
Negative conditioning		
General	8 (15%)	11 (16%)
Religious	10 (19%)	2 (3%)
Victim of sexual violence	2 (4%)	0 (0%)
Mentally ill	6 (11%)	1 (1%)
No cause identified	15 (28%)	42 (64%)

Note. The data are from Barnes (1986b).

II

ASSESSMENT AND TREATMENT

In Chapters 2–5, we have introduced the most common clinical problems that you will face in the practice of sex therapy. We have provided separate chapters for each phase of the sexual response cycle and a separate chapter on sexual pain disorders, for three reasons: (1) to enhance your understanding of these "pure" dysfunctions; (2) to provide you with a theoretical structure; and (3) to facilitate subsequent communication. We wish to point out that, in practice, sexual dysfunctions are rarely so cleanly defined. That is, it is sometimes quite challenging to determine where a desire problems ends and an arousal problem begins. Moreover, you can expect to see comorbidity—the co-occurrence of two or more dysfunctions. Sometimes this results by chance, and occasionally it is the case that one disorder (the primary disorder) "causes" a second disorder (the secondary disorder). An example has been mentioned in Chapter 5: Dyspareunia can set the stage for the development of vaginismus. Similarly, in men, it is not uncommon for erectile difficulties to lead to secondary desire disorders.

Now that you have a basic understanding of the sexual dysfunctions, we turn our attention to the practical tasks of assessment and treatment. In Chapter 6 we present a guide to the biopsychosocial assessment of the sexual dysfunctions. Although we emphasize the assessment interview, we also discuss the use of psychological questionnaires and inventories, as well as psychophysiological and medical assessments. In Chapters 7 and 8 we discuss treatment options. Chapter 7 is devoted to sex therapy proper. In this chapter we discuss the components of sex therapy, including the use of homework, sensate focus exercises, masturbation, erotica, client education, cognitive restructuring, and stimulus control. Process issues, and techniques for specific problems, are also discussed. Chapter 8 provides an overview of the most common medical interventions for the treatment of the sexual dysfunctions. Throughout this chapter, we suggest ways in which sex therapy may be integrated with these medical approaches to increase the likelihood of a successful outcome.

6

Assessment

The purpose of this chapter is to provide a guide to the assessment of the sexual dysfunctions. In this chapter, we assume that you are the primary treatment provider. (In Chapter 8 we provide information for situations in which you might serve as a consultant.) Therefore, in this chapter, we provide information on the use of interviewing, self-report questionnaires, and psychophysiological procedures; we also discuss how to supplement your psychosocial evaluation with data from a medical evaluation. Results from your assessment should allow you to describe the problem, formulate a working hypothesis of its etiology (i.e., predisposing, precipitating, and maintaining factors), identify therapeutic goals, provide feedback to the client, and establish baseline functioning from which to evaluate the efficacy of treatment.

Interviewing

The Importance of Listening

In our work, we find that careful listening in the context of clinical interviewing serves as the cornerstone of the assessment process. This view is not unique, of course, to the domain of the sexual dysfunctions. Indeed, many fine articles, chapters, and books have been written on skillful interviewing (e.g., Morganstern, 1988; Pope, 1979; Sullivan, 1954; Turkat, 1986). We recommend that you study these works for the general information and insights they provide about interviewing. In this chapter, however, we focus our discussion on the issues that pertain specifically to interviewing clients about sexual problems.

Despite its importance, not all health professionals know how to listen, especially when it comes to the sexual sphere. We have had numerous clients report to us that they had tried previously to discuss their sexual problems with their physicians or therapists, but were met with embarrassment or lack of interest; as a result, the clients did not pursue their concerns. For example, a 70-year-old female client recently told us that she tried to discuss her vaginal dryness problem with her physician. Unfortunately for our client, the physician avoided further discussion of this problem, and only later referred to it as her "other problem." She sensed his discomfort with the subject, and did not raise the problem again. She later told us, "You know, my doctor was too embarrassed to even say the word 'sex,' so he made me feel weird for asking about it."

Similarly, a 60-year-old gentleman, who had been widowed in the past year, mentioned to his physician that he was worried about his sexual functioning; this concern was especially relevant now that he had started dating again. The physician's response was to shift the conversation to the man's blood pressure and to avoid the sexual issue. The client told us that he dropped the subject and thought that he must have been inappropriate for asking: "I felt dumb and embarrassed for bringing up the subject."

Such reports from clients are unfortunately all too common, even in this supposedly enlightened era. It has been our experience that many health professionals are still unwilling, and/or too uncomfortable, to address a patient's sexual concerns. For those of you (physicians, counselors, and therapists) who are able to address such concerns, we provide the following guidelines.

Step-by-Step Details of Interviewing

Comprehensive and accurate assessment is crucial to formulating a helpful treatment program. However, obtaining meaningful information is a skill that involves far more than just asking the right questions. Assessment can be especially challenging, because most people are uncomfortable discussing their sexual behaviors. Our 70- and 60-year-old clients mentioned above were both nervous about discussing their sexual concerns; they needed relaxed, encouraging responses from their physicians. Furthermore, many individuals may have strong beliefs about what sexual conduct is acceptable or unacceptable, and they may be offended if a therapist's views do not agree with their own.

We begin by proposing that an interview will best serve the needs of the client if you obtain important information in a sensitive and efficient manner. Toward this end, we believe that the crucial components of an effective clinical interview include (1) making assumptions (hypotheses) before the interview; (2) setting goals for the interview; (3) attending to process throughout the interview; and (4) following a specific structure and content during the interview.

Assessment should always begin with an appropriate introduction for the client(s). During this time the assessment structure and content should be outlined. We prefer to do this while both partners are present. For illustrative purposes, let us consider a fictitious couple, Mary and Bob. We might begin by saying:

"Today in this first interview I would like to obtain some background information. Then I would like to get an understanding of what issues brought you here today. I'd like to spend three meetings gathering information. My previous experience suggests that it is most helpful if I interview each of you, separately, for one session each. So, I'd like to begin today by interviewing you, Mary. While I do this, I'd like to ask Bob to complete some questionnaires that my secretary has for you. [Note: The use of self-report measures is discussed later in this chapter.] Next week when we meet, I'd like to interview Bob alone, and ask Mary to complete the questionnaires. Then, at our third session, I'd like to see both of you together. At the end of the third session, I will be able to provide you with my clinical impression and outline a therapy program for you, if this is indicated."

As the therapist, you should also mention your credentials and let the couple know that you are comfortable dealing with sexual problems. You should convey to the couple that overcoming sexual difficulties requires the cooperative efforts of both partners. This is necessary to address because such a couple often believes that (1) one person is to blame for the problems, and (2) it is the role of the therapist to identify and "cure" the "guilty/sick" one. After you have said this, however, it is important to interview each person separately following the introduction, to gather accurate information that is unencumbered by a partner's presence. Time can be wasted if the partners are always seen together. Many individuals have hidden stories (e.g., affairs, homosexual interests) that would never be revealed in the presence of their partners; yet this information is vital for developing a case formulation and planning the therapy program.

After the introductory remarks, the partners should be invited to ask any questions they might have. The remainder of the first session is then spent interviewing one of the partners alone. The next session is used to interview the other partner alone.

The third session can be used to assess the interaction of the couple. During this session, you can observe the partners communicate and interact with each other. Problems and strengths in communication readily emerge at this time—for example, you can assess how caring, hostile, honest, and so on, the couple appears to be. It is also important to determine how much trust each partner has in the other; we try to do this by comparing the amount of self-disclosure that occurs during the couple session with that in the earlier individual sessions. This third session is also designated to present an initial case formulation and provide an outline of the therapy plan.

SESSION 1

Assumptions. Assumptions are the hypotheses that a clinician makes in order to gather the most accurate information without wasting time and effort. Assumptions reflect the preferred direction of error. Thus, for example, it is better at the beginning to assume a low level of verbal understanding on the part of a client and thus to direct language to the client in a clear and concrete manner. Obviously, as a clinician learns more about a client, these assumptions are adjusted.

Other examples of useful assumptions include the following:

- Clients will be embarrassed and have difficulty discussing sexual matters.
- Clients will not understand medically correct terminology.
- Clients will be misinformed about sexual functioning.
- Clients will be in crisis and may be suicidal.
- Clients have not been open with each other and do not freely discuss sexual matters.

Goals. Goals are the desired outcomes established before each session to give the assessment procedure a focus. At times, the goals have to be adjusted as information is learned, to accommodate the needs of the client. However, adhering closely to the goals will help make the therapy more efficient by helping to minimize sidetracking.

Examples of the goals you might set for the first session include the following:

- Establishing rapport.
- Obtaining a general description of sexual problems.
- Obtaining a thorough psychosocial history.
- Obtaining a description of other life concerns, current stressors, and the like, to determine whether sex therapy is appropriate for the client/couple at this time.

With regard to the last-mentioned goal, there are no specific guidelines for making this determination. Thus, a therapist should determine, on a case-by-case basis, whether or not working on a sexual problem will benefit a client/couple. Certainly, if either partner is depressed and/or overly anxious, or if there is a great deal of anger or even hatred between a couple, then it is more appropriate to address nonsexual issues first. In some cases, sexual difficulties may be insignificant in light of other problems. Furthermore, effective assessment and therapy require a collaborative attitude among both partners and the therapist, which is compromised in the presence of such hostility. Similarly, there may be very dysfunctional communication between a couple, which must be addressed before sexual issues can be effectively addressed.

Process. "Process" is the term that describes the interaction between a client and a therapist; this interaction can either facilitate or inhibit the assessment. When we use the term "process," we also mean to include the physical setting (is it private? professional?), the therapist's appearance (intelligent, competent, trustworthy?), and the therapist's personal presentation (calm, friendly, accepting?), as well as the more common meanings of the term "process." It is clear that many clinicians feel uncomfortable in dealing with sexual problems. Personal feelings of shock and embarrassment will often show through attempts to be friendly and accepting. Mismanagement of these negative feelings could be divisive and create a barrier to effective therapy. If a therapist's feelings cannot be managed appropriately, then he or she should not be dealing with sexual problems. Clients readily discern embarrassment or incompetence—as our 60- and 70-year-old clients mentioned earlier did.

Additional examples of process factors that can sabotage assessment (and subsequent therapy as well) include differences between the therapist and clients in terms of age, gender, and/or ethnicity; and erotic attractions or interpersonal repulsions between therapist and client, or client and therapist.

Structure/Content. "Structure" and "content" refer to the ordering of questions to be asked, and the areas to be covered, respectively. In general, it is to the client's benefit for a therapist to get to the heart of the client's concerns. Thus, spending several sessions "breaking the ice" or "establishing a relationship" is not warranted in most cases.[1] However, it is useful to get a general sense of the client's history, especially as it relates to his or her sexual adjustment.

We do not advise following an invariant order of questions for all clients. Instead, the structure and content of the interview should reflect the needs of the client. There are frequently crisis issues that must be attended to before sexual matters can be addressed. Or it may be important to allow a client to digress beyond the usual structure, but only if the digression contributes ultimately to a better understanding of the client or the client's problem.

With this recognition of the need to individualize the interview structure and content to each client, we can nevertheless suggest an order that might be a useful beginning or "default" structure for your use.[2]

1. Start with nonthreatening demographics (e.g., age, marital status, who lives in household, current employment, educational background address, telephone number, etc.).

2. Continue with the open-ended question "What brings you here today?" Notice how freely and comfortably the client discusses sexual matters in general, and his or her particular difficulty. Use probes and directive comments to keep the client's report on target. Once you reach a general impression concerning the scope of the sexual problem, then move on to the detailed chronological history.

3. Obtain a psychosexual and psychosocial history.

a. *Childhood*. Ask about the family structure and experiences when client was a child. Also ask about social status, abuse or neglect,[3] first sexual experience (upsetting/pleasant?), parents' relationship, alcohol and substance use, messages about sex, and any other information that emerges as potentially relevant.

b. *Adolescence*. Inquire about relationships with peers, self-esteem and body image, dating, sexual experiences (both homosexual and heterosexual), menarche in females, success–failure in school, substance use, and any other information that emerges as potentially relevant.

c. *Adult*. Ask about significant relationships and events after age 20; try to address self-esteem, marriage/relationship history, sexual experiences, and so forth. Inquire about any unusual sexual experiences, as well as psychiatric history or treatment.

d. *Current sexual functioning*. Acquire details regarding sexual and nonsexual experiences in the current relationship, recent changes in sexual functioning and/or satisfaction, flexibility in sexual attitudes and behaviors, extramarital affairs, strengths and weaknesses of partner, likes and dislikes regarding the partner's sexual behavior, and so on.

4. Obtain a brief medical history.

a. Ask about significant childhood/teenage diseases, surgery, medical care, congenital disorders, and the like. Ask men and women about how they experienced secondary sex changes (particularly menarche, in the case of women).

b. Pay particular attention to the medical history after age 20; ask about any significant diseases, surgery, medical care, and so forth. Be sure to ask about the following: Has client received regular medical care? (If not, refer for medical workup.) Is client currently taking prescribed medication? Is client currently being treated for any medical problems? For women: Inquire about menstrual difficulties and, if appropriate, ask about the menopause.

5. Be sensitive to potential covert issues. Ask whether there are any issues that the client does not want discussed in front of his or her partner. What significant conflict exists (impressions of one's partner or hidden experiences)? *We believe strongly in creating an interview environment in which each partner can be assured of confidentiality.* Without separate confidential interviews, crucial information may remain hidden. For example, consider the case of Mr. and Mrs. L:

Mr. and Mrs. L, aged 45 and 42, respectively, had been married 10 years; they had one son, aged 8. Both had some college education and were successfully employed in middle-level management positions. When they were together at the onset of the first interview, both agreed that the problem was Mr. L's loss of interest in sex and his delayed ejaculation. This had reportedly begun about 1 year ago and had gotten worse, especially over the past few months. Both felt that this might be related to the stress in Mr. L's job and to his diabetes (which was occasionally out of control). Mrs. L reported that at one time his diabetes was so much out of control that he fainted; he could not be awakened and had to be taken to the hospital. After a discussion of the assessment structure and therapy process, Mrs. L left the consulting room and retired to the waiting room.

At this point, Mr. L said that he was relieved that the therapist was meeting with him alone, because he had to relate something that his wife was unaware of. He had been taking intravenous heroin for about a year and was well aware that heroin caused delayed ejaculation. The "fainting" episode that his wife described was actually due to an overdose of heroin. He felt that he was not addicted to heroin, and he had stopped taking it 3 weeks prior to beginning therapy, but he recognized that he was still vulnerable. Mr. L would never have revealed his heroin problem if he had not met with the therapist alone. He was not prepared to discuss it with his wife; he was convinced that she would leave him if she ever found out.

This case is a good example of the need for initial separate and confidential interviews. The partners are told that it is more helpful and efficient to complete the assessment this way, even though the overall therapeutic emphasis will be on the couple's interaction and communication. Furthermore, the partners are told at that time it may be helpful to deal with either person alone in order to work through specific issues. Making these statements at the outset establishes conditions that will allow for working through problems that present later during therapy.

6. Provide each client with a second opportunity to reveal anything he or she thinks may be relevant. In this regard, LoPiccolo and Heiman (1978)

recommend ending the interview by asking, "Is there anything else that you would like to tell me about your background that you feel bears on your sexual life?"

SESSION 2

The second interview is with the other partner. We ask this partner whether anything has changed since the first interview and whether his or her partner has discussed the first interview with him or her. The answers to these queries will yield information about a couple's interaction pattern, openness in communication, and ability to schedule time for important issues. It is also important to ask this partner whether there are any issues or questions that he or she would like addressed before the interview begins. This open-ended approach allows the discussion of process issues (such as a client's doubt about a therapist's qualifications), as well as important personal issues that may have an impact on the therapy (such as a client's affair or a death in the family).

Once the open-ended issues are dealt with, then the interview may move on to the interview proper. The interview follows the structure and content outline for the first interview.

SESSION 3

The third interview normally includes both partners. (An exception to this may occur if one individual's needs are so overwhelming that individual therapy is indicated prior to couples therapy.) The interview with both partners should begin in an open-ended manner to determine what changes and conversations may have occurred since the last session. A couple's response to this approach is important diagnostically, because it provides an understanding of how the couple approaches and discusses important problematic topics. You can observe which partner takes responsibility for what, and how effectively each person communicates his or her needs. Consider, also, that a couple may be overwhelmed with recently occurring problems or stressors, such as job loss or death in the family. Obviously, it is important to acknowledge extratreatment issues that may preoccupy clients and distract them from the current focus of the assessment. The remainder of the third session should be spent providing your formulation, identifying treatment goals (sexual and nonsexual), outlining therapy plans, and explaining details regarding the initial stages of therapy. To further facilitate rapport, maximize therapy compliance, and avoid backsliding, you should ask each partner how each feels about the plan and what problems each anticipates as barriers to progress.

The third assessment session should follow this outline:

Assumptions. As before, it is useful to begin with some assumptions. For example, you may find it helpful to assume the following:

- Couple has not discussed previous interviews.
- Couple has trouble discussing sexual matters and is embarrassed.
- There may still be a crisis.
- Correct terminology is still not well understood.
- Sexual attitudes are well developed, rigid, and conservative.
- Avoidance of sex will occur because of fear and discomfort.

Goals. Similarly, you should establish goals for this session; possible goals include the following:

- Review your own observations and discuss inconsistencies with couple's assumptions and observations.
- Outline and begin therapy plan.
- Obtain couple's commitment to follow the therapy plan by discussing potential compliance problems ahead of time.
- Influence couple to begin conceptualizing problem as learned and without blame.

Process. Process issues continue to be important. Thus you may want to cover these points:

- Ask couple whether there are any developments since your last meeting.
- Ask couple what they have discussed: why or why not?
- Ask whether there are any doubts or issues to be discussed before therapy begins.
- Ask the couple whether there are any anticipated difficulties in participating in therapy with you as therapist (are there concerns regarding the therapist's gender, age, or race?).

Interview Structure and Content. The third session may be ordered as follows.

1. After consideration of process issues, begin the interview by defining the problem, indicating possible contributing factors, and acknowledging that you will continue to collect information as therapy starts. Ask each partner to comment on and clarify any misunderstandings or disagreements.

2. Ask each partner to discuss his or her reaction to a sexual encounter when it is thought to be a failure.

3. Outline the therapy plan; if possible, try to discuss all stages of therapy. Emphasize, in detail, what the first stage will involve—this will establish hope. Be sure to ask the couple to identify any anticipated problems, and to commit to the initial step (i.e., set a specific date and time for your next meeting).

For many clients, further assessment information will be needed, such as psychological testing, psychophysiological assessment, and/or medical evaluation. If this is the case, then therapy instructions may have to be postponed until the assessment picture is completed. (Later in this chapter we discuss the integration of interview data with information obtained from other methods.) It is very important to explain the nature of and need for further assessment so that a client does not get discouraged or frustrated.

Conte (1986) points out that the interview is the earliest and most common procedure for assessing sexual problems. Over the years, as our clinical sophistication and knowledge base have increased, the interview procedure for assessment of sexual problems has become more structured and standardized. Thus, today's interviewing methods are yielding more valuable information than ever before; we are more knowledgeable about the complexities of sexual functioning and understand the need for assessment procedures that go beyond the interview. The remainder of this chapter focuses on the use of self-report questionnaires, psychophysiological techniques, and medical procedures that are available to supplement the interview and complete a comprehensive assessment.

Self-Report Questionnaires

Self-report questionnaires are "standardized paper-and-pencil questionnaires that can be filled out by the client in a relatively short period of time, that can be easily administered and scored by the practitioner, and that give fairly accurate pictures of the client's condition at any point in time and/or over a period of many administrations" (Corcoran & Fischer, 1987, p. 9). These questionnaires have many potential advantages. First, they provide extensive information at little cost; thus, they are cost-effective. Second, they allow a client to organize his or her thoughts in a reflective, considered way that is not always possible with the time constraints of an interview. Third, self-report questionnaires permit clients to disclose sensitive information that they might not reveal during a "live" interaction, or that they might find difficult to verbalize (Corcoran & Fischer, 1987). Fourth, self-report questionnaires allow you to assess a client's progress over time, making treatment evaluation more precise and less prone to therapist-related biases. Fifth, self-report questionnaires allow you to compare your client to other individuals (with the help of established norms); thus, in difficult diagnostic cases, these questionnaires can provide a known metric against which to make judgments. Sixth, questionnaires can serve as an additional stimulus that encourages a client to think through aspects of his or her sexuality. Seventh, if used after the interview, self-report questionnaires can be used to evaluate the validity of a diagnostic or etiological formulation (see Carey et al., 1984). Alternatively, if used before the interview, self-report measures can serve as screening devices that help you as the interviewer to be more efficient in getting to the heart of the presenting complaint.

Despite their many potential advantages, however, self-report questionnaires have not been widely used in sexuality assessments. Conte (1983, 1986) suggests that one reason for this disuse is that many questionnaires have been developed in the context of research projects for very specific purposes, and thus have limited clinical utility. There is certainly some truth to this view. It is probably also true that using questionnaires in a careful way may appear time-consuming and inconvenient in a busy practice. An additional reason for the limited use of self-report measures is that good instruments have been difficult to locate.

Locating Questionnaires on Your Own

Obtaining good questionnaires has been difficult in the past. Many research-oriented journals that provided psychometric information (e.g., reliability, validity) on new measures did not publish the actual questionnaires. Clinical sources that provided the items often did not provide psychometric characteristics. As a result, many practitioners have resorted to homemade instruments that are of dubious quality. Fortunately, it is now easier to learn about and obtain self-report questionnaires for clinical use.

Several professional journals provide an outlet for authors who wish to make their questionnaires available to other users. Of the journals available, we recommend *Psychological Assessment: A Journal of Consulting and Clinical Psychology*. This journal is available at most university libraries, or you can subscribe by writing to the American Psychological Association in Washington, DC. There are also several recent books devoted to the use of self-report questionnaires. For general clinical measures, we have found Corcoran and Fisher's (1987) book, *Measures for Clinical Practice: A Sourcebook*, to be quite useful. For measures related to physical health and adjustment, we recommend McDowell and Newell's (1987) book, *Measuring Health: A Guide to Rating Scales and Questionnaires*. Finally, for measures of sexual functioning, Davis, Yarber, and Davis's (1988) book, *Sexuality-Related Measures: A Compendium*, warrants your attention.

Evaluating Questionnaires

Once you learn of a questionnaire, you will want to evaluate it along several important dimensions.

1. *Psychometric strength*. Is it reliable (i.e., are the individual items consistent with one another, and are scores stable over time?) and valid (i.e., does it measure what it purports to measure, or is it measuring some other construct, such as intelligence or social desirability)? These criteria may seem overly technical, but we would encourage you not to overlook them. A measure that is not reliable and/or not valid is not only worthless, but it could also distort your understanding of your client.

2. *Clinical relevance*. Does the measure address the clinical issues at hand? For example, if you are concerned primarily with evaluating a client's level of sexual desire, it would not be fruitful to ask him or her to complete the Minnesota Multiphasic Personality Inventory (MMPI; a global personality measure), or even the Sexual Opinion Survey (SOS)—because these instruments provide no information on desire. Also, it is true that many instruments are not intended for clinical use and have little or no clinical utility; however, there are also a large number of well-conceived and useful measures. You need to determine the clinical relevance for each measure you use with each client on a case-by-case basis.

3. *Practicality*. Is the questionnaire at a reading and vocabulary level appropriate for your clients? We have found that many questionnaires use vocabulary that is beyond most clients. One source for information on reading levels of a variety of sexually relevant questionnaires is a paper by Jensen, Witcher, and Upton (1987). Moreover, there now exists user-friendly computer software that can assess reading level on most personal computers.

4. *Comparability*. Are there normative data against which to compare your client's scores? Here you will need to be sure that the normative sample is appropriate for your clients. Thus, if a questionnaire was normed with males aged 50–70 years, and your clients tend to be young females, the normative data are probably not useful. Also, be aware that many questionnaires have been normed on college students, who may not be representative of your clients.

5. *Cost*. Does the measure cost you or your client too much time and/or money to use? Some instruments (e.g., the MMPI) are so long that many clients find them annoying and, as a result, do not respond in a cooperative fashion. Other measures are expensive to obtain and/or administer. You should know, however, that many measures are in the public domain and can be used for free.

Given these criteria, we have identified several worthwhile measures that you may want to consider for use in your work.

Specific Self-Report Questionnaires

SEXUAL INTERACTION INVENTORY

As stated previously, we typically see sexual partners together. Thus, we are very concerned with the interaction between the partners about sexual matters. Therefore, we have used the Sexual Interaction Inventory (SII; LoPiccolo & Steger, 1974) to corroborate and supplement information obtained in the interview. The SII consists of 17 heterosexual behaviors (see Table 6-1), each of which are rated by both partners along six dimensions (see Table 6-2). Thus, the final questionnaire contains 102 questions that measure both satisfaction with, and frequency of, sexual behavior in heterosexual[4] couples. The SII is particularly valuable for assessing problem areas within a couple's interaction and for assessing treatment outcome over time.

According to Jensen et al. (1987), the instructions for the SII are at a sixth-grade reading level; unfortunately, however, the items themselves are at the college level. Research suggests that the SII is valid and reliable (see LoPiccolo & Steger, 1974). Most people can complete the SII in less than 30 minutes, and it can be scored in about half that time. Finally, the SII is relatively inexpensive; at the time of this writing, it can be purchased for $10

TABLE 6-1. Behaviors Listed in the Sexual Interaction Inventory (SII)

1. The male seeing the female when she is nude.
2. The female seeing the male when he is nude.
3. The male and the female kissing for one minute continuously.
4. The male giving the female a body massage, not touching her breasts or genitals.
5. The female giving the male a body massage, not touching his breasts or genitals.
6. The male caressing the female's breasts with his hands.
7. The male caressing the female's breasts with his mouth.
8. The male caressing the female's genitals with his hands.
9. The male caressing the female's genitals with his hands until she reaches orgasm.
10. The female caressing the male's genitals with her hands.
11. The female caressing the male's genitals with her hands until he ejaculates.
12. The male caressing the female's genitals with his mouth.
13. The male caressing the female's genitals with his mouth until she reaches orgasm.
14. The female caressing the male's genitals with her mouth.
15. The female caressing the male's genitals with her mouth until he ejaculates.
16. The male and female having intercourse.
17. The male and female having intercourse with both of them having an orgasm.

Note. From "The Sexual Interaction Inventory: A New Instrument for Assessment of Sexual Dysfunction" by J. LoPiccolo and J. C. Steger, 1974, *Archives of Sexual Behavior, 3,* 585–595. Copyright 1974 by Plenum Publishing Corporation. Reprinted by permission of the authors and publisher.

TABLE 6-2. Ratings Used in the Sexual Interaction Inventory (SII)

For each of the 17 items above [see Table 6-1], the client is asked to rate the behavior along the following six dimensions:

When you and your mate engage in sexual behavior, does this particular activity usually occur? How often would you like this activity to occur? ("Sexual behavior" refers to any type of physical contact which is intended to be sexual by either you or your mate.)

a. Currently occurs:
   1. Never
   2. Rarely (10% of the time)
   3. Occasionally (25% of the time)
   4. Fairly often (50% of the time)
   5. Usually (75% of the time)
   6. Always

b. I would like it to occur:
   1. Never
   2. Rarely (10% of the time)
   3. Occasionally (25% of the time)
   4. Fairly often (50% of the time)
   5. Usually (75% of the time)
   6. Always

How pleasant do you currently find this activity to be? How pleasant do you think your mate finds this activity to be?

c. I find this activity:
   1. Extremely unpleasant
   2. Moderately unpleasant
   3. Slightly unpleasant
   4. Slightly pleasant
   5. Moderately pleasant
   6. Extremely pleasant

d. I think that my mate finds this activity:
   1. Extremely unpleasant
   2. Moderately unpleasant
   3. Slightly unpleasant
   4. Slightly pleasant
   5. Moderately pleasant
   6. Extremely pleasant

How would you like to respond to this activity? How would you like your mate to respond? (In other words, how pleasant do you think this activity *ideally should be,* for you and your mate?)

e. I would like to find this activity:
   1. Extremely unpleasant
   2. Moderately unpleasant
   3. Slightly unpleasant
   4. Slightly pleasant
   5. Moderately pleasant
   6. Extremely pleasant

TABLE 6-2. *(Continued)*

f. I would like my mate to find this activity:
   1. Extremely unpleasant
   2. Moderately unpleasant
   3. Slightly unpleasant
   4. Slightly pleasant
   5. Moderately pleasant
   6. Extremely pleasant

Note. From "The Sexual Interaction Inventory: A New Instrument for Assessment of Sexual Dysfunction" by J. LoPiccolo and J. C. Steger, 1974, *Archives of Sexual Behavior, 3,* 585–595. Copyright 1974 by Plenum Publishing Corporation. Reprinted by permission of the authors and publisher.

from Joseph LoPiccolo, PhD, Department of Psychology, University of Missouri, Columbus, MO 65211.

DYADIC ADJUSTMENT SCALE

The Dyadic Adjustment Scale (DAS; Spanier, 1976) is particularly valuable for assessing problem areas within a couple's interaction outside of the sexual domain. The DAS consists of a list of 32 items (see Table 6-3) designed to assess the quality of the relationship as perceived by married or cohabiting couples. As with the SII, each partner completes the questionnaire separately. Scoring yields four subscales and a total score; however, we tend to use only the total score in our work. It provides a general measure of marital/cohabiting satisfaction. According to Jensen et al. (1987), the instructions of the DAS are at a seventh-grade reading level, whereas the items themselves are at the eighth-grade reading level; thus, it should be possible to use the DAS with most clients. Research suggests that the DAS is valid and reliable (see Spanier, 1976). Most people can complete the DAS in 15 minutes, and it can be scored in about 5 minutes. The DAS is in the public domain and therefore can be used free of charge.

DEROGATIS SEXUAL FUNCTIONING INDEX

Although we focus on the couple, it is also important to understand the individual separately from the couple. To obtain extensive information on the individual, we use the Derogatis Sexual Functioning Index (DSFI; Derogatis & Melisaratos, 1979). The DSFI is a widely used, omnibus scale of sexual

TABLE 6-3. The Dyadic Adjustment Scale

Most persons have disagreements in their relationships. Please indicate below the approximate extent of agreement or disagreement between you and your partner for each item on the following list.

	Always agree	Almost always agree	Occasionally disagree	Frequently disagree	Almost always disagree	Always disagree
1. Handling family finances	5	4	3	2	1	0
2. Matters of recreation	5	4	3	2	1	0
3. Religious matters	5	4	3	2	1	0
4. Demonstrations of affection	5	4	3	2	1	0
5. Friends	5	4	3	2	1	0
6. Sex relations	5	4	3	2	1	0
7. Conventionality (correct or proper behavior)	5	4	3	2	1	0
8. Philosophy of life	5	4	3	2	1	0
9. Ways of dealing with parents or in-laws	5	4	3	2	1	0
10. Aims, goals, and things believed important	5	4	3	2	1	0
11. Amount of time spent together	5	4	3	2	1	0
12. Making major decisions	5	4	3	2	1	0
13. Household tasks	5	4	3	2	1	0
14. Leisure-time interests and activities	5	4	3	2	1	0
15. Career decisions	5	4	3	2	1	0

	All the time	Most of the time	More often than not	Occasionally	Rarely	Never
16. How often do you discuss or have you considered divorce, separation, or terminating your relationship?	0	1	2	3	4	5
17. How often do you or your mate leave the house after a fight?	0	1	2	3	4	5
18. In general, how often do you think that things between you and your partner are going well?	5	4	3	2	1	0
19. Do you confide in your mate?	5	4	3	2	1	0
20. Do you ever regret that you married (or lived together)?	0	1	2	3	4	5
21. How often do you and your partner quarrel?	0	1	2	3	4	5
22. How often do you and your mate "get on each other's nerves"?	0	1	2	3	4	5

23. Do you kiss your mate?

Every day	Almost every day	Occasionally	Rarely	Never
4	3	2	1	0

24. Do you and your mate engage in outside interests together?

All of them	Most of them	Some of them	Very few of them	None of them
4	3	2	1	0

How often would you say the following occur between you and your mate:

	Never	Less than once a month	Once or twice a month	Once or twice a week	Once a day	More often
25. Have a stimulating exchange of ideas	0	1	2	3	4	5
26. Laugh together	0	1	2	3	4	5
27. Calmly discuss something	0	1	2	3	4	5
28. Work together on a project	0	1	2	3	4	5

These are some things about which couples sometimes agree and sometimes disagree. Indicate if either item below caused differences of opinions or were problems in your relationship during the past few weeks. (Check yes or no.)

	Yes	No	
29.	0	1	Being too tired for sex
30.	0	1	Not showing love

31. The dots on the following line represent different degrees of happiness in your relationship. The point, "happy," represents the degree of happiness of most relationships. Please circle the dot that best describes the degree of happiness, all things considered, of your relationship.

0	1	2	3	4	5	6
•	•	•	•	•	•	•
Extremely unhappy	Fairly unhappy	A little unhappy	Happy	Very happy	Extremely happy	Perfect

32. Which of the following statements best describes how you feel about the future of your relationship:

5   I want desperately for my relationship to succeed and would go to almost any lengths to see that it does.
4   I want very much for my relationship to succeed and will do all that I can to see that it does.
3   I want very much for my relationship to succeed and will do my fair share to see that it does.
2   It would be nice if my relationship succeeded, and I can't do much more than I am doing now to help it succeed.
1   It would be nice if it succeeded, but I refuse to do any more than I am doing now to keep the relationship going.
0   My relationship can never succeed, and there is no more that I can do to keep the relationship going.

Note. From "Measuring Dyadic Adjustment: New Scales for Assessing the Quality of Marriage and Similar Dyads" by G. B. Spanier, 1976, *Journal of Marriage and the Family, 38*, 15–28. Copyright 1976 by the National Council on Family Relations. Reprinted by permission of the publisher.

functioning. It contains 245 items that measure 10 domains considered to be essential to effective sexual functioning: Information, Experience, Drive, Attitudes, Psychological Symptoms,[5] Affect, Gender-Role Definition, Fantasy, Body Image, and Sexual Satisfaction. According to Jensen et al. (1987), the instructions of the DSFI are at a ninth-grade reading level, whereas the items themselves are at the college level. Research suggests that the DSFI is reliable and valid, and norms are available (see Derogatis, 1975). Most people can complete the DSFI within 45 minutes; scoring, however, is complicated. The DSFI can be purchased from Leonard R. Derogatis, PhD, Clinical Psychometric Research, Baltimore, MD.

SEXUAL OPINION SURVEY

The SOS (Fisher, 1988; Fisher, Byrne, White, & Kelley, 1988) is also used to aid our understanding of the individual. The SOS consists of 21 items intended to assess "affective and evaluative responses to a range of sexual stimuli (autosexual, heterosexual, and homosexual behavior; sexual fantasy; visual sexual stimuli)" (Fisher, 1988, p. 34). Each of these 21 items describes a sexual situation, and a negative or positive affective response; clients then indicate the extent to which they agree (or disagree) with the affective response. Research suggests that the SOS is valid and reliable, and norms are available (see Fisher et al., 1988). Most people can complete the SOS in 10 minutes or less, and it can be scored in about half that time. It is our understanding that the SOS is in the public domain, so it can be used for free.

OTHER MEASURES

There are a number of other excellent measures that you might want to consider adopting in your work. Conte's (1983) review and the Davis et al. (1988) volume are good sources for other measures to consider. We also recommend that you obtain a good medical history screening questionnaire (these are often available from local health maintenance organizations) if you do not already have access to your client's medical chart.

Concluding Comments on the Use of Self-Report Questionnaires

Although we encourage you to use carefully selected self-report questionnaires in your work, we also wish to be clear about their limitations. Such measures should never be used blindly, or without a careful interview.

Moreover, we wish to be clear about "traditional" psychological measures such as the MMPI (Hathaway & McKinley, 1967) or the Rorschach inkblot test (Exner, 1986). These measures have *not* been found useful for diagnosing the presence of sexual dysfunction or for delineating its etiology (Conte, 1986). Therefore, we discourage their use, unless it is for some other purpose for which that instrument has been demonstrated to be reliable and valid (see Anastasi, 1988, for further discussion of this topic).

Psychophysiological Assessment

Psychophysiology permits inferences about psychological processes that are based upon physiological measures (Cacioppo & Tassinary, 1990). Thus, if used appropriately, these measures can be powerful tools in your assessment armamentarium. Among other strengths, psychophysiological measures tend to be less susceptible to the distortions and biases that can occur with interviews and questionnaires. In addition, psychophysiological measures permit a better understanding of the physiological underpinnings, and sometimes the actual mechanisms, of a dysfunction.

In practice, psychophysiological methods[6] are used infrequently, and tend to be used primarily with men. The infrequent use of psychophysiological methods reflects several factors. First, these methods require a significant amount of technical skill to achieve a minimal level of competence. Most training programs simply do not provide the requisite opportunities to acquire such skill. Second, psychophysiological recording apparatus and supplies are expensive. It is unlikely that you could get started for less than $1,000, and a state-of-the-art assessment laboratory can cost $15,000 or more. Third, the external validity of laboratory-based sexual measures has been challenged (Heiman, 1978). Although debatable, this point has discouraged some practitioners. Finally, several of the factors that are involved in sexual functioning (e.g., relationship quality) occur at a different level of analysis.

The limited use of psychophysiological measures with women is also the product of several influences. Hoon (1979) suggested that this reflects (1) sexist biases among sex researchers and clinicians, (2) a culture-wide failure to recognize how widespread sexual problems are, and (3) a lack of technology for assessing sexual problems of women. Since Hoon's review article, some progress has been made (see Geer, 1987; Rosen & Beck, 1988), and additional progress is anticipated. At the present time, however, little clinically relevant work with women is being done.

The two psychophysiological methods most commonly employed with men are nocturnal penile tumescence (NPT) and daytime arousal studies.

Nocturnal Penile Tumescence

The physiological recording of NPT, usually in a full sleep laboratory or center, has been considered the "gold standard" of differential diagnosis in men. Briefly, the rationale for this procedure is as follows: If a man can obtain an erection during sleep (which most men do on four or five occasions per night[7]), but cannot obtain an erection during partner stimulation, it is assumed that the source of the erectile dysfunction is "psychogenic" (sometimes referred to as "functional"). In contrast, if a man cannot obtain an erection at night, it has been assumed that his dysfunction is "organic."[8]

Despite the promise of NPT, there are several important challenges to its use and interpretation. An extended discussion of these challenges is provided elsewhere (see Meisler & Carey, 1990), and we wish to mention only two here. First, from a purely technical viewpoint, recent data indicate that NPT may be influenced by sleep problems (e.g., apnea, hypopnea, or periodic leg movements) not routinely assessed in the typical NPT evaluation. These sleep parameters may produce artifacts that can interfere with interpretation of NPT tracings. Second, from a practical perspective, NPT monitoring is very costly. The typical procedure requires expensive equipment, is labor-intensive, and necessitates that a client spend two or three nights in a sleep center. As a result, this assessment procedure is well beyond the financial means of most clients. Even when a client can afford it, NPT requires a full sleep laboratory and a well-trained technical staff—resources rarely found outside of major research hospitals.[9]

Fortunately, however, there is a much more affordable and perhaps more valid psychophysiological assessment procedure that you may want to consider.

Daytime Arousal Evaluation

Measuring sexual arousal directly (i.e., in response to erotic stimulation) can be extremely valuable; indeed, it is the lack of such a response that is often reported as the problem in erectile dysfunction. Psychophysiological measurement of sexual arousal offers an objective view of a person's response to erotic stimuli. Psychophysiological studies (Libman et al., 1989; Sakheim, Barlow, Abrahamson, & Beck, 1987; Wincze et al., 1988) have provided valuable information for the assessment process.[10] For example, Wincze et al. (1988) found that exposing some dysfunctional men to erotic stimulation resulted in full erection responses, even though those men reported an inability to obtain an erection. Such data can be critically helpful in formulating a case.

Current psychophysiological procedures are technically challenging, expensive, and ethically complex. Because of these (and other) considerations, we have elected not to present a step-by-step guide to establishing a laboratory.[11] Nevertheless, we wish to provide a brief overview of these procedures for your information.

In brief, our procedure uses videotapes of erotic stimulation presented for approximately 8 to 10 minutes.[12] Throughout the procedure, the client is seated in a separate room in privacy. Stimuli are selected carefully so that they are appropriate to a person's sexual orientation and exclude material a client might find offensive.[13] Using a mercury strain gauge, we can measure precisely the amount of tumescence and the point in the videotape at which the tumescence appears. The debriefing following this assessment procedure can be especially valuable; we use it to help us to understand the client's cognitive reaction to erotic stimulation. We ask questions about the client's ability to concentrate on the erotic stimuli and his emotional reaction to the stimuli. For example, one 56-year-old male client experiencing erectile difficulties expressed detachment from the erotic stimulation: "That stuff doesn't bother me. I know they are just acting, and I need the real thing." Further inquiry revealed that this client had very limited use of erotic fantasy and, in fact, felt it was "wrong" to fantasize. The conflict between his "obligation" to have sex with his wife and his restricted views about sexual expressions later became the focus of therapy.

To repeat: When you see your first client, it is unlikely that you will have the technical expertise or laboratory equipment needed to conduct a psychophysiological assessment. However, if you anticipate that you will be conducting a large number of assessments, we would encourage you to obtain this equipment, and to seek further supervised clinical training.

Medical Evaluation

In addition to the information you obtain from the interview, self-report questionnaires, and psychophysiological evaluation, you will also need to know (1) when (and how) to refer a client for medical testing; and (2) how to interpret, and integrate into your case formulation, the results of the most common medical tests.

As mentioned earlier, information about a patient's medical history and visits to physicians should be a routine part of your initial screening interview. As we have also discussed previously, your interview may be supplemented with a medical history questionnaire that asks for basic information about chronic and acute medical conditions, medication use, surgical history, congenital disorders, hospitalizations, significant medical problems within the extended family, and visits to physicians. This will save you time during your interview, and help to alert you to important medical considerations.

Even when you have conducted a careful interview and collected additional information with self-report questionnaires, it may be necessary to refer your client for further medical evaluation. Indeed, we believe that it is good practice to refer any client for a medical workup if he or she has not recently been examined. Clients who describe pain, discomfort, bleeding, discharge, or any other unusual symptoms that have not been recently evaluated should be referred to a physician before proceeding with a psychosocially oriented treatment approach. In our view, it is best to be conservative, and to refer to a physician if there is any concern whatsoever.

When a client has had a recent medical evaluation and the dysfunction is manifested only under certain circumstances, or with certain partners, then it is less likely that further medical evaluation is necessary. However, you should continue to be vigilant for complications that may require additional medical consultation.

What to Look for in a Medical Consultant

It is extremely important to select your medical consultants with great care. Your selection should be based upon the following considerations.

1. Select a physician who is willing to work cooperatively with you and to respect your contributions. We discourage you from working with a physician who takes over the case and begins treatment without consulting you. For example, if you refer a client for evaluation of Male Erectile Disorder, you should expect that the consultant will get back to you before she or he starts treating the client with vasoactive agents. Such a treatment may frighten your client and undermine your credibility with him.

2. Try to find a physician who is willing, within reasonable limits, to educate you regarding his or her specialty. Professionals differ with regard to their ability to communicate knowledge, as well as in their interest in educating others. Many welcome the chance to share their expertise and, in so doing, to educate their colleagues and clients.

3. Try to assess the consultant's interpersonal skills or, as they are traditionally referred to, his or her "bedside manners." It would reflect negatively on your judgment if you referred your client to a physician who is aloof, cold, or even insulting. We have heard reports regarding all types of unprofessional behavior. For example, one report was of a physician grabbing an overweight male client in the abdomen and stating, "You are too fat to have sex, so why bother?" We have also known of physicians who have encouraged clients to have extramarital affairs to solve their sexual problems.

4. Try to determine the physician's competence and comfort with sexual problems. Medicine is a large and complex field; being trained as a physician, even as a genital specialist (i.e., in gynecology or urology), does not guarantee current knowledge or comfort with sexual problems. It is extremely important to discuss with potential consultants their self-efficacy and comfort

in dealing with sexual complaints. If possible, it is worthwhile to check with other experienced sex therapists regarding good consultants.

When you deem it important to obtain additional medical evaluation, you will need to coordinate this referral. We suggest a two-stage approach. First, we have found it helpful to call the physician. If you are calling a physician for the first time, you may want to tell the receptionist that you have a patient referral; ask whether you can have the "back number," as most physicians have a separate line for such personal calls. If you do not go to this extra trouble, you may have to wait several days for a return call as most physicians are tremendously busy. Once you have established telephone contact, and determined that the physician is an appropriate referral, you will want to provide him or her with a brief written report to guide the assessment.

It is important that your written referral be brief and outline the specific reason for your referral. Again, avoid psychojargon! Here is an example of a letter referring one of our clients to a physician.

Re: Mrs. Jane Smith
    D.O.B. 6/5/61

Dear Dr. Parker,

I am writing to request an evaluation of Mrs. Jane Smith regarding her complaint of painful intercourse. Based upon a clinical interview (8/9/90), I can share the following background information with you:

Mrs. Smith is a bright, successful health care worker; she has been married for 3 years. She reports that she does not enjoy sexual relations and almost always experiences pain during intercourse. Her only sexual relations have been with her husband; although she says she loves him, she cannot relax during sex with him.

Mrs. Smith has not had a gynecological examination for 3 years; she agrees that it is important to determine the role of medical conditions in her sexual problem. I would greatly appreciate it if you would examine Mrs. Smith and inform me of any medical factors that may be affecting her sexual functioning.

Sincerely,

Interpreting Medical Test Results

After you have referred a patient for a medical consultation, you will need to integrate the results of this evaluation into your assessment. To do this, you need to be able to interpret test results. A nonphysician should, of course, rely on a physician's interpretation of medical test results. However, we believe that there at least three reasons why you should learn the basics about the most common procedures, tests, and results. First, this knowledge will help you to obtain the most crucial information in an efficient manner when you communicate with your consultants. Second, this knowledge will allow you to prepare clients for the tests they are likely to undergo, and to discuss the results of these tests as they affect your formulation and treatment planning. Third, such knowledge will enhance your understanding of your client, which will help you to be a better therapist. To get you started, we discuss briefly several common procedures and results below. In addition, we can recommend Pinckney and Pinckney's (1986) book, *The Patient's Guide to Medical Tests,* for further information.

PENILE–BRACHIAL INDEX

Men who are being evaluated for erectile difficulties will often undergo a penile blood pressure examination. The penile–brachial index is an expression of the relationship between the brachial systolic pressure and penile blood pressure. This relationship is expressed as the ratio of penile systolic blood pressure to brachial blood pressure. Normally, the pressures should be about equal, and yield a ratio of 1.0. If the penile pressure is less (i.e., representative of a decreased blood flow), the ratio will be less than 1.0. Most professionals in the field accept a level below 0.7 as abnormal, indicating vascular impairment of the caliber that would contribute to erectile problems. Typically, ratios are obtained for both the right and left dorsal arteries of the penis. Both need to be in the normal range to rule out a vascular etiology. Finally, like most diagnostic procedures, this measure is not completely reliable, and it should not be the sole measure used to determine vascular function.

ENDOCRINE MEASURES

Hormonal levels may be important to the sexual health of both men and women. In interpreting the results of hormonal levels, several factors are important. First, it is important to remember that levels may vary, depending on the assay procedure used; thus, levels typically vary somewhat across laboratories. Second, values should be understood as falling along a continuum of possible values, and the concept of a normal range is important. Third, it is critical to know the measurement units that are being used.

In women, estradiol is considered important. Typically, results are presented in picograms per milliliter (i.e., pg/ml). Because estradiol values fluctuate with the phases of the menstrual cycle, menstrual phase should be known when the sample is obtained and interpreted. The normal range of plasma estradiol during the first 10 days of the cycle averages 50 pg/ml;

during the last 20 days, it averages 125 pg/ml. (Men normally average 20 pg/ml at all times.) Values below the normal range for a particular phase may adversely affect vaginal lubrication.

In men, testosterone and prolactin are considered important. For testosterone, values are typically expressed in nanograms per deciliter (ng/dl) or in nanograms per milliliter (ng/ml). In laboratories that we work with, the normal range in men is usually from 280 to 1100 ng/dl, or from 2.8 to 11.0 ng/ml. (The normal range in women is 6.0–86.0 ng/dl.) Testosterone values need to be obtained during the early morning. This is because testosterone in males responds to a diurnal cycle, with the highest values recorded during the morning. You should also know that testosterone values are usually expressed as total testosterone; this includes both bioavailable and inactive testosterone. The bioavailable testosterone that influence sexual behavior is a fraction of the total and is composed of both free testosterone and albumin-bound testosterone.

Prolactin is a pituitary hormone that causes the breasts to enlarge and to secrete milk; it is also believed to be important for evaluating sexual desire in men. Specifically, higher levels of prolactin have been associated with decreased sexual desire. The normal range for prolactin in men and women (except for women during pregnancy and while nursing, when higher levels are observed) is 0–20 ng/ml. A value greater than 20 ng/ml warrants a repeat test, because it may intimate, among other conditions, the presence of a pituitary tumor.

Integrating Multiple Data Sources into a Coherent Case Formulation

We have mentioned at the beginning of this chapter that one of the goals of the assessment is to develop a coherent case formulation (i.e., a working hypothesis of the etiology of the problem). This formulation should relate all aspects of a client's complaints to one another and explain why the individual has developed these difficulties (Carey et al., 1984). One purpose of this formulation is to aid you in the development of a treatment plan. A second purpose is to communicate to your clients that (1) their problem is an understandable one, given their physiology, medical history, life experiences, and so forth (i.e., they are not crazy); (2) there is reason for hope and optimism; and (3) you have a conceptual "road map" and rationale upon which to build a therapeutic plan. Finally, developing a case formulation allows to check with the client to see whether you have obtained all the necessary information, and whether the information that you have is correct.

One of the more challenging aspects of sex therapy is integrating multiple levels of influence (i.e., biological, psychological, dyadic, cultural) into a coherent case formulation. Despite its difficulty, a biopsychosocial case formulation captures the richness of sexual function and dysfunction. A client is more likely to agree to try a psychosocial approach if you recognize that biological causes are not irrelevant, but that they may be overridden or compensated for. A client is also more likely to agree to try a psychosocial approach if you inquire about and recognize specific dyadic and sociocultural influences. You need to be sensitive to specific rituals and traditions that a couple has established, as well as to ethnic, cultural, or religious issues.

Your case formulation should include biological, psychological, and social areas even if you believe that one area does not contribute to the problem at the moment. It is always hard to predict the future, and you will have laid the groundwork should additional information become available and/or future developments occur. Moreover, this comprehensive approach to case formulation will give the client confidence that you have considered all possibilities. Indirectly, you communicate to the client that he or she should also think about the problem in a multifaceted, biopsychosocial framework.

To illustrate how you might present your formulation to a couple, we provide the following example.

"Mr. and Mrs. Russell, I want to review with you all of the information that I have gathered; please correct me if I state anything that you believe to be a mistake. I also want to present to you an approach that I think will help you with the erection problem. Here, too, I welcome your input.

"First, let me review the information that I have. The medical tests that Dr. Mitchell completed tells me that you, Mr. Russell, are in pretty good health. Dr. Mitchell did report, however, that the blood pressure in your penis was a little low, and this might explain some of your problem. This biological difficulty means that psychological and relationship conditions have to be ideal for your penis to work; this is because your physical response does not appear to be as strong as it used to be. However, I believe that your penis will function if Mrs. Russell and you can work together to create the right environment. This is good news because it means we can try to improve the situation without surgery. If this doesn't work, then we can discuss the pros and cons of surgery.

"I'd also like to say a few things about the psychology of this situation. It seems, from my discussion with both of you, that Mr. Russell gets frustrated when he wants to please you, Mrs. Russell, but is unable. Mr. Russell, you can get very upset when you are unable to obtain an erection. It even seems that sometimes you defeat yourself before you even get warmed up. As you heard with your own ears today, what Mrs. Russell wants most of all are your affection, hugs, and kind words. Whether or not you have an erection does not seem to be the crucial aspect to her. This is a relief for you to know. We can talk more about pleasing Mrs. Russell, but it is good to know that the absence of an erection will not ruin her day!

"Mr. Russell, it also seems that you bring a lot of worries with you—some from your work—and this may interfere with your ability to enjoy the caressing that Mrs.

Russell provides. To counter these influences, I'd like to teach you how to be more relaxed at all times, including during sexual activities. Also, we can discuss in more detail ways to set things up so that you have sex only at less stressful times. As another approach, we will work toward an emphasis on sexual pleasure rather than sexual performance.

"Mrs. Russell, you have mentioned that you don't always say what you want, when having sex or even when deciding what to watch on TV! We can work on helping you to feel more comfortable expressing your needs and desires; this will help Mr. Russell to understand you better. It will also take some of the pressure he feels off of him.

"I also know, from our discussions, that you are a deeply religious couple. I understand that both of you feel very uncomfortable with regard to masturbation and viewing erotic material. Although the use of masturbation and erotic material is helpful to some people, it will not be necessary for us to use either.

"Let me stop at this point, and listen to your reaction to my comments."

This sample formulation illustrates how we try to integrate biological, psychological, and social factors for a particular case. In general, we find that this approach gives the clients confidence that you have considered all possibilities, and that you are not just providing a "packaged" treatment program. Instead, this approach makes clear to clients that all data are considered, and that a specialized, customized treatment is adopted.

Special Challenges to Assessment

Before ending this chapter, we want to acknowledge that the assessment process is not without its pitfalls, potholes, and problems. We have already alluded to the technical skills, cost, and other obstacles to conducting a state-of-the-art assessment. We now turn our attention to more prosaic challenges to the assessment process.

The Uncooperative Partner

In a small number of our cases, a client will enter therapy without the full cooperation of his or her partner. Some of these clients have partners who are reported to be shy but cooperative; in other cases, the partner believes that the problem is the client's and refuses to participate. This always presents a difficult situation, and one in which you can never be sure whether you have all the pertinent facts. To help an uncooperative partner become engaged in therapy, you can suggest talking to the partner by phone. If there is still refusal, then you can suggest reading material that is pertinent to the problem.

Crucial components of therapeutic change (e.g., effective communica-tion, cognitive restructuring, and dispelling blame) can almost never be achieved when one partner refuses to participate. This is especially true when the uncooperative partner is purported to be angry and blaming. You can, of course, offer some therapeutic benefit to the participant client by providing etiological explanations and information, clearing up misunderstandings, putting the problem in perspective, and outlining strategies for change. However, you must also describe the limitations of therapy and try not to shift blame or fuel anger toward the absent partner. The end result of therapy is often a client who has an improved understanding of the problem and feels better about himself or herself, but still has a dysfunctional relationship with his or her partner.

Single Clients

Clients without partners who are experiencing sexual dysfunction problems may require a few special considerations; in general, however, most of what has been discussed is applicable to these clients. It is common for a single client to enter therapy after having experienced a "sexual failure." For men this may have been an experience of premature ejaculation or erection failure, whereas for women this is likely to have been vaginismus, dyspareunia, or loss of desire. Regardless of the nature of the problem, single clients are likely to enter therapy with low self-esteem, sexual insecurities, and avoidance of social interactions. You must be sensitive to these likely areas of concern and spend more time in identifying barriers that may impede social interactions.

Some single clients offer to bring in a casual partner to help with the therapy process. Our general approach is to allow a partner to participate only if there is a genuine commitment. The reason for this is to protect the client, since assessment and therapy require the revelation and open discussion of vulnerabilities and intimacies that the client may later regret having discussed. We have had some occasions when married clients offered to bring in lovers rather than their marriage partners. This situation presents obvious legal and ethical concerns that are in your best interests to avoid. We will counsel clients on the pros and cons of legal separation and divorce. If a client chooses to take no action, then the limitations and value of therapy must be fully discussed with the client.

Gay Clients

Single gay clients or gay couples should be approached no differently from single heterosexual clients or heterosexual couples. Gay clients who are perfectly comfortable with their homosexuality are likely to present with sexual dysfunction concerns similar to those of heterosexual clients. However, if you are heterosexual and are uncomfortable treating homosexuals, then you should refer them to another therapist. Also, if a homosexual client is uncomfortable with the idea of a heterosexual therapist, then a referral to a gay therapist may also be a good idea.

Concluding Comments

The assessment procedure necessary for accurate diagnosis of sexual dysfunction has definitely become more complex in recent years. We now understand that most sexual problems present with an interplay of medical and psychosocial factors, and demand a wide range of expert diagnostic input. This is an expensive and, at times, a long-drawn-out process; we look forward to more streamlining in the future.

A comprehensive assessment interview cannot be separated from therapy. Within the assessment process, a client's attitudes are often challenged, new information is learned, and misunderstandings are corrected. By asking the client about various factors that influence his or her sexual response, you are helping the client to view the sexual problem as a state rather than as an unchangeable trait. This conceptualization is important to restore optimism to the client and to his or her partner. Similarly therapeutic is the reduction or removal of blame for the sexual problem. Assessment solicits information from each partner; it thus helps redirect blame and guilt, and focuses the couple's energies on solving problems. Assessment also facilitates the breakdown of barriers to communication. This process is begun during the assessment, since the client is asked to discuss details of his or her own sexual behavior and details of his or her partner's sexual behavior. Clients observe you as the therapist discussing sexual matters in an open and nonthreatening manner, and this models effective communication.

Thus, through the assessment process, couples are exposed to an appropriate communication style and are encouraged to discuss sexual matters in a constructive, rather than a destructive or avoidant, manner. It is not surprising that many couples report positive change in their attitudes and, in some cases, in actual sexual behavior following assessment and before therapy proper begins.

Notes

[1] In some extreme cases, often where prior relationships have been quite unstable, it will be necessary to devote several sessions to establishing trust.

[2] The outline provided here is meant solely as a guide. This suggested order should not be followed blindly, but should be modified depending upon the clinical circumstances. You may

also want to review other such outlines that have been published (e.g., Hawton, 1985; LoPiccolo & Heiman, 1978).

[3] When asking about sexual abuse or trauma, we encourage you to follow the recommendation of Dr. Judith Becker, an expert in this area. Becker (1989) recommends that you ask clients whether they have ever been the recipients of *unwanted* sexual acts. Use of the word "unwanted" allows clients to report experiences that they might not reveal if asked about "rape" or "abuse." In this regard, it should be mentioned that many women are reluctant to identify sexual violations committed by boyfriends, husbands, and others who are known to them. We also wish to alert you to the potential importance of *vicarious* experiences, as illustrated by the case history presented in Chapter 2.

[4] The fact that the SII is intended for use only with heterosexual couples is a limiting factor.

[5] The Psychological Symptoms subtest is a distinct psychological instrument termed the Brief Symptom Inventory (BSI; Derogatis & Spencer, 1982). Scores on the BSI yield nine subscales (Somatization, Obsessive–Compulsive, Interpersonal Sensitivity, Depression, Anxiety, Hostility, Phobic Anxiety, Paranoid Ideation, and Psychoticism), as well as three global indices (Global Severity Index, Positive Symptom Distress Index, and Positive Symptom Total). The BSI may come in handy with clients for whom you suspect some interfering psychopathology.

[6] We use the term "psychophysiological" in the narrow sense of noninvasive, surface measures. Certainly, one can construe the assessment of hormonal levels in the blood as a psychophysiological measure. However, we refer to measures that are invasive and/or that require medical expertise and supervision as "medical measures" (see later section).

[7] It is interesting that most men misattribute the NPT response to having a full bladder. This misattribution undoubtedly developed because when men wake up at night to urinate, they often have erections, which then detumescence after urination. We have heard physicians speak of "full-bladder erections," showing that this misunderstanding is widespread and not confined to less educated people. It is interesting that most men do not see an inconsistency in their logic, based on lack of erection during the daytime when they have to urinate.

[8] Although this rationale is widely accepted, recent challenges to its validity have been made (see Meisler & Carey, 1990). For example, evidence now exists suggesting that the NPT response may be absent during clinical depression (Roose, Glassman, Walsh, & Cullen, 1982).

[9] In lieu of a full NPT examination, some professionals have used the snap gauge to assess nocturnal erections. The snap gauge tells you how many bands are broken during a night's sleep; the more bands that have been broken, the greater that evidence of nocturnal erections. Despite the apparent usefulness of the snap gauge, however, it cannot be recommended confidently because of the false-negative problem (i.e., men who do not have erections, but also have no organic pathology). This is discussed further in Meisler and Carey (1990).

[10] This is an especially valuable approach for assessing men who do not masturbate and do not use erotica on a regular basis.

[11] For readers who wish to pursue this further, we recommend Rosen and Beck (1988) as a guide.

[12] The viewing time is longer than is often noted in research studies, but in our clinical settings it allows a person to relax and get mentally involved in the stimulus presentation.

[13] We use the interview, the SII, and the SOS to help us to determine which stimuli are most appropriate.

7

Psychosocial Approaches to Treatment

Before you begin, you should know and be prepared for the fact that sex therapy remains widely misunderstood. Schoener (1990) points out that the human potential movement of the late 1960s fostered the development of sensitivity groups, which challenged the traditional boundaries of therapy. Physical contact between therapist and client occurred and was rationalized as "therapy." The permissibility of physical contact between client and therapist was supported further by the development of sex therapy as a formal treatment modality during the early 1970s:

> This new field of sex therapy received considerable media attention throughout much of the 1970's; unintentionally it brought about increased confusion among consumers. Because much of the public was unable to distinguish between psychotherapy and sex therapy, it is my impression that many potential consumers of psychotherapy services believed that erotic contact or touching by the therapist was proper if the client was being treated for a sexual problem. Over the past 14 years numerous clients have described this confusion to us. (Schoener, 1990, pp. 15–16)

The use of surrogates as part of treatment for sexual problems further contributed to the notion that the experience of sexual behavior within the context of therapy was permissible and expected (see Wolfe, 1978). Despite the uproar and protests from the therapeutic community over such practices, such public images remain (Schoener, 1990). Thus, we have had clients who have asked us directly whether sexual surrogates will be provided as part of therapy. In addition, clients have at times asked us why we were asking questions about their background or about their partners; it had been their understanding that the purpose of sex therapy was to teach them sexual techniques. Clearly, many clients who wish to participate in sex therapy do not understand what this treatment involves; thus (and this is our key point), *it is critically important that you explain the content and process of therapy to each new client.*

In this chapter, we attempt to demystify and de-eroticize the process of sex therapy by clarifying what is actually done. This chapter covers general strategies for approaching any sexual dysfunction problem, as well as details of specific techniques.

Strategy for Approaching Sex Therapy

The outline presented in Chapter 6 for conducting a comprehensive assessment interview applies to the therapy as well. Thus, we recommend that you make assumptions, set goals, attend to process issues, and follow a planned structure. We develop each of these recommendations below.

Assumptions

As in the case of assessment, it is helpful to begin therapy with a set of assumptions. These assumptions are educated guesses (i.e., hypotheses) that you make in order to facilitate efficient and effective progress. Some helpful assumptions that may prepare you for common problems are as follows:

- The client has a narrow definition of sex (e.g., "sex = intercourse"); he or she will focus on performance as a marker of success.
- The client has stereotyped views of masculine and feminine sex roles; these views will interfere with the assimilation of new information.
- The client does not understand the ingredients conducive to sexual arousal (e.g., favorable times to have sex, interfering factors, etc.).
- The client has a pattern of avoidance of sexual interactions; as a result, he or she may unintentionally sabotage therapy.

By making these assumptions *a priori,* you will be prepared for potential pitfalls in the therapeutic process, and will increase the likelihood of success. Of course, if the assumptions prove to be inaccurate, you can adjust your approach. In every case, an inaccurate assumption indicates a therapeutic gain.

Goals

In our view, the primary goal of therapy should be *to create or restore mutual sexual comfort and satisfaction.* More specific goals should be established only after the completion of a comprehensive assessment. We have found that clients often enter therapy with very specific goals, but that after the assessment new goals need to be established. For example, a couple with severe communication problems may enter therapy with the goal of having the female partner experience coital orgasm. This goal, established by the couple, is not likely to be reached as long as angry conflict exists between the partners. It is your task as the therapist to help the couple to understand the psychological as well as the mechanical factors that contribute to satisfactory arousal and sexual enjoyment; in so doing, new goals are established.

New goals must be presented to the couple in such a way that the partners understand that in order to reach their goals, they must first work on preliminary goals. Moreover, it is important for the couple to understand that achieving these preliminary goals may cause discomfort. We encourage clients to conceptualize these preliminary goals as "stepping stones" or "building a foundation." Finally, and very importantly, goals should be discussed openly with the couple.

As a therapist, you need to be careful not to establish goals that increase performance anxiety. For example, goals such as "increasing erection firmness," "producing orgasm," or "controlling ejaculation" may actually exacerbate the problem, especially if performance anxiety is a factor inhibiting the response. If such performance-related outcomes do occur, they should be looked upon as pleasant side effects secondary to achievement of the goal of increasing mutual pleasure.

Process

Many important interpersonal and interactive nuances can occur during therapy. Although these are not part of the planned therapy program, they can be crucial to therapy success. Factors such as your appearance, the appearance of your office, and your educational credentials may be important to a client. Being responsive to client requests for information, and returning phone calls promptly, also facilitate a positive rapport. These factors are present in any therapeutic interaction and are not the special domain of sex therapy.

Sex therapy brings with it its own set of important process issues:

1. The discussion of sensitive and potentially embarrassing material requires special sensitivity. It is common for a client to say, "I have never told this to anyone else before." Your reaction to such information is crucial and can either encourage or discourage further discussion. As noted in Chapter 6, we have had clients say, "I tried to tell this to my doctor, but he appeared so uncomfortable that I couldn't discuss it." You can encourage further discussion by acknowledging that the client may find it difficult to discuss sexual topics, by reassuring the client of your experience in dealing with sexual problems, and by appearing calm.

2. Careful attention should also be paid to the development of therapist–client feelings (i.e., transference and countertransference). Keep in mind that intimate discussion about sexual issues with a caring therapist may set the stage for sexual fantasies and attractions. As a therapist, you must be aware of the potentially seductive nature of the therapy process (especially with a single client) and avoid the personalization of the therapist–client relationship. If you suspect that the client is behaving in a seductive manner, then the therapy should address this issue. If you feel attracted to your client or find yourself behaving in a seductive manner, you should consult with a colleague immediately. Ask him or her to help you to assess the magnitude of the problem and to devise a strategy for working through this countertransference. The colleague may encourage you to discuss the problem with your client or to refer the client to another therapist. We wish to make it clear, however, that *sexual intimacy between a client and therapist is never acceptable or justifiable under any circumstances*.

3. If you are working alone (i.e., without a cotherapist) with heterosexual couples, you *must* avoid the appearance of taking sides. A couple will often make the assumption that a therapist is aligned with the same-gender client. This issue should be discussed at the beginning of therapy, and throughout therapy as needed, to counteract such assumptions. Similarly, if you are working alone with a single client of the other gender, you must reassure the client that you are experienced in dealing with other-gender sexual problems. In both client situations (couple or single), clients may make false assumptions about a therapist's knowledge or biases, based solely on a therapist's gender.

Other process issues are encountered in sex therapy, but these three issues seem to be the most common and important ones.

Structure and Content

The next consideration in sex therapy is the structure and content of therapy itself. As noted in Chapter 6, therapy begins during the assessment when key target problems are identified. So, for example, if relationship issues are of sufficient magnitude to interfere with progress, these must be treated first. If relationship issues are not destructive or interfering, then sex therapy can begin. From our perspective, therapy can be construed as having three stages.

STAGE I

The first stage of sex therapy usually focuses on some or all of the following goals: acquiring knowledge, negotiating sexual differences, identifying desired sexual behaviors (and approaches to sex), and acknowledging performance anxiety. Depending on the extent of a couple's or individual's problems, this first stage of therapy may include anywhere from one session to several sessions. Basically, Stage I therapy is focused on assuring that proper knowledge, goals, and motivation exist to proceed with actual therapy strategy.

STAGE II

The second stage of therapy involves the active work on more specific sexual goals identified during Stage I. This may include, for example, practicing new approaches and behaviors to reduce performance anxiety, using fantasy training to increase arousal, and practicing communication to reduce misunderstanding and express sexual desires. Cognitive approaches to improve maladaptive beliefs also occur during this stage.

STAGE III

The third stage of therapy involves a review of treatment process and outcomes (to consolidate gains and gain a sense of accomplishment), planning for treatment generalization, and relapse prevention. Stage III should begin when Stage II programs appear to be successful and moving along with only minimal therapist guidance. We begin this stage with a review of how the sexual problem developed, what the couple or individual was experiencing at the beginning of therapy, what goals were established, and what goals were achieved. Next, we discuss anticipated pitfalls in the future (that might lead to a recurrence of problems), and a review of the strategy to deal with such problems.

The discussion above has outlined elements of a comprehensive approach to sex therapy. The following material provides the details of the therapeutic procedures that are commonly found in most approaches to sexual dysfunction problems.

General Components of Therapy

There are several procedures that tend to be therapeutically useful for most sexual dysfunctions. In the next section we discuss five of these: sensate focus, education, stimulus control, cognitive restructuring, and communication training.

Sensate Focus

Just as the interview serves as the cornerstone of sex assessment, sensate focus serves as the cornerstone for sex therapy. The sensate focus approach and procedures were initially developed by Masters and Johnson (1970), and can be used to address a number of aspects of improving an individual's or couple's sexual behavior.

PRINCIPLES

The most important principle of sensate focus involves helping the client or couple to develop a heightened awareness of, and to *focus* on, *sensations* rather than performance—thus, "sensate focus." By doing this, a person or couple reduces anxiety by striving toward something that is immediately achievable (i.e., enjoying touching), rather than striving toward a goal (e.g., erection, orgasm, controlled ejaculation) that may not be achievable; the latter increases the risk of "failure" and embarrassment.

Second, sensate focus involves a structured but flexible approach to therapy. Sensate focus is structured in that clients are given explicit instructions for intimacy; if these instructions are followed, the clients/partners will gradually regain confidence in themselves and in their relationship. Although it is structured in the sense that couples know what is expected of them, sensate focus is very flexible in that it can be accommodated to any couple's unique circumstances. It is critical that, as a therapist, you do not forget to accommodate the procedures (described later) to the specific needs of your clients.

Third, sensate focus is a gradual approach to change. It is anticipated that change will take time, and there is no effort to rush ahead. One example of this principle is that clients discontinue intercourse early in therapy, so that they can relearn the "basics" of being affectionate, receiving pleasure, and so on. For some clients, intercourse will not be reintroduced into their sexual repertoire for weeks or even months! The gradual approach can be off-putting to some because it can seem slow, so special care is needed in explaining the importance of this approach to clients.

Fourth, sensate focus therapy and home exercises need to be conducted in a shared and nonthreatening environment. As the therapist, you need to attend to both partners in a couple to be sure that the exercises are proceeding at a nonthreatening pace.

You should be mindful of the principles behind sensate focus as you proceed. The procedures outlined below, and in other sources, are not intended to be followed in a cookbook-type fashion. Rather, they are proffered as a guide and should only be followed as long as they are consistent with the spirit of the principles just outlined.

PROCEDURES

As intimated above, the actual procedures of sensate focus involve encouraging partners to approach intimate physical and emotional involvement with each other in a gradual, nonthreatening manner.[1] The general operating procedure involves homework, which encourages the couple to engage in sexually related exercises, and ongoing therapy sessions, which are used to discuss the exercises, emotions triggered by these exercises, problems, and so forth.

Homework involves the provision of explicit instructions to the clients; these instructions require practice of some exercises outside of the therapeutic sessions. It is made clear to the clients that the homework will be reviewed and modified (as necessary) at each session. The homework exercises can be broken down into four "steps"; these steps are typically followed in a sequential fashion, but there are no absolutes here. Whether each step should be included, and how much time should be devoted to each, are clinical judgments.

The first step of sensate focus typically includes "nongenital pleasuring" (i.e., touching) while both partners are dressed in comfortable clothing. The least threatening behaviors may include back rubs or holding hands. Variations in the amount of clothing worn, the length of sessions, who initiates, the types of behaviors participated in, and the frequency of sessions should all be discussed in the therapy sessions before a couple goes home to practice. The partners should begin their physical involvement at a level that is acceptable to both.

Because many couples will find this to be a somewhat slow and indirect method (to say the least), you must emphasize right from the start that (1) they are going through a necessary process in order to address their long-term goal, but that (2) the short-term goal is to focus on sensations and not performance. Discuss with each couple the mechanics of the approach, including structured versus unstructured approach, frequency, potentially interfering factors, and anticipation of any problems.

Even if you give what you believe to be a clear explanation of the nonperformance aspects of sensate focus, some clients will miss the point! So we try to be particularly explicit and often tell clients: "The next time you have a therapy session, I will *not* ask you about erections or orgasms; what I will ask you about is your ability to concentrate on receiving and giving pleasure, and on your ability to enjoy what you are doing." We repeat this message with couples because most couples are performance-oriented (i.e., they focus on erection and orgasm); unless they are disabused of this notion, they will retain performance criteria during the sensate focus exercises.

At this point, you might also discuss with the client or couple the concept of performance anxiety. This should include exposing "all-or-none" thinking (e.g., "sex = intercourse") and other factors that interfere with enjoyable sex.

The application of sensate focus cannot proceed unless the partners understand this concept, acknowledge that it applies to them, and appreciate the need for a different approach in thinking and behavior.

The second step, typically, will involve "genital pleasuring." During this phase of therapy, partners are encouraged to extend gentle touching to the genital and breast regions. Partners are encouraged to caress each other, in turn, in a way that is pleasurable. As before, the couple should be discouraged from focusing on performance-related goals (i.e., erection, orgasm, etc.). As the therapy progresses through sensate focus, you should review factors that facilitate or inhibit goals. Discussing these factors with the partners in a nonjudgmental way can help them feel more in control of their own progress and less like pupils in a classroom.

Once a couple becomes comfortable with genital touching and is ready to resume sexual intercourse, we find it necessary to emphasize that even sexual intercourse can be broken down into several behaviors. Thus, we might encourage some couples to engage in "containment without thrusting." That is, the receptive partner (i.e., the woman in heterosexual couples) permits penetration and controls all aspects of this exercise. For example, the depth of penetration and the amount of time spent on penetration can be varied. Again, we encourage flexibility and variation in order to remove pressure associated with a couple's tendency to think in "all-or-none" terms.

A common problem with this stage of sensate focus is that therapists rigidly adhere to the proscription on intercourse (Lipsius, 1987). If employed mechanically, proscription of intercourse can lead to loss of erotic feelings, loss of spontaneity, unnecessary frustration, and increase in resistance. Our approach to the proscription issue is to discuss with the couple all of the potential benefits and liabilities of proscription, and to point out that the couple is working on a process that will build for the future. Pressure to ensure that a couple adheres to a proscription is dependent to a large degree on clinical judgment.

In our view, a proscriptive approach may help a couple resume physical contact under certain circumstances. Three circumstances that come to mind are the following: (1) A couple is very stressed by "sexual performance," (2) there are a lot of interfering performance-oriented thoughts, and/or (3) the couple has avoided all physical contact. On the other hand, couples who have not approached sexual relations so rigidly or with such intense emotional reactions may benefit from a general understanding of the purpose of sensate focus, but with a more relaxed attitude toward proscription.

The final step of sensate focus proper includes thrusting and intercourse. Again, it is usually a good idea to encourage the receptive partner to initiate the movement, and for movements to be slow and gradual. As always, the couple is encouraged to focus on the sensations associated with intercourse, and not to be concerned about orgasm. The partners might try experimenting with different positions, and not only assume the same position(s) they have used prior to therapy.

These are the general procedures that constitute what is commonly referred to as sensate focus. Several authorities have elaborated the basics provided here (e.g., Hawton, 1985; Kaplan, 1974; Masters & Johnson, 1970); you may want to consult these references once you have worked comfortably with the steps as described above. At this point, however, we want to identify some of the potential problems that you are likely to encounter.

PITFALLS OF SENSATE FOCUS

The sensate focus procedure has potential applications and benefits for many of the problems encountered by sex therapists. Unfortunately, the procedures are often misunderstood and misapplied. It is not unusual for couples to enter therapy and report that they had tried to "abstain from sex" or "just fondle" and this did not work. Recently, a new couple enrolled in therapy for the purpose of dealing with erectile difficulties. In reponse to a question about past therapy, the husband of the couple explained that they had previously participated in sex therapy and had tried sensate focus. The approach used was "not to have sex for a 2-week period." The couple had no understanding of the purpose of the procedure or the guidelines for their behavior. They left their previous therapy very dissatisfied.

We constantly encounter variations of the misapplication of sensate focus. It is a very simplistic procedure on the surface and a very effective strategy, but is easily misapplied and misunderstood by both therapist and client. McCarthy (1985) has pointed out a number of the common mistakes in the use of sensate focus homework assignments.

The most common mistake that therapists make is not explaining the details of the procedure and not engaging the couple in the decision-making process of the application. This often results in noncompliance. A second common mistake is demanding performance as part of the procedure (e.g., "The next step in the procedure is to stimulate your partner in the genital area to the point of orgasm"). This type of statement may increase performance anxiety, especially in a vulnerable person. It would be preferable to state, "You have done well so far in concentrating on your sensations and feelings as you and your partner stimulate each other. Thus far you have included genital caressing. What do you feel the next step should be?" This approach allows a variety of responses without an anticipation of sexual failure or pressure. One additional mistake some therapists make involves premature termination of the sensate focus approach when a couple is noncompliant or encounters difficulties. Premature termination only serves to reinforce avoidance. Difficulties should be discussed at length, and barriers to progress should be identified and removed. Generally, we allow 3 weeks of noncompliance before changing procedures.

Another opportunity for disaster presents itself when therapy moves into the arena of "homework procedures." At this time, there exists a potential conflict between being natural and unstructured, and being mechanistic and structured. Most couples and individuals express a preference to approach homework assignments in a "natural, unstructured" manner. With this approach, you describe the procedures involved and the principles behind the procedures, but leave it up to the couple to schedule other details, such as the frequency and times for "practice." Although this may intuitively be the preferred strategy, you can expect couples to return to therapy without having carried out the assignment! The reason for this is that all too often there is a long history of sexual avoidance; thus, the individual or couple cannot get started without raising anxiety levels unacceptably high.

Thus, we usually explain the pluses and minuses of structured versus unstructured strategies before providing homework exercises. The couple can then choose a strategy and, in so doing, can be fully aware of the potential for noncompliance. At times, a client may "try out" a certain strategy, and upon failure may adopt a different approach. In addition to exploring the issue of structured versus unstructured practice, you should explore other potential obstacles to carrying out therapy procedures—for example, relatives living in the house, work schedules, medical concerns, and travel plans. Once these potential obstacles are identified, and solutions generated, then the rationale and details of homework can begin.

BENEFITS OF SENSATE FOCUS

There are many benefits that may result from the sensate focus procedure. New behaviors may be learned, along with new approaches to sexual interactions. We have dealt with couples who have had very narrow approaches to sex. It is not unusual, for example, for a couple to report that they engage in no touching behavior at all. They may kiss once, then have intercourse! We have even encountered couples who view foreplay as "something that kids do." For such a couple, sensate focus offers a structured opportunity to challenge established habits that may be restricting pleasure and causing sex problems.

Sensate focus may also help to change clients' perception of their partners. A common problem we run into is that many men approach sexual intimacy with intercourse as the only goal. In a heterosexual couple, the female partner may begin to see herself as an object of her partner's pleasure and not as a companion who is loved. The sensate focus procedure can help partners to focus on each other with mutual affection rather than as objects of arousal.

Sensate focus can also be quite diagnostic. Difficulties that emerge often carry important information about other problems that a couple is having. These other problems often cannot be addressed through sensate focus itself.

CONCLUDING COMMENTS

Sensate focus should be viewed as one part of a total treatment approach; it is not a complete therapy in itself. Thus, communication issues, faulty attitudes that interfere with sexual enjoyment, and nonsexual marital conflicts are examples of therapy concerns that may be dealt with concomitantly with sensate focus. Sensate focus is a procedure that has multiple benefits and can be used as part of a treatment program for every category of sexual dysfunction problems.

Education

Education (i.e., providing information) may be the most common component of sex therapy. Information can help to correct myths and to reverse misunderstandings that adversely affect sexual functioning. For example, the belief that foreplay is for kids or that intercourse is the only true form of sex can be devastating to a middle-aged or elderly male and his partner. Similarly, the belief that the erection must appear first (i.e., *before* sexual activity) in order to signal sexual interest and desire can limit a person's sexual opportunities. The net effect of these beliefs is that a male who does not obtain an erection prior to a sexual interaction will not participate in sex. We have known many men and women who have avoided sexual interactions for years, partly because of an adherence to these beliefs.

Education about the normal changes in male and female functioning due to aging can be used to support the important and "normal" role of foreplay in adult sexual activity. The belief that foreplay is for kids may have had its origin in the common Italian practice of *carezza;* this term refers to the nonintercourse sexual play activity practiced by Italian youths. In some parts of Italy it is still a ceremony to "show the sheets" to the bridegroom's father after the wedding night. Blood must appear on the sheets to reassure the father that his son has married a virgin.

Zilbergeld (1978) lists other common myths that you may want to attend to:

- Men should not have (or at least not express) certain feelings.
- In sex, as elsewhere, it's performance that counts.
- The man must take charge of and orchestrate sex.
- A man always wants and is ready to have sex.
- All physical contact must lead to sex.

• Sex equals intercourse.
• Sex requires an erection.
• Good sex is a linear progression of increasing excitement terminated only by orgasm.
• Sex should be natural and spontaneous.

In addition to debunking myths, you can often serve a valuable role by providing new information. For example, giving an elderly woman information about the use of vaginal lubricants (e.g., Replens, Astaglide, Today, and Lubrin or Condom Mate suppositories) may alleviate her pain during intercourse. Also, pointing out to a couple or individual that biological factors may play a role in the dysfunction can relieve guilt or blame. It is likewise helpful to provide correct information about anatomy[2] and physiology, as well as normative sexual behavior. In this regard, we are reminded of one client who entered therapy with very low self-esteem. The source of his distress was a "problem" with premature ejaculation: He confessed that he usually reached orgasm within 15–20 minutes of vaginal penetration. He was surprised, to say the least, to learn that the latency to orgasm during intercourse among American men typically ranges from 2 to 7 minutes (Kinsey et al., 1948).

Given that education can be therapeutic, the question arises: How can you best educate a client in the context of sex therapy? Here, as elsewhere, we advise flexibility. Some clients like to read and request suggestions for readings. Other clients prefer to ask questions during therapy. Still others will be reluctant to ask for information directly; for these clients, you will need to take advantage of naturally occurring opportunites to give an impromptu "lecture."

Fortunately, for clients who like to read, there are many excellent books available. We can recommend several titles (see below), and we encourage you to develop your own reading list. You may want to purchase several copies of your favorite guides and have them available to loan out (be careful, however; you may not get them back!). Alternatively, you might identify one or two local bookstores and ply them with purchasing suggestions. In any event, we advise that you read any book that you recommend to a client and be prepared to discuss its contents during the sessions.

RECOMMENDED READINGS FOR CLIENTS

Barbach, L. G. (1975). *For yourself: The fulfillment of female sexuality*. New York: Signet.
Barbach, L. G. (1981). *For each other: Sharing sexual intimacy*. Garden City, NY: Doubleday.
Boston Women's Health Collective. (1984). *The new our bodies, ourselves*. New York: Simon & Schuster.

Comfort, A. (1972). *The joy of sex.* New York: Crown.

Gagnon, J. H. (1977). *Human sexualities.* Glenview, IL: Scott, Foresman.

Gottman, J., Notarius, C., Gonso, J., & Markman, H. (1976). *A couple's guide to communication.* Champaign, IL: Research Press.

Heiman, J. R., & LoPiccolo, J. (1988). *Becoming orgasmic: A sexual and personal growth program for women* (rev. ed.). New York: Prentice Hall.

Kilmann, P. R., & Mills, K. H. (1983). *All about sex therapy.* New York: Plenum.

McCarthy, B., & McCarthy, E. (1984). *Sexual awareness: Enhancing sexual pleasure.* New York: Caroll & Graf.

Schover, L. R. (1984). *Prime time: Sexual health for men over fifty.* New York: Holt, Rinehart & Winston.

Zilbergeld, B. (1978). *Male sexuality: A guide to sexual fulfillment.* New York: Bantam.

Finally, given our culture's captivation with technology, you may want to consider using videotaped educational material. A good source for such materials is Focus International, 14 Oregon Drive, Huntington Station, NY 11746-2627.

Stimulus Control and Scheduling

We know that awkward circumstances are not conducive to relaxed, enjoyable sexual relations. When taken to an extreme, such circumstances can contribute to sexual dysfunction. Consider the following example (one to which we have alluded in Chapter 3): A client of ours complained of loss of erection not only with his wife, but with his very sensuous and eager girlfriend. He wanted to know why this happened. During the assessment interview he was asked about the circumstances under which sex occurred; he reported that the first time he attempted sexual intercourse with his girlfriend, he was in the back seat of a Volkswagen in a church parking lot! With horrified churchgoing onlookers walking by, it was easy *for us* to understand why he lost his erection. However, our client had not identified his circumstances as a source of interference.

"Stimulus control" refers to efforts to establish a pleasant, relaxing environment that is conducive to sexual expression, thereby minimizing interfering circumstances. Even simple suggestions such as arranging for a babysitter, cleaning up the bedroom, or putting on relaxing music can be helpful; surprisingly, these suggestions are not obvious to some clients. Clients sometimes need to be reminded of the efforts they made during courtship to "set the mood." Once ensconced in a relationship, many forget to attend to these preparations, or think that they are unimportant.

Likewise, many couples do not set aside a time for sexual expression. Commonly, couples attempt sex under the pressure of "the first free moment during a busy week." They expect good sex to be spontaneous and unplanned.

Again, many will have forgotten all the planning that went into "spontaneous" sexual expression during courtship. We often encourage clients to schedule a time for sex, and to plan for it with as much effort as they might for any other special event in their lives. We remind them that anticipation fuels desire.

Cognitive Restructuring

Two forms of cognitive restructuring can be helpful: challenging negative attitudes and reducing interfering thoughts.

CHALLENGING NEGATIVE ATTITUDES

Exposing and helping a client to change negative attitudes is a complex therapeutic task. One of the differences between a myth (or misunderstanding) and a negative attitude is that the latter is held onto tenaciously, despite compelling data to the contrary. For example, a woman may have very negative feelings toward men and believe that men cannot be trusted. This attitude may be the result of a previous relationship in which the woman's partner was unfaithful. In this woman's current relationship, she may interpret her partner's erectile failure as evidence of being unfaithful. If it is clear that the erection failure is due to other factors, it may take considerable therapeutic effort to address her general negative and untrusting attitude toward men.

Similarly, a male may have a negative attitude toward women; for example, he may perceive all women as manipulative and financially motivated. His "lack of desire" may be a reflection of his fear of making a commitment and being manipulated. Again, you may have to address this attitude before working directly on the sexual problem. In all cases, this should be approached with caution—a client may be very defensive and have a great deal invested in holding onto a negative belief. You may have to deal with such issues in individual therapy before couples therapy can proceed.

REDUCING INTERFERING THOUGHTS

Sometimes you will need to help a client reduce intrusive images or thoughts that are interfering with sexual enjoyment. A man who worries about the firmness of his erection, or one who worries about having sex with a new partner in the bed that he and his recently deceased wife had sex in for 30 years, is likely to encounter interfering thoughts and sexual problems. The presenting problem may be loss of erection, loss of desire, or delayed ejaculation, but the source of the problem is the interfering thoughts. Similarly, a woman who worries about her sick child, or about professional responsibilities and commitments, may lose her sexual desire or be unable to achieve orgasm. It is always intriguing that, despite the obvious presence of interfering thoughts, many clients ignore or dismiss such thoughts as contributors to sexual difficulties; instead, they focus on the perception of their own, or their partners', inadequacy.

To deal with interfering thoughts, you must first help the client identify the presence of such thoughts. Once such thoughts are identified, and it is agreed that interfering thoughts do occur in association with sexual behavior, then you must help the client reduce the occurrence of such thoughts. It is often helpful to give the client alternative thoughts to focus on during sexual activity. For example, focusing on body parts or a sequence of sexual activities is usually more conducive to arousal. However, you should be prepared for such suggestions to lead to discussions about whether or not it is "normal" or "healthy" to fantasize about sex (or about sex with another partner) during actual sexual activity. Some clients feel very strongly that fantasizing is tantamount to cheating on one's partner. Obviously, such discussions have to be approached with a great deal of care and sensitivity. We also find it helpful to have clients read the chapter on sexual fantasies in McCarthy's (1988) book, *Male Sexual Awareness.*

It may also be helpful to a client to suggest compartmentalizing thoughts. Specific times during the day should be set aside to focus on worrying and problem solving; other times should be set aside for pleasant thoughts and sexual thoughts. Putting such categories of thoughts on schedule may help teach a client to eliminate negative thinking during sexual time periods.

CONCLUDING COMMENTS

Negative beliefs and interfering thoughts can present impediments to sexual expression and enjoyment. In some cases, it will be possible to address these cognitive difficulties as a part of the sex therapy itself. In other cases, however, more intensive cognitive restructuring may be needed, usually in the context of individual therapy. Because cognitive therapy techniques and process can be quite involved and quite useful, we recommend that you familiarize yourself with more detailed accounts of these methods (e.g., Beck, 1976; Ellis, 1962; Meichenbaum, 1977).

Communication Training

Communication problems are frequently encountered when dealing with sexual dysfunction. In our practice, we have developed a handout for clients that serves as both an assessment tool and a therapeutic guide. The handout is a 10-page pamphlet that describes common couples' communication problems and provides suggestions about how to overcome these problems. The typical problems in communication include the following:

1. Off beam: Partners start to discuss one problem and drift into another.
2. Mind reading: Partners guess the meaning of each other's statements because they think they know each other so well.
3. "Kitchen sink": Partners start discussing one problem and bring in every other problem.
4. "Yes, but": Each partner listens but continues to think that the other is wrong.
5. Cross-complaining: Each response contains a new complaint.
6. Standoff: Partners tend to repeat the same argument over and over without progress or resolution.

We have found it both time-saving and effective to hand out the communication pamphlet to couples at the first sign of communication problems. We typically instruct clients to read the handout independently (we give one to each partner) and to check off those problems that seem to apply to their relationship. We then discuss the various areas of communication difficulties, often with examples from their own experiences. It is very important for you to establish from the beginning that the review of the examples is designed to look at the process of communication, and not to illustrate or determine who was right or wrong.

As the therapist, you should serve as a model of good communication during all sessions. This is achieved by actively listening, displaying empathy, asking clients to express themselves clearly, and other such social and communication skills. In addition, you should continually look for improvement in communication skills and point these out to a couple when they occur. It is helpful for you to inform the couple that, throughout the therapy, communication skills will be continually monitored and addressed when appropriate. If this is stated at the outset, an individual will not feel picked on when a communication issue is raised.

In many cases, sexual dysfunction problems cannot be addressed until communication improves. In such cases, we often point out that sexual expression is a specific form of communication and that it will be enhanced by focusing on general communication training.

Much has been written on communication training for couples; for further training, we recommend the excellent works by Beck (1988) and Gottman, Notarius, Gonso, and Markman (1976). The latter is also useful as a guide for clients.

Procedures for Specific Problems

As indicated in the previous section, many common procedures and circumstances are encountered in the treatment of almost all sexual problems. This section deals with procedures for specific problems.

Desire Disorders

Low sexual desire in men or women can be related to a number of factors (see Chapter 2). Therefore, during the assessment, you must first determine whether the problem is situational (i.e., specific to the client's current situation and functioning) or generalized (i.e., a more pervasive problem). A careful assessment should identify potential etiological factors. For example, is low desire due to a long-standing negative attitude toward sex? And, if so, is this due to sexual trauma or poor parental role modeling? Is low sexual desire due to one particular partner or set of circumstances, or is the low desire present in all sexual situations? In addition, low desire may be the end product of severe performance anxiety, in which a person has selectively ignored and avoided erotic stimuli because of the threat such stimuli pose. As always, a careful assessment is essential to formulating the problem and planning treatment.

GENERALIZED HYPOACTIVE SEXUAL DESIRE DISORDER

When low desire is a product of long-standing attitudinal and experiential factors, therapy must focus on processing the source and reaction to the important background influences. The client must develop an understanding of the influences on his or her low desire. Insight alone rarely results in any positive change, and increasing desire may only develop following positive sexual experiences. However, even when positive experiences are encouraged through sensate focus, long-standing desire problems can be resistant to change. Exposure to erotic and/or masturbatory training may also be used in resistant cases to promote change.

Use of Erotic Materials. "Erotica" may be defined as depiction of consensual sexual relations, whereas "pornography" is depiction of coercive sexual relations. Use of erotic materials should proceed only after a thorough discussion with the client. Objections to pornography, particularly the objectification and degradation of women, should be addressed so that there are no barriers to accepting and experiencing erotic stimuli. When you are confident that your client can use erotic stimuli without negative objections, then the nature of and details of exposure should be worked out. Use of erotica should be approached as a sexual experience, and attention should be paid to mood, setting, and other important ingredients of a satisfying encounter. It is also crucial to advise the client to view erotica without being a movie or literary critic! We have had clients return after viewing erotica and comment on the poor cinematography. Developing your own library of materials that you have previewed, so that you can make knowledgeable recommendations to clients, is a good idea.

Masturbation Training. Masturbation training with fantasy must be approached in a fashion similar to the use of erotica. Negative attitudes must be explored first, and then detailed attention must be paid to maximizing a positive sexual experience. It must also not be assumed that the client knows how to masturbate. Recently, we had a client who reported to us a lack of success in attempting to masturbate. When he was asked how he masturbated, he reported that he masturbated with his hand open so that his palm rubbed against the underside of his penis. In addition, he reported putting honey on his penis as a "lubricant." He thought he read somewhere that honey was a good lubricant. Another male client who reported difficulty with masturbation put his penis between the palms of both hands; he then rubbed his penis back and forth, much in the way a Boy Scout might try to start a fire with a stick! Specific instructions with pictures helped both of these clients to learn how to masturbate successfully. Carefully prepared and sensitive educational videotapes are also available from Focus International (see "Education" section earlier in this chapter).

Masturbation training helps some clients to become much more sensitive to the necessary conditions for a positive sexual experience. In clients who lack desire and sexual confidence, masturbation training can lead to positive experiences, which build both desire and confidence.

SITUATIONAL HYPOACTIVE SEXUAL DESIRE DISORDER

When low desire is linked only to a current partner or circumstance, change can usually be achieved more easily. Solving the problems with the current partner or circumstance must be addressed first; then a return of sexual desire can be facilitated. If increase in desire does not follow a resolution of current problems, then sensate focus, exposure to erotica, or masturbatory training may be helpful.

An often overlooked circumstantial cause of low desire is habituation. This is especially true of couples who are in long-term relationships and who always approach sex in the same fashion. With a recent case of situational

Hypoactive Sexual Desire Disorder, we initially had some difficulty in pinpointing the cause. The partners seemed to be very compatible and communicated effectively. They also were relatively liberal, and approached sex with a lot of creativity and variety. During one session, which the male partner attended alone because his partner was on a business trip, he was asked whether there was anything he hadn't discussed that bothered him about his wife.

"You know what really bugs me? She goes around the house completely nude all the time. As soon as she comes home from work, she strips down to her bare ass and stays that way all night. She also never wears underwear and even tells our friends about this. She tells me that I'm a prude if I'm not naked and, if we sit next to each other, I have to hold her hand or else she will hold my penis. I hate that! Also, she never closes the bathroom door when she goes to the bathroom and comes right in when I'm going. There is no privacy whatsoever in our home."

As an example of habituating to a partner, this case was somewhat extreme; however, we often encounter couples who are completely open with their toileting behavior and nudity. Although there is certainly nothing morally or ethically wrong with this, it is not uncommon for such openness to lead to habituation. Theoretically, this is consistent with Stoller's (1975) view that novelty and risk are the motivating forces behind sexual desire and arousal. Thus, whether a couple is very conservative or very liberal in their approach to sexual relations, habituation can be a factor contributing to low desire.

Another common expression of situational Hypoactive Sexual Desire Disorder occurs in partners with different levels of desire. Initially this difference may be masked, because one partner (usually the less desirous) accommodates to the other. Over time, however, some resentment develops and the problem surfaces. In such a couple, it is common for the less desirous partner to be labeled as the "client." As it turns out, however, there is simply a discrepancy between a *relatively* low-desire partner and a *relatively* high-desire partner. In such a couple, you can expect communication and problem-solving skills to be poor; these will require attention before the partners can begin to negotiate a sexual pattern that is mutually acceptable and satisfying.

We have often found that low sexual desire is a result of partner incompatibility. Partners, whether married or unmarried, homosexual or heterosexual, may have difficulty in articulating to each other that there is little or no sexual attraction between them. There may be unresolved anger or there may be incompatibility just because a couple has "grown apart." At any rate, it is common for the role of the therapist to shift to helping a couple identify and deal with their incompatibility separate from the sexual issue. The focus on low sexual desire may have been the catalyst that brought a couple to therapy to deal with their negative or neutral feelings toward each other. In separate interviews with each partner, you can often elicit descriptions and feelings of desire for other persons or for circumstances separate from the partner. Your role may then be to help the partners accept their low desire for each other and to put this information into perspective. This does not necessarily result in separation for a couple and may even lead to a peaceful acceptance of their situation.

Male Erectile Disorder

More is now known about Male Erectile Disorder than any other sexual dysfunction. Thanks to extensive, multidisciplinary research, we now have an understanding of the biopsychosocial mechanisms of erectile dysfunction. The medical aspects of treatment are thoroughly addressed in the following chapter. It should be pointed out, however, that even in cases where significant organic factors have been identified, psychological factors may also be present and must be considered in treatment.

Once a comprehensive assessment has been completed and the relative contributions of organic and psychogenic factors can be determined, a specific treatment program can be designed. As the therapist, you should also be aware that erection problems may have evolved as a result of premature ejaculation, delayed ejaculation, or lack of desire. All of these potential problem areas should be thoroughly explored, along with the comprehensive medical and psychosocial assessment of the erection problem.

Treatment may include any of the treatment approaches we have already discussed. Indeed, the approach to treating Male Erectile Disorder has in the past relied largely upon relationship approaches, particularly sensate focus. Given current knowledge, we are now more sensitive to including in our treatment approach consideration of the individual factors discussed in Chapter 3 and outlined by Barlow (1986).

Most males who experience erectile difficulties become very upset with themselves and fear ridicule from their partners. In heterosexual males, fears of homosexuality may emerge; that is, heterosexual men often interpret difficulty in obtaining or maintaining an erection as a sign that they are gay. In both homosexual and heterosexual males, erection difficulties raise fears regarding masculinity. Regardless of the precipitating factors, most cases of Male Erectile Disorder are maintained by interfering thoughts that may precede and occur during sexual relations. As we explain to our clients, these interfering thoughts are not erotic or sexy thoughts; moreover, they decrease arousal and inhibit erection. In a nondysfunctional man, thoughts preceding and occurring during sexual relations usually focus on his partner's or his own body parts, seductive behaviors, and anticipations of arousal and pleasure. In contrast, the dysfunctional male is preoccupied with worries regarding the firmness of his erection; images of his partner being disappointed, angry, or ridiculing; and distinct feelings of anxiety and depression.

The treatment of Male Erectile Disorder must address the interfering thoughts by helping the man to "restructure" his thoughts—that is, to focus on sexually facilitating thoughts rather than on sexually inhibiting ones. The term "performance anxiety" (cf. Masters & Johnson, 1970) is often applied to the dysfunctional thinking, but focusing on anxiety can be misleading. Several studies have shown that anxiety can actually facilitate rather than inhibit arousal (Barlow et al., 1983; Hoon et al., 1977; Wolchik et al., 1980). Indeed, Barlow (1986, 1988) has presented compelling evidence that the thought processes of dysfunctional males contribute to the erectile difficulties.

One way to help the client to refocus his thinking onto more positive thoughts is to have him recall his thought content during past satisfying sexual experiences. This usually sensitizes him to the types of thoughts he should concentrate on. If he has difficulty remembering positive sexual thoughts, you may wish to help him with "typical" helpful thoughts. This is an instance where exposure to erotic literature or videotapes may be helpful.

Once your client is able to readily identify the positive sexual thinking process, he is ready for sensate focus. You can now establish the goal (during sensate focus) to be positive sexual thinking, rather than achieving or maintaining an erection. Remember, the client is likely to focus on his erection, and to report success or failure on this basis during sensate focus. Your job is to return his focus onto erotic thoughts and images, not the erection.

Throughout the treatment process, you should continually monitor and attend to interfering thoughts, communication, conducive erotic environment, feelings of comfort, and good partner relationship. You must also help your client to avoid performance-oriented approaches to sex by accepting a broad definition of sex. That is, the goal is to help the client to see that sex is more than just intercourse; instead, sex involves a wide range of behaviors. We find the use of a menu analogy to be very helpful as a way of reducing performance pressure and to broaden the definition of sex. With this analogy, clients are told to conceptualize sex as a meal and to pick and choose from the menu, depending upon their appetite and taste.[3] Appetite and taste for sex may be expected to vary from occasion to occasion and person to person.

Even in cases where there is clearly an organic basis for the erectile problem, the issues mentioned above should be considered in treatment. Negative, interfering thoughts (especially in long-standing problems) may be present in any cases of Male Erectile Disorder.

When a partner is involved in treatment, it is also important to consider the partner's cognitions concerning the dysfunction. Just as the man with erectile difficulty harbors negative associations around this problem, so too, the partner can be expected to have negative cognitions. Typical partner responses may include the following:

- "I'm no longer attractive."
- "He doesn't love me any more."
- "He must be having an affair with someone else."
- "He isn't trying; he doesn't want to have sex with me."

We always ask the partner what he or she thinks is the cause of the erectile problem. It is very important to help to clear up possible misunderstandings before proceeding to an intervention, such as sensate focus exercises. If potential misunderstandings are not addressed, it is likely that they will arise again and sabotage treatment progress.

One final note: As with other disorders, *never* assume that a couple is approaching sexual relations in a manner that is conducive to arousal! On many occasions we have encountered clients who never kiss, touch, fondle, stroke, or hug prior to attempting intercourse; yet these clients expect an erection to emerge once they attempt intromission! Inquire about the details of the foreplay, as well as the erotic environment. Is each partner satisfied with what has been occurring?

Inhibited Female Orgasm

Inhibited Female Orgasm (see Chapter 4) can be a very frustrating dysfunction that can easily evolve into a total avoidance of sexual relations. Because of the strong association with performance anxiety, sensate focus is often advised. In many cases, however, the suspicion is a lack of sufficient erotic input, often associated with distracting and interfering thoughts. Directed use of masturbation with appropriate focus on erotica is sometimes helpful. As in the case of other dysfunctions, it is necessary to conduct a detailed assessment to determine whether the problem has always existed (i.e., lifelong and/or generalized) or is associated with a current problem or condition (i.e., acquired and/or situational).

The book *Becoming Orgasmic* (Heiman & LoPiccolo, 1988) outlines in detail a program for helping women to learn masturbation and to become orgasmic. This is a revised edition of a widely acclaimed earlier volume; it provides excellent information, and its approach to the problem is considered state-of-the-art. Today's therapists give more consideration to cognitive factors and less to the mechanics of masturbation.

We have found in many instances that Inhibited Female Orgasm is associated with negative feelings toward sex (in general), oneself, or one's partner. With some clients, we have also encountered fears regarding fainting, losing control, or increased vulnerability. Rarely, in our experience, is the difficulty just a problem of poor sexual technique. In order to use a procedure such as masturbation training, you should first explore in detail whether negative cognitions/affects are present. It would be a strategic blunder to suggest masturbation training without first assessing the woman's and her partner's beliefs about the nature of the problem and the acceptibility of masturbation. Once these feelings have been explored, and both partners are comfortable, the physiology of orgasm should be explained and masturbation training initiated.

Premature Ejaculation

Complaints of premature ejaculation are often associated with misunderstandings about sex and are also often "smoke screens" for relationship problems. Common misunderstandings include an unrealistic expectation about the length of time thrusting should last before ejaculation, and the belief that sex ends as soon as ejaculation occurs.

In many cases of premature ejaculation, we direct our initial discussion to the question, "Why do you have sex?" After some thought, a number of reasons are suggested by clients. "To have pleasure" or "because it feels good" may be the most common response. We point out that people have sex for a variety of reasons: to experience pleasure, to express love and affection, to make up after an argument, to have children, to make oneself feel better, to please a partner, and so on. Moreover, the reason will change from occasion to occasion. The goal of this general discussion is to impress upon our clients that pleasure or pleasuring, and all of the other reasons we have sex, are not dependent on the length of time between intromission and orgasm. Furthermore, the length of time a man "lasts" should be looked upon as but one small part of the whole sexual exchange. Indeed, the primary goal of this question and related discussion is to encourage the couple to focus on general pleasuring rather than orgasm. We encourage the partners to continue having intercourse even after ejaculation.[4] This takes the pressure off the timing of ejaculation, and properly puts the emphasis on the total sexual relationship. This approach almost always results in a couple's reporting a more satisfying relationship. Interestingly, even though we do not focus on the length of time between intromission and ejaculation, this time interval usually increases.

A second question that we ask premature ejaculators and their partners is "What do you believe is causing the problem?" As is the case with all sexual problems, the meaning attributed to the problem by each partner should be thoroughly explored. In some cases of premature ejaculation, the female partner may express anger because her sexual needs are going unmet. Similarly, some women may believe that their men have more control over ejaculation than is truly the case; they may interpret their partners' haste as the men's way of being thoughtless or inconsiderate. However, we have yet to have a client who can control his ejaculation so expertly that he can purposely reach orgasm quickly in order to hurt his partner's feelings. On the contrary, most men who seek treatment for premature ejaculation want desperately to increase their latency and to please their partners. They tend to be embarrassed and confused about their difficulty.

More often than not, focus on premature ejaculation is a misdirection from the real problem, which is a stressed relationship. In such cases, therapy directed at improving a stressed relationship will also improve the premature ejaculation. When you believe that a couple has no sexual misunderstandings and has a compatible relationship, then the well-known "squeeze technique" can be applied (Masters & Johnson, 1970). The squeeze technique involves instructing the male to masturbate to a point that he feels would result in ejaculation if he continued. He should pause in the masturbation at this point and squeeze the head of his penis along the coronal ridge by placing his forefinger and middle finger on one side of his penis and his thumb opposite on the other side. The squeeze is recommended to be firm and to last about 10 seconds. By repeating this process several times before allowing ejaculation to occur, and by practicing this procedure over a number of sessions, the man will learn to control his ejaculation.

Another procedure that is sometimes advised for controlling premature ejaculation is the "start–stop," or "pause," technique (Semans, 1956). This technique is the precursor to the squeeze technique but without the squeeze. The couple is asked to practice foreplay and penile stimulation to the point prior to ejeculation. The male with premature ejaculation signals his partner when to stop so that his arousal level can subside. Stimulation is then resumed after a pause, and the process is repeated at least three times before allowing ejaculation to occur. It is important to instruct the male to enjoy his sensations and to learn to identify the various levels of arousal that he experiences. Even though this technique has been around for 35 years it is still considered a viable option that is widely used as one component of a total therapy approach.

When suggesting these techniques, however, you should take care not to depict ejaculation control as a complete solution of the couple's problem. Ejaculation control should be viewed as *part* of, and not the totality of, satisfying sex.

Vaginismus and Dyspareunia

For both vaginismus and dyspareunia, a complete medical evaluation is advised to rule out any possible organic factors. The most common nonorganic etiological explanation of vaginismus and dyspareunia is founded in prior sexual trauma and negative sexual messages. Overcoming these problems often involves the complex task of reviewing and processing negative attitudes about sex. Once the client is comfortable with a positive attitude toward sexual relations, then it is possible to initiate an *in vivo* desensitization procedure involving gradual insertion of a finger or dilator into the vaginal opening. It is probably more convenient and easier for most women to practice insertion using their own fingers. Some women, however, are more comfortable using a graduated set of dilators, perhaps because of phobic reactions to their genital area (Leslie R. Schover, personal communication, December 30, 1990). The dilators may be obtained from a medical supply firm and come in graduated thicknesses.

The strategy should be thoroughly discussed and reviewed with a client before actually suggesting it. It may be helpful to approach the topic by saying, "Some women who have difficulty with penetration have found that by practicing insertion very gradually they can overcome the problem. How would you feel about the technique of practicing insertion while you are alone and in the complete privacy of your home?" Once a woman has agreed to try, you should explain that she (the client) is in complete control of the procedures. It should be emphasized that the depth of penetration and length of time of penetration can be controlled and varied by the client. The client should approach this while bathing or while relaxed on her bed. She should start by inserting her little finger or the narrowest dilator, and only when she is comfortable with inserting a dilator for a period of 5 minutes should she move on to the next size. A vaginal lubricant can be advised. Over a number of sessions, she should work up to inserting two fingers or the largest dilator for a few minutes. Because many women will have strong objections to touching their genitals or masturbating, this exercise has to be put into perspective and distinguished from masturbation.

As a woman becomes more comfortable with insertion, her partner can be included in the procedure. Again, it should be emphasized that the woman must be in complete control of the procedure and that she can stop the procedure at any time. Moreover, the insertion process should be approached gradually with partial penetration and withdrawal. This process is usually started with digital penetration; over a number of sessions, the couple moves toward penile insertion. Use of vaginal lubricants may be a useful addition to the insertion procedures.

Additional Considerations in Sex Therapy

Religious and Cultural Concerns

Occasionally you may encounter a client whose religious or cultural beliefs clash with a healthy approach to sex. For example, masturbatory conditioning or even sensate focus may be objected to by some religious viewpoints. You should, of course, always be sensitive to the possibility of such issues and never proceed with therapy until religious and culturally based beliefs related to sexual practice are thoroughly explored.

We have found that at times a client's misinterpretation of a religious belief has stood in the way of therapy. In such cases it is helpful to refer the client to an appropriate member of the clergy who can interpret the belief system and work in consultation with you.

Alcohol and Drug Abuse

Alcohol and drug abuse can adversely affect sexual functioning on a biological basis, as we describe in more detail in Chapter 9. There can also be an adverse effect interpersonally and psychologically. We have found that it is futile to work on sexual problems when there is an ongoing substance abuse problem. The substance abuse problem in almost all cases must be treated first and must be under control before a consistent program for sexual dysfunction can be implemented.

Major Psychological Disorders

It is not unusual for some of the clients you will be working with to present with major psychological disorders. Individuals with personality disorders or neurotic disorders may be very challenging as you attempt to address their sexual concerns. Sometimes the psychological problems may be so overwhelming that a focus on the sexual issues is inappropriate or even impossible. At other times, focusing on a client's sexual concerns will alleviate the neurotic or personality disorder symptoms. Psychological testing and a careful psychosocial interview will help you to decide which problem is most important to work on. We have found that when psychological symptoms interfere with progress in a session, then the focus must switch to the treatment of the neurotic problem or personality disorder. We have conducted therapy by shifting our focus of attention depending on a client's needs. Obviously, if such an approach interferes with progress in both areas then a concentrated effort must be made on the psychological problems until they are under control.

We have found that attempting to work with individuals manifesting psychotic symptoms or organic brain syndrome is extremely difficult and, for the most part, unsuccessful. Such clients may not be able to understand or focus on the important aspects of therapy, and the therapist may even exacerbate the psychiatric symptoms by discussing sexual problems. Although we do not dismiss such clients as a policy, individuals with symptoms of psychosis or organic brain syndrome should undergo thorough neuropsychological testing. Consultation with a neuropsychologists will often give valuable information as to the capabilities of a client to retain and process instructions and sexual information. Management with therapeutic medications is often necessary, but you should understand the potential impact that such medications may have on sexual functioning. When symptomatology is very manifest, treatment of sexual problems is not advised.

Spacing of Sessions and Length of Therapy

Our general approach to most sexual dysfunction problems is to space sessions at weekly intervals. If possible, we will see clients at a more accelerated pace during the initial assessment, but in our experience weekly sessions allow for homework practice without losing continuity. The spacing of sessions should be re-evaluated regularly to determine whether a different schedule will better serve the couple, for whatever reason, without disrupting the flow of therapy. If a couple or individual is very compliant in following therapy instructions, then spacing sessions every 2, 3, or even 4 weeks is possible once progress has been clearly established. When sessions are widely spaced, instructions should be given that will allow for phone contact and even emergency sessions if needed. Most of our clients have been able to successfully reach therapy goals within 15 sessions.

Case Examples

As pointed out in Chapter 6, assessment is much more complex today than it was in the past and often requires a multidisciplinary effort. Therapy for sexual problems has also increased in complexity and often must take into account other medical and psychological treatment issues. We believe it is a fitting conclusion to this chapter to briefly describe four cases that we dealt with in a typical week, to illustrate the variety of problems a sex therapist may be called upon to deal with.

Case 1

A 32-year-old multiple sclerosis victim and his wife attended therapy together to explore their sexual options. They had been married for 10 years; 3 years ago he had started experiencing severe erectile dysfunction. He had obtained a semirigid penile implant 6 months ago; however, after 2 months he could not tolerate the prosthesis due to extreme sensitivity and had the prosthesis removed. He now asked whether he should try an inflatable prosthesis or explore other options.

Case 2

Mr. Z was a 62-year-old factory worker; his wife of 37 years had died of a heart attack 6 months ago. Currently he was dating a 50-year-old woman, but reported that he was having difficulty maintaining an erection. Furthermore, later in the interview he revealed that he and his late wife had not even attempted intercourse in the last 16 years because of his wife's dislike of any sexual activity. After receiving a careful explanation of the psychological factors influencing his sexual response, Mr. Z replied, "Is that all you can tell me? I thought you would teach me exercises to overcome my problem."

Case 3

Mr. and Mrs. J stated that their goal in therapy was to help Mrs. J to achieve coital orgasms. Both partners were in their late 20s, were college-educated, and were successful in professional careers. Mrs. J was very teary during the session, and the couple argued angrily over issues that appeared to be related to control. Both insisted, however, that they did not wish to deal with marital issues, but wanted instructions to overcome the sexual problem.

Case 4

Mr. M was 65 years old and had been divorced from his second wife for 5 years. He was now dating a 49-year-old woman, and he was experiencing "soft" erections during most attempts at intercourse. He had had a myocardial infarction 2 years ago and was currently taking Lopressor. In addition, he said he had a "nervous stomach" and was taking Tagamet.

The four cases above were challenging and complex; each required sensitivity and knowledge of therapeutic options. Cases 1 and 4 also required an understanding of multiple sclerosis, myocardial infarction, and gastric ulcer. It is becoming commonplace for the sex therapist to demonstrate familiarity with these and other medical conditions, and to combine medical and psychological interventions in order to assist a client. Therefore, in the next chapter, we discuss these issues in more detail.

Notes

[1] Theoretically, the procedure of breaking down a complex response into small steps may be a form of operant shaping (since an individual will gain a sense of reinforcement through successes); this may also be conceptualized as an *in vivo* desensitization procedure when anxiety reduction is the goal.

[2] To aid with education about anatomy, you may want to purchase medical illustration books or even three-dimensional anatomical models. Although the former can be found in most medical school bookstores, the latter can be more difficult to obtain. If you are interested in purchasing models, you can write to Jim Jackson and Company, 33 Richdale Avenue, Cambridge, MA 02140, for a recent catalog of reproductive anatomy models.

[3] We thank Toby Simon from Brown University Health Services for this clever idea.

[4] Although this technique may be helpful for focusing a couple's attention on pleasure rather than performance, this may not be a desirable procedure for couples practicing "safer sex." If he does not withdraw after ejaculating, a man wearing a condom may lose the condom as detumescence begins. For men wearing condoms during sexual relations, the squeeze technique or stop–start procedure may be preferable.

8

Integrating Psychosocial with Medical Approaches to Assessment and Treatment

The previous two chapters on assessment and treatment have assumed that you are the primary caregiver, and that a psychosocial approach is being implemented. Although most of us prefer this role, most sex therapy practices also include a fair amount of consultation with other professionals, particularly physicians. In the role of consultant, you will typically be asked to provide two types of services: (1) to conduct a psychosocial evaluation as part of a comprehensive assessment (often as a screen prior to a medical intervention), and/or (2) to facilitate psychosocial adjustment to a medical treatment. In this chapter, we discuss these two roles; we begin by reminding you of the "medical model," and overviewing the most common medical approaches to sexual rehabilitation.

The Medical Model Is Alive and Well

The belief "If it is broken, the doctor can fix it" is perhaps nowhere more strongly held than in the treatment of sexual dysfunctions. This is especially true of men who experience erectile difficulties. Even after many men have been told directly that their sexual problem has no organic basis, we have often heard the reply, "But can you give me a pill to help me out?" Indeed, such requests are understandable given the plethora of advertisements in "men's magazines" that mislead men by promising success through a pill. Witness the following illustration:

For a Better Erection That Will Astound You
and Delight Your Partner
ERECTION PILLS

Results are immediate and long-lasting. Don't leave her unsatisfied. Erection Pills can make even the limpest of men powerful. Give her what she's craving. Be the big man you always wanted to be. This preparation is a must for those of you who have been having difficulties in obtaining and maintaining a fulfilling erection. Instant action guaranteed. Your money back if not completely satisfied.

BUY ERECTION PILLS, ONLY $6.95

Inadvertently, some physicians may have also contributed to the emphasis on medically based treatment. Public presentations and professional writings repeatedly dichotomize sexual problems into organic and psychogenic categories. The assumption is that the problem has an organic basis, then it has to have an organic solution. This approach does not recognize that many sexual problems emerge from a combination of organic and psychogenic factors; even when the etiology is clearly organic, the best solution may be partly or completely psychological in nature.

As an example of how such a biomedical "fix" can be flawed, consider the following: A woman complains of vaginal dryness and discomfort during sexual intercourse. A purely (blindly) medical-model approach to treating this problem would probably involve only the prescription of vaginal lubricants. Although such a treatment may be necessary, it may not be sufficient. Perhaps the woman is not sexually aroused because she feels that the relationship, outside as well as inside the bedroom, is unsatisfactory. She would be aroused if her partner expressed affection at other times, and was more sensitive to her needs. Because these issues are not addressed by a lubricant, it is likely that the woman will remain unaroused and uncomfortable despite an appropriate (albeit incomplete) treatment.

Similarly, for some men, sexual relations can be dutiful and devoid of satisfying pleasure. The lack of the erection response as a result of diabetes or some other disease process may be met with mixed emotions. That is, a man may feel a loss of masculinity along with the erectile dysfunction; however, this "failure" may provide an acceptable excuse to avoid unsatisfying sexual relations and may be welcomed by both partners. A physician who sees the problem only as a loss of erection may be doing his or her patient a disservice by suggesting a medical solution such as a penile implant. The real solution may be to provide the couple with information and to help them overcome restrictive attitudes that have hampered their ability to enjoy sensual pleasure in the past.

Tiefer (1986) points out that the problem of erectile loss is as much a problem of masculine identity as it is sexual. A man who suffers erectile failure is often not bemoaning the loss of sexual pleasure or a meaningful level of intimacy with his partner; rather, he is concerned about "not function-ing as a real man." The patient's quest for "potency" may pressure the physician into offering a medical solution. Physicians who are largely un-trained in psychological principles may feel ill prepared to address such matters; they may, under constant pressure from their clients, acquiesce to a man's fantasy solution. As Tiefer (1986) points out, "A medical explanation for erectile difficulties relieves men of blame and thus permits them to maintain some masculine self-esteem even in the presence of impotence" (p. 591).

How to Participate Constructively in the Medical Approach to Sexual Health

As a psychosocial consultant to a medical team, you will have an opportunity to affect the system. The extent of your influence will depend upon your ability to work constructively with physicians and to understand the medical approach, as well as upon your skills as a psychosocial assessor and therapist. Therefore, we devote the remainder of this chapter to discussing how to work with physicians and how to help patients to use the most common medical interventions.

To be initially invited to serve as a consultant, you must gain the respect of physicians as a nonphysician therapist and must be able to contribute to the physicians' care of their patients. Respect may come from the physicians' knowledge of your work and your professional reputation. If you are affiliated with a university or medical school, a certain amount of respect is inherent in your position. If you are not affiliated with a university or medical school, we suggest you build your reputation through contacting and meeting with physi-cians who are likely to be interested in your services. Regardless of your institutional location, efforts should be made to inform physicians who are most likely to be referral sources (e.g., urologists, gynecologists, family or general practitioners) that you are interested in treating individuals with sexual problems. If given the opportunity to speak before a group of physi-cians on the topic of human sexuality, do not decline! This is one of the best opportunities to meet physicians and convey to them your expertise.

Once you have been able to arrange a meeting with a physician, you should convey to him or her that you are interested in being a referral source for patients who may require more prolonged psychological/therapeutic in-tervention. In addition, let the physician know that you may also be called upon to complete a psychosocial evaluation when there is a question of possible psychological or social (i.e., relationship) factors that may be affect-ing patients' sexual functioning. The physician will find you useful (1) if you can speak to him or her without psychological jargon, (2) if you understand the basic medical aspects of sexual dysfunction, and (3) if you are able to give the physician useful and timely feedback that will help in his or her treatment.

You will not be perceived as useful if the physician refers a patient to you but never hears back from you. Your written reports to physicians should contain only the most essential psychosocial history; they should be as brief and to the point as possible. A busy physician has little time for or interest in reading a lengthy report that contains psychological jargon and unsupported inferences to parent–child conflict. We suggest that you prepare a succinct one-page report that focuses on identifying the major psychological factors affecting sexual functioning; also include the treatment plan that you will be recommending (and implementing). As an example, consider the following:

Re: Mr. Robert Quigley
    D.O.B. 12/24/43

Dear Dr. Mitchell,

Thank you for referring Mr. Quigley to me to evaluate his erectile dysfunction. I met with Mr. Quigley on July 31, 1990, and I met separately with his wife on August 7, 1990. Mr. and Mrs. Quigley agree that erectile difficulties began about 2.5 years ago, but that the problem has only recently been addressed because of Mrs. Quigley's insistence.

Mr. Quigley reports experiencing firm nighttime erections; he is also able to experience full erections during masturbation. Based on this information and the absence of any clear-cut medical factors (as noted in your evaluation report and referral), I suspect that Mr. Quigley's erection problem is most likely psychogenic. In this regard, it is noteworthy that Mr. Quigley is a hard-driving and anxious executive who worries excessively about business matters. This worry may have initially led to his sexual problem; subsequently, he has become preoccupied with his sexual performance and places great demands upon himself. This is a common psychological cause for erectile difficulties. Moreover, he has been avoiding sexual encounters in an effort to minimize further disappointment; this avoidance pattern only serves to maintain his difficulty.

I believe Mr. and Mrs. Quigley will benefit from sex therapy, and they have both agreed to participate. There does not appear to be any need for further medical evaluation at this time, but I will keep you informed of Mr. Quigley's progress. Thank you for referring this interesting patient.

Sincerely,

How to Help Patients to Use Medical Interventions: General Suggestions

Medical assessment can describe three possible sets of circumstances that relate to a patient's sexual functioning: (1) There is clearly no medical condition affecting sexual functioning; (2) there exist some signs and symp-

toms of a medical condition that may interfere with sexual functioning; and
(3) there is clear-cut evidence of one or more medical conditions that are
probably interfering with sexual functioning. Under any of these circumstances, medical intervention may be considered. For example, even when the
problem appears to be primarily psychogenic, a noninvasive medical solution
(e.g., vacuum device) may be used. At issue is the intensity with which a
patient sees the medical intervention as a solution to all of his or her sexual
problems. Tiefer (1986) and Schover (1989) both caution therapists about
patients who are insistent on a medical solution for their sexual problems. The
danger is that in seeking a medical solution, such a patient may be less likely
to address important psychosocial issues that may also have an impact on
sexual functioning.

In order to help a patient utilize a medical intervention to enhance sexual
functioning, the medical intervention must be discussed in the context of a
broad definition of sexuality. Thus, although a woman experiencing painful
intercourse may benefit from the use of a lubricant, or a man experiencing
erection failure may benefit from vasoactive injections, the use of any medical
intervention should be viewed as one component of a therapeutic approach
designed to enhance sexual enjoyment. As the therapist, you should be
cautious about encouraging a patient to embrace the medical solution if
important personal or interpersonal issues remain unresolved. Only when you
are confident that your patient can put the medical intervention into perspective should you endorse such an intervention. Schover (1989, p. 93) has
suggested the following criteria for screening penile implant candidates who
do not need sex therapy:

1. Good general psychological coping.
2. Good skills for both partners in initiating sex and requesting specific
   techniques during lovemaking.
3. Agreement between partners on sexual frequency and variety of
   sexual techniques.
4. Good skills in expressing nonsexual affection.
5. If in a committed relationship, good satisfaction for both partners.
6. History of continuing noncoital sex to orgasm for both partners in
   spite of the erection problem.
7. If over age 50, good knowledge about sexuality and aging and how to
   compensate for minor changes.
8. No sexual dysfunctions other than erectile dysfunction.
9. Clear organic cause for the erectile dysfunction.

We believe that these same criteria are applicable to the treatment of any
sexual problem when any medical intervention is considered. If a patient
meets Schover's (1989) criteria, then it is advisable to proceed with the *option*

of a medical intervention. If a patient does not meet the criteria, then you should focus on the deficits before suggesting the addition of a medical intervention. Typically, such therapy focuses on providing information, communication skills, and sexual skills training (see Chapter 7) before proceeding medically.

Suggestions for Specific Medical Interventions

This section describes the types of supplemental medical interventions that may be helpful for your patients.

Pharmacological Approaches

The pharmacological treatments for sexual problems fall into three categories: (1) hormonal therapy (e.g., low testosterone in males treated by injection of testosterone enanthate, or estrogen deficiency in women treated by estrogen replacement therapy); (2) vasoactive treatments (e.g., erectile dysfunction treated with papaverine, phentolamine, or prostaglandin E1); and (3) alpha-adrenoreceptor blockers (e.g., yohimbine).

HORMONE THERAPY

Low testosterone or elevated prolactin and gonadotropins are hypothesized hormonal causes for sexual dysfunction in men. Although the mechanisms by which such hormonal imbalances affect desire or erection remain to be elucidated, testosterone replacement may be suggested by urologists as a treatment for these difficulties. When improvement is seen, it may be due to a placebo effect as much as to a true pharmacological effect. The widespread use of testosterone is most likely influenced by the suspected positive relationship between testosterone and sexual functioning in men and the small likelihood of side effects. Thus, the philosophy in using testosterone in treating male sexual dysfunction seems to be that it may help to overcome the problem and it cannot hurt. Certainly, there is little evidence that the short-term use of testosterone is harmful, although long-term use in older men may put them at greater risk for hyperplasia (i.e., abnormal growth) of prostate cells (Rous, 1988).

Hormonal problems that affect sexual functioning in women most commonly occur during menopause or postmenopause. (They can also occur prematurely as a result of surgical treatment for cancer; for more information, see Chapter 9.) Women experiencing lowered levels of estrogen may be susceptible to shrinking and thinning of the vagina, a loss of tissue elasticity, and lessened vaginal lubrication during sexual arousal (Masters, Johnson, & Kolodny, 1988). The decrease in vaginal lubrication often results in dyspareunia if an artificial lubricant is not used. Research investigating the effects of hormone replacement therapy on sexual outcomes has been reviewed by Walling, Anderson, and Johnson (1990). These authors concluded that estrogen therapy leads to significant gynecological improvements (e.g., reduced atrophic vaginitis) which may, in turn, allow sexual functioning to return to normal. Progestogen therapy, on the other hand, provides few if any direct sexual benefits, but it is useful because it reduces the risk of endometrial hyperplasia that can occur with estrogen therapy alone. Finally, androgen therapy has been used to enhance sexual desire in postmenopausal women. Much remains to be known about which women are likely to require (and respond to) hormone replacement therapy as well as what type, dose, duration, and route of administration will prove optimal. A good source to help you to stay up to date on new developments in this area is the *Archives of Sexual Behavior*.

VASOACTIVE THERAPY

During the past decade, use of intracorporeal injections of vasodilators for the diagnosis and treatment of male erectile problems has increased. The injection of phenoxybenzamine into the corpus cavernosum of the penis was first reported by Brindley (1983) as inducing successful erections. Phenoxybenzamine, however, is painful to inject and slowly produces turgidity that may result in penis enlargement for up to 3 days (Althof et al., 1987). Clinicians have found that papaverine is preferable because it is active within 15 minutes of injection and produces an erection that lasts 1 to 4 hours if the appropriate dosage is used.

Although papaverine produces desirable erections in men with psychogenic erectile failure and mild to moderate organic erectile failure, there are some problems with its use. Althof et al. (1987) point out that no long-term follow-up studies have evaluated the impact of this treatment procedure on sexual and psychosocial functioning. In a short-term follow-up study, Althof et al. (1987) found that within 6 months of home-based (i.e., self-injection) therapy, 35% of the men in the program had dropped out. Unfortunately, the authors did not complete a detailed study of why individuals dropped out. It is suspected that many may have dropped out early because of objections to the injection procedure itself. Of those who remained in the program, 26% reported periodic bruising at the injection site, and plaque-like nodules were detected in 21% of the patients.

From our patients using home-based injections of papaverine, we have heard complaints of decreased desire and orgasmic problems following treatment; in contrast, we have also found that others benefit from this procedure. Consider the following example:

Mr. and Mrs. W were referred for sex therapy by their urologist because Mr. W complained of lack of orgasm during papaverine therapy. Mr. W had experienced erectile failure for 5 years prior to undertaking papaverine self-injection home therapy. Mr. W had vascular-based erectile dysfunction. The papaverine injections always produced an erection; however, after about 2 months, he started experiencing lack of orgasm during intercourse. This problem then led to critical self-examination and partner concern. Over the next 6 months, sexual relations declined from two times per week to no relations at all during the 2 months prior to entering sex therapy.

During the initial interview, it became clear that Mr. W often participated in sexual intercourse "just to please" his partner. He was not always interested in sex and decreased the amount of foreplay because "the erection was there and foreplay was unnecessary."

Mr. and Mrs. W had not participated in therapy prior to papaverine self-injection. Such therapy might have helped them to utilize the papaverine procedure in a more advantageous manner, and might have prevented problems. During such educational sessions, we alert couples (or single men) to the problems that can occur if they have intercourse when it is not really desired; we also encourage couples and individuals to continue to participate in non-coitus-oriented sex. Papaverine injections leading to sexual intercourse should be viewed as an addition to an otherwise active and satisfying sexual relationship. When sexual intercourse is the only time that a couple is sexually expressive and affectionate, problems generally emerge (as they did with Mr. and Mrs. W).

One additional concern regarding papaverine injections involves the impact that such injections can have on the partner. That is, for most individuals, it is very arousing and affirming to watch their partners' arousal grow as a result of their own sexual attraction or skills. Relatedly, women are often distressed by their partner's lack of erection because it initiates a fear that they are no longer attractive or sexually desirable to their partners and cannot "turn them on." If erections are caused by injection rather than foreplay, then a primary source of psychological feedback may be lost. Previously, such feedback has reassured a woman of her desirability. The consequences may be a decline in the woman's arousal; thus, partners can be encouraged to communicate that they are attracted to and desirous of each other.

Althof et al. (1987) point out that self-injection may enhance sex therapy programs for "carefully selected couples." Although the criteria for "carefully selected" were not specified, presumably the couples should not be upset by injection; should have a good premorbid sexual relationship; should communicate well; and should not focus on intercourse as the only goal in sexual interactions (cf. Schover, 1989).

Unfortunately, much of the research evaluating the effectiveness of self-injection therapy has tended to focus on the mechanical operation and utility of the erection, rather than on the psychological factors that might enhance or inhibit the desirability and acceptance of this procedure. For example, in a recent study, Watters et al. (1988) followed 62 patients who self-injected for 3 to 21 months. This study made no attempt to identify the psychological profile, the partner relationship, or the sexual behavior of the 62 men. Only the final disposition (e.g., "improving," "cured," or medical side effects) were described. Similarly, studies by Waldhauser and Schramek (1988) and Stief and Wetterauer (1988) seem most concerned with which vasoactive agent is most likely to produce the firmest erection in the shortest amount of time with the fewest side effects. It is perhaps because of side effects such as priapism (i.e., an erection that does not detumesce) and corporeal fibrosis (i.e., formation of fibrous tissue) that other agents must be investigated (Nelson, 1988). Regardless of which vasoactive agent is used, we would like to emphasize that the role of the sex therapist is to help select patients who can benefit most from this procedure and to help patients put vasoactive therapy in perspective as a part of their total program.

ALPHA-ADRENORECEPTOR BLOCKERS

One additional area of pharmacological treatment of sexual problems is the use of the alpha-adrenoreceptor blocker yohimbine. Its trade name is Yocon, and on the street it is known as "yo-yo." It has a half-life of 35 minutes (Morales et al., 1987) and produces many peripheral autonomic changes (e.g., increased heart rate and blood pressure). Yohimbine is believed to work by increasing blood flow into the penis and decreasing outflow (Meyer, 1988).

Although the search for an effective aphrodisiac has been conducted for centuries, there is as yet no reliable pharmacological agent that will either cure erectile failure or increase sexual desire. Yohimbine is certainly a far cry from an aphrodisiac, but recently gained notoriety through Julian Davidson's work with rats (Clark, Smith, & Davidson, 1984), in which he demonstrated an increase in sexual activity of laboratory rats that ingested yohimbine. Davidson (personal communication, September 18, 1986) has reported that he received numerous telephone calls and correspondence from the world press following the publication of his article. He was appropriately cautious with his presentations of the data, but the world press seemed anxious to extrapolate every applied implication possible. Yohimbine has actually been investigated for over 25 years for its effect on sexual behavior, but only received widespread attention subsequent to the Clark et al. (1984) article.

A number of studies have attempted to clarify the exact impact of yohimbine on sexually functional and dysfunctional men (Lording, 1978; Morales, Surridge, Marshall, & Fenemore, 1982; Morales et al., 1987; Susset et al., 1989). In a very recent study, Susset et al. (1989) found a modest impact on the sexual functioning of a population of Veterans complaining of erectile failure. Those who responded best to the medication were younger men with less organicity and with relatively recent onset of erectile problems.

Surgery

Currently, there are three surgical approaches to correcting male erectile problems: (1) the implantable penile prosthesis, (2) penile arterial revascularization, and (3) penile venous ligation. As in the case of pharmacological approaches to sexual dysfunctions, there is a gap in the literature regarding the psychological concomitants of surgical intervention (Mendoza & Silverman, 1987). The surgical perspective has focused almost entirely on improvement in surgical procedures to produce a firmer and more natural erection with the fewest medical complications. In evaluating the effectiveness of surgical procedures, infection rates, mechanical malfunction, and medical complications are reported. When patient satisfaction is included in the evaluation process, it is almost always presented in global terms of "satisfied" or "not satisfied." Schover (1989) points out that such an approach to assessment is flawed because of the principle of cognitive dissonance (i.e., the more effort that a man expends, and the more difficulty he endures in order to reach the goal, the more he may be expected to value that attainment, regardless of the "objective" outcome). Thus, men who go through the pain and expense of surgery will be likely to take a positive view of their postoperative functioning.

This section on surgical approaches is focused entirely on male sexual problems, since at present no commonly used surgical procedures are employed to improve female sexual functioning.[1]

THE IMPLANTABLE PENILE PROSTHESIS

Surgical procedures to improve male sexual functioning have existed since the beginning of the 20th century. Credit for the development of the modern penile prosthesis is given to Small, Carrion, and Gordon (1975) for the semirigid silicone prosthesis, and to Scott, Bradley, and Timm (1973) for the inflatable prosthesis. These devices were considerable improvements over the earlier devices, which utilized rib cartilage, were prone to ulceration, and lacked malleability. The use of the semirigid silicone rod or the inflatable prosthesis provides a close semblance to normal functioning, with an acceptable level of side effects.

It has only been in the last few years that the importance of psychosocial factors in implant surgery has been addressed (e.g., Krauss, Lantinga, Carey, Meisler, & Kelly, 1989; Meisler, Carey, Krauss, & Lantinga, 1988; Pedersen, Tiefer, Ruiz & Melman, 1988; Schover, 1989; Tiefer, Pedersen, & Melman, 1988). Of great importance has been the identification of predictors of positive outcome. As mentioned above, Schover (1989) has outlined factors associated with positive outcome following penile implant. Meisler et al. (1988) offer additional support for Schover's (1989) observation; they describe a case in which poor psychological coping and poor marital adjustment prior to the implant was associated with a negative postsurgical adjustment. More research is needed to develop a body of convincing evidence against penile implants without careful psychological screening.

The collaborative relationship between sex therapists and urologists is extremely important in the screening of potential implant patients. Some urologists may look upon psychologists only in terms of a resource for screening out poor candidates and treating psychopathology. However, as Schover's (1989) work suggests, even in cases with a clear organic basis there is a need to attend to subtle factors related to overall sexual and relationship skills. Furthermore, it is important to assess a patient's sexual expectations, attitudes, and knowledge. For example, if a man is single and he has avoided all social and sexual contact (because he believes that a firm erection is essential for a relationship with any woman), then that man is a poor candidate for surgery. Such a man is likely to have complaints and insecurities about the size and firmness of his "implanted" penis; he is also likely to engage in sexual activity to "prove" masculinity, rather than because he is involved in a close and loving relationship with a partner. The desire to prove one's masculinity through sexual expression often results in other (e.g., orgasmic) problems.

As a sex therapist, you can assist in the assessment and treatment of potential implant patients because of your skills in interviewing and psychological assessment; moreover, you can take the time that most surgeons do not have to extract the subtle information necessary for accurate screening. In some cases, it is only necessary to ask more detailed questions to arrive at an accurate presurgical decision. For example, the following patient was recently referred by a urologist for presurgical evaluation.

Mr. S, a 71-year-old man, had been married for 40 years to his 79-year-old wife. He reported that he and his wife were from the "old school" (i.e., they entered marriage at a young age without any sexual experience or knowledge). It took them several years after marriage to complete sexual intercourse because he "did not know where to put it." Although the couple had three children, Mr. S reported that his wife always dreaded sex; she never initiated sex; and even when she did participate in sex, she never moved or touched him.

Currently, when Mr S attempted to initiate sex, he was unable to obtain an erection prior to sexual activity. As is common, he and his wife interpreted that as his problem. She adamantly refused to touch him on the penis and would make remarks about her lack of interest whenever he showed the slightest physical affection.

Mr. S reported that he did obtain early-morning erections occasionally; however, even if there were no morning responses, Mr. S would still be inappropriate for an implant operation. The long-standing negative and unsatisfactory sexual relationship was predictive of a poor outcome with a penile implant. Mrs. S was invited and encouraged to attend counseling sessions, but she refused.

The case of Mr. and Mrs. S represents inappropriate circumstances for an implant; yet it should be noted that Mr. S was seriously considered as a candidate and would have obtained the implant if he was advised to do so by the consulting sex therapist. On the surface, Mr. S was an appropriate candidate, in that he could not obtain an erection; he was married; he was 71 years old; and he had diabetes. These factors would be enough evidence for many urologists to proceed with an implant. There were a number of psychosocial factors, however, that upon closer scrutiny contraindicated surgery: The poor marriage, the expectation on Mr. S's part that sexual intercourse would improve the relationship, and the total lack of physical affection predicted a poor outcome.

VASCULAR SURGERY

As discussed in Chapter 3, there are two categories of vascular problems that may affect erectile functioning: arterial (i.e., inflow) decrease and/or venous (i.e., outflow) increase. Arterial problems result when there is a narrowing or blockage of the pudendal or dorsal penile arteries, which supply blood to the corpora cavernosa. The engorgement of blood into the corpora cavernosa is necessary for the erection to occur. In order for the erection to be maintained, blood has to be "trapped" in the corpora cavernosa at a certain pressure. If too much blood circulates out of the penis or "leaks," the erection will subside. This is a problem of venous leakage.

Surgical procedures to correct both arterial and venous problems have been employed since the early part of this century, with somewhat uncertain results (Hawatmeh, Houttuin, Gregory, & Purcell, 1983). Advances in the understanding of the physiology of the erection response have led to improved surgical procedures with some claims of success (Balko et al., 1986; Bennett,

1988; Lewis, 1988). However, long-term follow-up studies are lacking in this area; although the immediate results of vascular surgery are often successful, follow-up evaluation 6 to 9 months after surgery often reports high failure rates. Lewis (1988) reviewed the literature on venous surgery and concluded that failure occurs in about 50% of the cases. More recently, Melman and Rossman (1989) have reported a failure rate of about 90% with venous surgery at 9 months after surgery. They conclude that there may be a defect in the active veno-occlusive mechanism in these patients, which the surgery does not correct. Although vascular surgery holds some promise, there is still much room for improvement.

The psychological consideration for vascular surgery candidates should be similar to that for implant surgery candidates. A cost–benefit analysis should be made, and presurgical therapy should be considered for patients who do not demonstrate the positive predictors outlined by Schover (1989). Patients who have avoided all sexual interactions for several months or more, or patients who show evidence of marital difficulties, could benefit from presurgical therapy.

An important difference exists between vascular surgery and either implant or vasoactive injection; namely, if the vascular surgery is successful, then "natural" functioning is restored. Thus, men who undergo successful vascular surgery will obtain erections only when (1) there is sufficient erotic stimulation, and (2) they desire sex. On the other hand, men with implants or vasoactive injections may participate in sex without sufficient erotic stimulation or feelings of desire. Sex under such conditions, as discussed above, may be highly unsatisfactory and iatrogenic for the implanted or injected male and his partner.

Vacuum Device Therapy

The use of vacuum devices for assisting men to obtain erections has been sanctioned by the medical profession for a relatively short period of time, even though such devices have been patented since 1977 (Nadig, Ware, & Blumoff, 1986). Several devices are currently being marketed; most work by creating a vacuum in a cylinder, which is placed over the penis. The vacuum draws blood into the corpora cavernosa of the penis; this blood is then trapped by placing a constricting "rubber band" around the base of the penis.

Although such a procedure "works" (i.e., produces an erection) for most men (even those whose erection difficulties are organically based), it is not without problems. First, it takes some dexterity to manipulate the pumping device in the manner needed to complete a seal around the base of the penis. Second, once the desired degree of tumescence is reached (some men report pain in the penis during the pumping process), the constricting band must be slipped off the cylinder and onto the base of the penis; in this process, the band itself may cause some discomfort. Third, ecchymosis (i.e., bruises) and petechiae (i.e., red spots) are reported in some men, although these are reversed with a period of disuse.

Nadig et al. (1986, p. 130) describe how the erection created by the vacuum device differs from a naturally occurring erection:

1. Blood flow into the penis decreases while the rubber bands are in place.
2. Penile skin temperature falls as a result of decreased arterial blood flow.
3. Congestion of extracorporeal penile tissue occurs, indicated by distention of superficial veins and cyanosis of the penis and by the observation that penile circumference increased more with this device (mean = 4.3 cm) than during normal erections (mean = 2.8 cm).
4. The penis is rigid only distal to the constrictive bands and thus pivots at its base.
5. The ejaculate is trapped in the proximal urethra until the bands are removed.

In spite of these problems, several short-term follow-up studies have reported about 80% satisfaction with the vacuum devices (Nadig et al., 1986; Viosca & Griner, 1988; Witherington, 1988). There is now a need for more long-term studies (i.e., lasting a year or more) that will critically evaluate the impact of such a device on the sexual satisfaction of the man and his partner.

We would advise that men who are considering vacuum devices go through the same psychological screening that implant candidates do. It is important that the man and his partner have realistic expectations for the use of the device and do not expect it to solve relationship problems. All of the considerations for implant therapy candidates raised by Schover (1989) apply to the vacuum device candidate.

The vacuum device may be used as a good diagnostic tool for implant candidates about whom there is some doubt. Because the vacuum device is noninvasive, there are fewer problems that may occur if the device does not work out. If a man and his partner have difficulty with or complaints about the use of the vacuum device, it is likely that they would also have difficulty with the implant.

Concluding Comments

This chapter makes it clear that sexual problems for men and women have historically been divided into medical (organic) and psychological (functional) camps. Such an artificial division has often led to incomplete and, at

times, inappropriate intervention strategies. The most obvious problem has
been in cases of male erectile failure diagnosed as organically based. Many of
these men have received penile implants as remedies for their sexual problem,
when a larger problem existed in their attitude toward sex or in their relationship with their partners. Some recent follow-up studies with implant patients
are pointing to significant rates of dissatisfaction, presumably because these
other problems remain unsolved with an implant.

Also of concern is that therapists dealing with men and women experiencing sexual problems have to take great care not to impose their own
values on their clients. For example, it may be tempting for a liberal therapist
to encourage his or her conservative client to expand his or her sexual
repertoire (e.g., to take the emphasis away from intercourse). Although the
aim may be noble, the therapist has to be sensitive to the possible distress that
this suggestion might cause the client and his or her partner. Some clients may
be so wedded to their beliefs and sexual mores that the only acceptable
solution (to them) is to restore a firm erection for intercourse. As disappointing as this may be to the therapist, it must be considered for some clients. The
sensitive therapist should keep all options open, and weigh the advantages and
disadvantages of each therapeutic solution against the likelihood of (client and
partner) satisfaction and/or potential problems. Thus, it is wrong to encourage
an implant even when the problem is organically based if there exists unrealistic expectations about the benefits of such a solution; it is equally wrong to
deny an implant just because there exists rigid and narrow-minded thinking
about sexual relations. The use of the vacuum device or vasoactive injections
may be a cautious first intervention strategy for those cases in which implant
surgery is considered. Thus, we encourage a "least invasive" approach as a
first step.

Comparatively little emphasis has been placed on medical solutions for
female sexual problems. Breast augmentation surgery may be similar to
penile implant surgery if one considers that such surgery will presumably
increase sexual desirability and self-esteem; however, it is dissimilar in that
breast surgery is not used for the purpose of overcoming sexual dysfunction.
Thus, a therapist may be concerned about a woman's sexual expectations
following breast augmentation, but it is unlikely that the problem would be
considered in the context of sexual dysfunction therapy.

Women do not seek out vascular devices or vasoactive agents to overcome sexual problems. Although corrective surgery to change a woman's
vaginal opening is done, this is relatively rare. Women also do not typically
seek out "a pill" to increase sexual desire, although some may argue that "*the*
pill" (i.e., a contraceptive) does just that. In all, women are less likely than
men to be the targets of medical intervention for sexual dysfunction problems.
This, however, may be as much a reflection of societal values as of anatomical differences.

Research on the outcome of medical intervention for sexual problems is beginning to address psychological satisfaction, rather than focusing entirely on the integrity of the procedure itself. Thus, the firmness and natural appearance of the penis after implant surgery may not be very important if the implant recipient and his partner are still having difficulty communicating and battling about sex. Prospective, longitudinal research that looks at psychological factors in the context of medical treatments is needed.

Note

[1] The surgical treatment of dyspareunia caused by vulvar vestibulitis, as noted in Chapter 5, remains an infrequent procedure.

III

SPECIAL TOPICS

In Part I of this book, we introduced the sexual dysfunctions in a straightforward and uncomplicated fashion. In Part II, we provided guidelines for the assessment and treatment of these straightforward difficulties. Throughout both sections we have alluded to complicating factors and complex cases. In the third and final section of this book, we provide additional information on this more advanced material. Specifically, in Chapter 9 we present an overview of three sets of factors that can complicate the assessment and treatment of sexual dysfunctions—namely, chronic illness, fear of sexually transmitted diseases, and substance abuse. Although these factors are not the only ones that can complicate the life of a sex therapist, they may be the most common. In Chapter 10 we supplement this material by providing detailed information on six cases that we have seen in clinical practice. Each case has been selected for its didactic value. For each one, we provide information on etiology, assessment, and treatment.

In Chapter 11, we conclude by providing you with information regarding your continued professional development and accreditation. We recognize, and we hope that you understand, that we have just scratched the surface of what you need to know. Continued development is essential. We also include material that we hope that you will find of use in establishing a practice in sex therapy.

SPECIAL TOPICS

9

Obstacles to Sexual Functioning and Satisfaction

Sexual health (i.e., functioning and satisfaction) represents the last link of a long chain of physiological and psychological processes. Thus, there are many opportunities for things to go wrong. In this chapter, we explore three conditions that have the potential to disrupt sexual functioning and satisfaction: fear of sexually transmitted diseases, substance abuse, and chronic illness.

Fear of Sexually Transmitted Diseases

In our view, sexual functioning and satisfaction will be maximized to the extent that sexual activity occurs in a context of positive expectancies. When individuals fear negative consequences as a result of being sexually expressive, then there is risk of sexual dysfunction and dissatisfaction. This risk is most salient when being sexually active can threaten one's life.

No book written about sexuality in the 1990s would be complete if it did not mention acquired immune deficiency syndrome (AIDS). AIDS is a severe disruption of the body's immune system, caused by the human immunodeficiency virus (HIV); AIDS was first diagnosed in 1981. Shortly thereafter, reports began to appear, initially in New York and California, about complications of AIDS such as pneumocystis carinii and Kaposi's sarcoma (a type of skin cancer). AIDS became, and remains today, a death sentence. Since then, a worldwide epidemic[1] has begun, which now casts a considerable shadow over sexual expression. It is beyond the scope of this book to provide technical information on AIDS or other sexually transmitted diseases (STDs)[2]; instead, our focus is on the relationship between AIDS and other STDs on the one hand, and sexual expression and behavior on the other.

Single gay men were targeted early as the population at greatest risk for HIV infection. Great efforts were made by members of the gay community to change their high-risk sexual practices. Indeed, tremendous changes have been made. Kyle (1989) summarizes:

Most gay men will tell you that life in the age of AIDS has severely ruptured the very fabric of their sexual lives. Various sexual proclivities that once produced some of the most spontaneous and erotic experiences are now relegated to the far corners of one's memory. Sex has become sharing space and frantic voyeurism. Masturbation, hand in hand with a vivid imagination, a ready supply of pornographic videotapes and ample 976 [sic] [telephone] numbers has replaced sensuality as the Saturday night modis operandi. (p. 276)

Recent studies have documented the changes that have taken place. In general, gay sexual behavior now involves less risky sexual behaviors and an increased use of condoms (Connell & Kippax, 1990; Richwald et al., 1988). Unfortunately, a minority of young, less educated, and lower-income gay men continue to participate in high-risk sexual practices (Richwald et al., 1988).

In contrast, the heterosexual community has modified only some of its high risk sexual practices. For example, DeBuono, Zinner, Daamen, and McCormack (1990) found that anal intercourse and involvement with multiple partners have *not* changed among well-educated heterosexual women since 1975; however, the use of condoms has increased significantly over the last decade. In interpreting such data, Baldwin and Baldwin (1988) suggest that AIDS education that focuses on providing information only will not result in behavior changes. They predict that behavioral change is likely only if AIDS programs emphasize lifestyle habits and social responsibility.

Despite the limited lifestyle changes that have occurred, people are concerned about AIDS. Clinicians report that clients are more concerned than ever before about STDs (Masters et al., 1988). It is not unusual for individuals to inquire about AIDS testing in new partners. We have treated several couples who suspended sexual behavior until HIV testing was completed. In one case of ours, a man's erectile dysfunction was directly related to his fear that a former sexual partner of his wife's had AIDS. We suspect that this is not an isolated case and advise inquiring about such fears in clients.

As a sex therapist, you should be prepared to address your clients' concerns and questions. Information regarding HIV transmission, screening, and diagnosis is widely available through state and federal health organizations (e.g., New York State Department of Health, 1990).[3] Moreover, we encourage active counseling regarding "safer sex" practices, particularly the routine use of condoms; you should not assume that all clients will be aware of and/or using such safety procedures.

Syphilis and gonorrhea are perhaps the best known of the other STDs, although in recent years increasing attention and concern have been directed toward genital herpes and chlamydia. Genital herpes currently affects 40 million U.S. citizens with an additional 500,000 cases occurring annually (Masters et al., 1988). Chlamydia affects approximately 4 million U.S. citizens and is known to be the most common bacterial-like STD infection. In men, the chlamydia organism can cause epididymitis (i.e., infection of the epididymis) and nongonococcal urethritis (i.e., an infection of the urethral tube). This can cause painful urination or orgasm, and may affect the prostate; it can also cause tenderness in the testicle(s). For women, chlamydia not only can cause pain through pelvic inflammatory disease, but may also have adverse consequences for the reproductive processes. Often chlamydia is a "silent" disease, especially in women.

For all the STDs, there is usually physical discomfort and psychological distress, especially when one partner is responsible for transmitting the disease to the other partner. Having an STD, or being afraid of contracting one, can adversely affect sexual functioning. Some people will avoid sexual contacts; others will become overly concerned (even paranoid) about potential partners' sexual past; and still others will develop Hypoactive Sexual Desire Disorder. Relatedly, negative emotions such as worry, anger, and/or guilt may contribute to sexual dysfunction and dissatisfaction.

To help clients to minimize their risk for STDs, you might suggest that they follow Byer and Shainberg's (1991) recommendations: minimize the number of sexual partners, avoid high-risk activities (e.g., unprotected vaginal or anal intercourse) or sexual partners who engage in high-risk activities, remain alert to any symptoms of infection, use condoms in any situation other than a long-term monogamous relationship, wash with soap and water after every sexual contact, urinate after intercourse, and avoid anilingus.

A number of authors (e.g., Girardi, Keese, Traver, & Cooksey, 1988; Grant & Anns, 1988; Lamb, Clark, Drumheller, Frizzell, & Surrey, 1989; Morrison, 1989) have recently addressed the ethical issues related to psychotherapists and their treatment of people with AIDS and those infected with HIV. One important ethical issue is the duty to treat versus the justification for refusal to treat "undesirable" patients. For physicians, the American Medical Association has outlined straightforward guidelines stating that "a physician may not ethically refuse to treat a patient whose condition is within the physician's current realm of competence solely because the patient is seropositive" (American Medical Association, 1988, p. 1360). The situation for psychotherapists is less clear, however, because a psychotherapist's effectiveness may be diminished if he or she is unable to remain objective in treating the patient because of fears or prejudices. Although it is unfortunate that therapist prejudices and fears exist, it is important for us to be aware of our prejudices and fears, and to refer patients elsewhere when necessary.

Another difficult ethical dilemma exists when a therapist is caring for a patient who is HIV-positive (or fears that he or she might be HIV-positive) but refuses to inform his or her sexual partner of the risk: Should the therapist break confidentiality and warn the partner at risk? Is the therapist bound by the duty to warn as outlined in the *Tarasoff* case (*Tarasoff v. Regents of the University of California*, 1974, 1976)? There is no clear answer to these questions at this time. The argument *for* warning a sexual partner is that the sexual partner is at risk for his or her life because, at present, AIDS is always fatal and is transmitted by an exchange of bodily fluids which is likely to occur during unprotected sexual activity (Girardi et al., 1988). The argument *against* warning a sexual partner is that (1) a psychotherapist is not a medical doctor and does not have the medical expertise to determine such risk, and (2) the benefits of disclosure may not outweigh the detrimental effects (Girardi et al., 1988). On this second point, Morrison (1989) points out that there is public hysteria over the AIDS epidemic and that a disclosure that one is HIV-positive may be grounds for cancelation of insurance and may lead to loss of job, home, and friendship. There is also a concern that if disclosure were mandated by law, AIDS testing and treatment would be inhibited.

This is clearly a very complex issue and one that has been debated at great length by many experts. Although there are no definitive solutions to this ethical dilemma, we encourage you to consult the general guidelines currently available (e.g., Lamb et al., 1989).

Substance Abuse

In DSM-III-R, the Sexual Disorders (the group to which the Sexual Dysfunctions are assigned) form only one group of psychological disorders. There are, of course, a great many other disorders—to mention only the largest and most prevalent groups, Schizophrenia, Mood Disorders (i.e., Major Depression and Bipolar Disorder), Anxiety Disorders, Psychoactive Substance Abuse Disorders, and Personality Disorders. Many of these other psychological conditions can adversely affect sexual health and adjustment. In this section, we discuss the group of disorders that may be most likely to co-occur with sexual dysfunctions—namely, substance abuse.

A great deal has been written about both the physical and psychological impact of chronic alcoholism on sexual functioning (O'Farrell, 1990; Wilson, 1981). It is well documented that alcoholic men and women experience a high prevalence of sexual problems (e.g., Jensen, 1984; Klassen & Wilsnack, 1986; O'Farrell, 1990; Tan, Johnson, Lambie, Vijayasenan, & Whiteside, 1984). Male alcoholics are susceptible to low desire and erectile dysfunction, whereas female alcoholics are at increased risk for low desire, orgasmic dysfunction, and vaginismus.

The etiology of sexual dysfunctions in alcoholic men and women is complex. Liver disease, testicular atrophy, cardiovascular disease, and neuropathy are all possible organically based insults that could cause dysfunction. Psychologically, alcoholic men and women often have belief systems that are not conducive to sexual functioning. For example, many believe that alcohol makes them better lovers and facilitates sexual functioning (O'Farrell, 1990). In our discussions with men, we often hear them attribute aphrodisiac qualities to one type of alcohol or another. However, alcohol in all forms is a central nervous system depressant that can actually impair sexual functioning. Moreover, for both men and women, an increase in anxiety and a lack of desire may be associated with abstinence and sobriety. Although not confirmed by research, it is our clinical impression that the newly sober alcoholic experiences a hypervigilant state in which problem solving and worry are in the forefront of consciousness. Sobriety often brings with it a more acute worry about life's problems, as well as increased concern about sexual performance, the quality of one's relationship with one's partner, and so on. These interfering thoughts set the stage for the classic performance anxiety syndrome identified by Masters and Johnson (1970).

In a recent study, Fahrner (1987) reported that 75% of 116 alcoholic men complained of sexual dysfunction and dissatisfaction. In a 9-month follow-up, the same prevalence of sexual dysfunction existed, whether the men were abstinent during the previous 9 months or whether they were drinking. Only when the men were treated with sex therapy did they show improvement in their sexual problems. This study did not address the issue that abstinence may contribute to sexual dysfunction problems but it did confirm that there is a high prevalence of sexual problems in alcoholic men and that abstinence alone will not correct the problem. Similarly, Klassen and Wilsnack (1986) reported a high prevalence of sexual dysfunction in women drinkers.

For both men and women, there is a significant association between drinking behavior and sexual dysfunction. Because there are a number of possible etiological explanations of this association, it is important to explore sexual behavior before, during, and after drinking. Our most important piece of advice is quite simple: Do not treat the sexual problem if problem drinking is ongoing. Problem drinkers should be referred for substance abuse treatment before sex therapy is attempted.

There is far less known about the effects of illicit drugs on sexual behavior. Of course, there is a great deal of folklore suggesting that street drugs enhance sexual performance. Research does not support this notion, and suggests instead that illicit drugs contribute more to sexual dysfunction than they do to sexual enhancement (e.g., Cocores, Miller, Pottash, & Gold, 1988). It is our practice not to treat clients who are actively abusing drugs; again, we advocate referring these clients for treatment of the substance abuse problem as a necessary first step.

Chronic Illness and Sexual Functioning

Chronic illnesses shake the very foundation of physiological and psychological well-being. Illnesses as diverse as cancer, coronary artery disease, multiple sclerosis, end-stage renal disease, and diabetes share a common effect: They can result in multiple disabilities and require significant lifestyle adjustment; moreover, the medical and surgical treatments for these conditions often compromise a person's overall quality of life. In addition to these general effects of chronic illness, some illnesses and their treatments disturb the hormonal, vascular, or neurological integrity needed for sexual functioning. Illnesses and treatments can also involve damage to the genital structure, which impairs sexual functioning. Thus, there are both nonspecific and specific effects of chronic illnesses and their treatments.

This section has two parts. First, we overview the *general* effects associated with many chronic illnesses. Second, we present information regarding the *specific* effects of two of the most common conditions that compromise sexual functioning—namely, cancer and diabetes.[4] Our goal is to provide some background information about these conditions, and to make recommendations regarding therapeutic interventions when appropriate.

General Effects of Chronic Illnesses

Chronic illness is one of the most challenging stressors people confront. Demographers tell us that the population is slowly aging; as this occurs, we can expect more and more people to develop and have to live with chronic illnesses. Regardless of the specific illness, a number of general effects and changes can be anticipated.

To begin with, diagnosis of a chronic illness can produce a negative emotional response. Some people will become sad, despondent, discouraged, and even seriously depressed; others will become angry at the injustice and unfairness of fate or divine plan; still others will worry about the implications of their illness for themselves, their loved ones, and their future. Almost all people will be reminded of their mortality, and will mull over existential concerns; fear, anxiety, regret, and other disquieting emotions may ensue. Although such dysphoria is often a temporary and understandable adjustment reaction, rather than an instance of a major psychological disorder (see Derogatis et al., 1983), these negative emotions can initiate a more long-standing sexual difficulty.

A second general effect of chronic illness is physical discomfort. Many people with chronic disease will experience pain, fatigue, and lethargy. Sleep and eating patterns may be disrupted, especially when use of medications is needed. Relatedly, body image—the perception of how one appears to others, and the appraisal of one's attractiveness and desirability—is likely to be altered. No longer can the image of youth, health, and vigor be sustained (even if it was not true before); instead, a person may feel unattractive, undesirable, and unworthy. Many patients report that family and friends treat them differently, with "kid gloves." For some, there will be a stigma of fragility attached to chronic illness. Under these circumstances, and given our societal myth that sex is for the young and the healthy, many chronically ill will "retire" prematurely from the sexual sphere.

Being chronically ill is expensive as well. Expenses associated with transportation and lodging for treatment, hospital care, physicians' fees, medications, prostheses, and lost wages mount quickly; these costs can place considerable financial strain on many patients and their families. Some patients may find it difficult to remain employed and to obtain affordable medical and life insurance. Many patients must spend retirement savings or take out a second mortgage on their home to make ends meet. These financial strains make it difficult to enjoy the simple pleasures of life.

Being chronically ill is also time-consuming. Traveling back and forth to physicians, taking additional time to prepare special diets or to conduct additional hygiene protocols, receiving treatments, and getting extra rest leave precious little time for other activities, including sexual enjoyment.

Given the wide array of lifestyle changes and stressors that accompany a chronic illness, it is hardly surprising that sexual functioning may be impaired. Some may think, "So what? Doesn't the person have more important things to worry about?" Certainly the factors mentioned above are plenty to worry about and cope with; however, it is important to remember that sexual intimacy, in its broadest sense, can serve to buffer and even to sustain a person during these tough times. This thought has been eloquently expressed by Schover and Jensen (1988) in the preface to their excellent book, *Sexuality and Chronic Illness:*

> Sexuality is one of the most fundamental ways that humans share intimacy. Chronic illness, by interfering with a person's vitality, physical attractiveness, genital function, and social interactions, may create distance in relationships. Major diseases remind each of us that death is a solitary experience. To remain a sexual person, then, is to affirm life and one's connection with others. (p. v)

Mindful of this sentiment, we proceed to discuss two chronic illnesses (viz., cancer and diabetes) that occur frequently and often impair sexual function and satisfaction. For each disease, we provide information regarding the number of people affected, a brief overview of that disorder, and the most common sexual consequences.

Specific Effects of Cancer

Cancer is the second leading cause of death in the United States, accounting for 22% of all deaths. During 1990, it has been estimated that over 1 million new cases of cancer will be diagnosed, and that over 500,000 people will die from cancer. The leading cancer sites for men are the lung (20%), prostate (20%), and colon and rectum (15%); the pelvic cancers account for 45% of all male cancers. The leading cancer sites for women include the breast (29%), colon and rectum (15%), and lung (11%); cancers involving the breast or pelvic region account for 61% of all female cancers (Silverberg, Boring, & Squires, 1990).

Cancer is not really a single disease; instead, "cancer" refers to a large collection of related disorders that are characterized by the uncontrolled growth and movement of abnormal cells. These abnormal cancer cells (also known as "malignancies," "neoplasms," or "tumors") are distinguished from healthy cells by their ability for unlimited reproduction, a characteristic that eventually allows them to invade normal tissue. Initially, cancer cells tend to remain close to the site where they originated, in which case we say the cancer is "localized." If untreated, some cells from the original tumor may invade surrounding or distant tissue and organs, in which case we say the tumor has "metastasized." When cancer cells infiltrate the vital organs, death is the likely outcome. Treatments for cancers (including surgery, radiation, chemotherapy, immune therapy, and hormone therapy) are designed to destroy as many cancer cells as possible and/or to prevent their continued proliferation. Unless most or all of the cancer cells are destroyed, the probability is high that the surviving cancer cells will regenerate and spread.

Traditionally, the treatment of cancer has focused on the control of malignancy—that is, keeping the patient alive. With the tremendous progress that has taken place in the treatment of cancer, however, more ambitious goals are now possible. Today the quality of a patient's life has become a major focus for health professionals and patients (see Burish, Meyerowitz, Carey, & Morrow, 1987). This concern is especially true of cancers that have good prognoses, including breast, testicular, and prostate cancers.

Attending to the sexual needs of cancer patients might seem to be the responsibility of the surgeon or oncologist providing the treatment. In our experience, however, these professionals are usually too busy to address the patients' sexual rehabilitation needs. Also, at the time of their medical and surgical treatment, many patients are physically and psychologically overwhelmed, and they are unable to benefit from sexuality-based information and suggestions. Thus, patients may seek out your help months or years after they have been treated for cancer and left the hospital. With this in mind, we provide a brief overview of the types of cancer that pose the greatest threat to sexual functioning and satisfaction.[5]

BREAST CANCER

Breast cancer is the most common type of cancer in women, accounting for 29% of all female cancers.[6] Fortunately, if breast cancer is detected and treated early, 75% of all women are likely to survive 5 or more years postdiagnosis. Treatment typically involves one of the following: radical mastectomy (i.e., removal of the breast, surrounding lymph nodes, and underlying muscles), modified radical mastectomy (i.e., removal of the whole breast), partial mastectomy (i.e., removal of a part of the breast), or lumpectomy (i.e., removal of the tumor and immediately surrounding tissues only). Surgery may be supplemented with radiation and/or chemotherapy, especially when the cancer has metastasized.

Despite the good news regarding survival, we can expect psychological morbidity for a sizable number of patients. Loss of a breast has both direct and indirect consequences with regard to sexual functioning. One direct effect involves the loss of erotic sensation from the breast. Encouraging patients to develop new erotic zones, and reframing the loss as a chance to increase erotic sensitivity in other areas, may be helpful. In addition, some women will experience soreness and pain in one arm after a radical mastectomy. This may prove distracting and make it difficult to enjoy sexual activity. In such cases, encouraging patients to plan sexual activity just after taking pain medications may be advised. An indirect effect of a mastectomy is the loss of a body part that, in our culture, helps to determine one's sex appeal and overall femininity. Readjusting the self-image will require time and social support.

As a result of these effects, roughly 25% of all mastectomy patients will experience disruptive mood and sexual dysfunction for up to 1 year after the initial surgery (see Schain, 1987). The extent of this disruption depends in part on the nature of the surgery; that is, the less extensive operations tend to be associated with less dysphoria and sexual dysfunction (e.g., Sacks, Gerstein, & Mann, 1983; Sanger & Resnikoff, 1981). Not surprisingly, surgical techniques that conserve a woman's breast appears to minimize the threat to body image and feelings of sexual attractiveness and desirability (Schain, 1987). Of course, factors such as partner support and good couple communication can positively influence postsurgical sexual functioning and satisfaction.[7]

In addition to the mood and body image changes that commonly occur in women treated for breast cancer, those women who receive chemotherapy may be at increased risk for dyspareunia as a function of hormone depletion. (This reduced hormonal output may be temporary or permanent, depending upon the extent of the damage done to the ovaries.) Considerable care must be taken with regard to how this problem is handled. Controversy exists with respect to the advisability of hormone replacement therapy for the breast cancer patient (see Vessey, McPherson, Roberts, Neil, & Jones, 1985). Even the use of vaginal lubricants that contain estrogens is ill advised. Instead, nonestrogen (e.g., water-based) lubricants such as Astaglide or Lubrin are preferred.

PELVIC CANCERS IN WOMEN

Pelvic malignancies (including gynecological, bladder, and colorectal cancers) account for 33% of all cancers in women (Silverberg et al., 1990). As with breast cancer, cancers of the pelvis may be expected to have unique effects on sexual functioning through both direct (e.g., structural) and indirect (e.g., body image) changes. Most of the research on the sexual sequelae of pelvic cancers has focused on gynecological tumors.

Gynecological cancer includes malignancies of the uterus (cervix and corpus), ovary, and vulva. These cancers are usually treated surgically with hysterectomy (i.e., removal of the upper third of the vagina, the uterus, and the cervix), vulvectomy (i.e., removal of the labia minora and majora, and the clitoris), and oophorectomy (i.e., removal of one or both ovaries and the fallopian tubes). Surgery means direct structural change and, in many cases, altered sexual anatomy and physiology (e.g., reduced hormone production and premature menopause). Often these surgeries are supplemented by radiation and/or chemotherapy. These adjuvant therapies, as they are called, tend not to create as many structural changes, but do have systemic effects.

A number of helpful studies describing the effects of gynecological cancer and their treatments have been conducted by Dr. Barbara Andersen and her colleagues. A thorough review of Dr. Andersen's work is available in several recent papers (e.g., Andersen, 1985, 1987; Andersen & Hacker, 1983). Below, we summarize the findings of her most recent published study.

Andersen, Anderson, and deProsse (1989a, 1989b) compared 47 women with early-stage gynecological cancer (either uterine or ovarian cancer) to two control groups: (1) 18 women with benign gynecological disease (e.g., endometriosis), and (2) 57 healthy women. The cancer patients received surgery, radiotherapy, or combination therapy; the benign disease patients underwent surgery only; and the healthy women received no treatment. All subjects were interviewed and completed questionnaires prior to receiving any treatment, and again at 4-, 8-, and 12-month follow-up sessions. Information about sexual behavior (e.g., kissing, fantasy, intercourse), sexual functioning (i.e., desire, arousal, orgasm), and diagnosis of sexual dysfunction (using DSM-III) were collected. A brief summary of the results indicated the following:

1. There was a significant decline in the frequency of intercourse for the women with cancer and benign gynecological disease from the initial assessment to the 4-month follow-up; somewhat surprisingly, there were no dif-

ferences between the two disease groups. The diminished intercourse rates remained stable at the 8- and 12-month follow-ups.

2. Sexual arousal was also negatively affected, at all three follow-up times, for both disease groups compared to the healthy women.

3. There was a significant increase in the rate of sexual dysfunction diagnosed for the cancer group. For example, at the 12-month follow-up, 32% of the cancer patients, 13% of the benign patients, and only 9% of the healthy patients demonstrated desire difficulties. Similarly, arousal and orgasm dysfunctions were experienced by 29% and 29% of the cancer patients, 20% and 14% of the benign disease patients, and 9% and 6% of the healthy women, respectively. These data, in distinction to the intercourse data (see finding 1), suggest that cancer patients may be at increased risk compared to a comparison group of gynecological patients.

4. Forty-seven percent of the women with disease were diagnosed with dyspareunia at some time following treatment. This difficulty appeared to be related to a decrease in vaginal lubrication secondary to a surgery- or radiation-induced menopause. Fortunately, for many patients, this dyspareunia appeared to decline over time (as a result of hormone replacement therapy or use of vaginal lubricants).

Overall, Andersen et al. (1989a) noted that among women who had no sexual dysfunction prior to their cancer treatment, 50% were subsequently diagnosed with at least one dysfunction during the posttreatment year.

Bladder cancer, a relatively infrequent type of cancer in women, is typically treated surgically with a radical cystectomy and sometimes with radiation. Radical cystectomy involves removal of the bladder, urethra, uterus, ovaries, fallopian tubes, and anterior vaginal wall (Babaian, 1982). The vagina needs to be reconstructed as a result of this surgical procedure; the "neovagina," as it is called, is usually reduced in depth. As a result, many women may initially experience dyspareunia and altered sensations. Although the latter may simply require the couple to relearn new pleasure zones over time, the former can be addressed immediately. Schover (1988) recommends that women (1) make sure that they are very aroused before starting intercourse, (2) use generous amounts of water-based lubricating gels, (3) communicate to their partners if they experience any pain, and (4) try coital positions that allow them control over the movement. Of course, patients should also be encouraged to keep their physicians informed regarding pain, because genital pain is sometimes a sign of cancer recurrence.

Equally important for subsequent sexual and general adjustment are the psychological scars that can occur following cystectomy. That is, women may feel that they have lost their womanhood and that they are no longer attractive. In one of the few studies addressing sexual function in women undergoing radical cystectomy, Schover and von Eschenbach (1985) interviewed nine sexually active women about their sexual function before and after surgery. (Six of the women also received preoperative radiotherapy.)

Seven of the nine resumed sexual activity after surgery, and all experienced dyspareunia during initial intercourse attempts. Fortunately, six of the seven active patients were able to manage the pain at follow-up. Also, for these women, there were no changes in the pleasure or type of stimulation needed to reach orgasm. In general, Schover encourages couples to begin noncoital sexual activity as soon as the wife feels a return of sexual desire. Once the vagina has healed fully, intercourse may be resumed, although dyspareunia may require special treatment. In this regard, the use of vaginal hormone cream, vaginal dilation with a set of graduated dilators, and Kegel exercises (to help a woman increase awareness of muscle tension that may contribute to the dyspareunia) are recommended.

Colorectal cancer, including cancers of the large intestine and rectum, account for roughly 15% of all cancers in women. The standard surgical treatment involves an abdominoperineal resection (i.e., removal of the lower colon and rectum, and creation of a colostomy). A "colostomy" is an artificial opening between the bowel and the body's surface for the purpose of waste elimination. (For some women, it will also be necessary to remove the uterus, ovaries, and part of the vagina as well. When this more extensive surgery is required, a neovagina—see above—must be created using skin grafts.) Typically, genital sensation is preserved, as the pelvic nerves are not damaged; thus, orgasm remains possible. Finally, for some women, adjuvant radiation and/or chemotherapy may be required (Cohen, Kaufman, & Kadish, 1986).

Even for the most resilient individual, having an abdominoperineal resection can have a profound impact on body image and sexual adjustment. Many women will become very embarrassed over their changed appearance. Gloeckner (1983) quotes one woman regarding her feelings about her husband seeing her stoma for the first time:

> "I didn't show him . . . it was my surgeon who asked me if my husband had seen it, and I said 'No.' And that was a good year or so—it took me that long. The doctor said, 'Don't you think it's time you showed him?' And it went just fine. I don't know what he expected but he showed no fear or concern or anything like that. What I was afraid of was that he might find it repulsive. And he didn't have that at all." (p. 185)

Because of their fears, some women may even think that sex is over for them. Thus, an important role for a sex therapist is to encourage patients and their spouses to discuss these concerns, and to dispel myths (e.g., that sex will be harmful to either partner or will cause the cancer to recur). Technical advice regarding positions for greater comfort during lovemaking is helpful, as are suggestions regarding the use of towels and rubber undersheets to minimize spillage. Schover (1988b) encourages her patients to focus on their positive features, to confront negative thoughts, and to stay active as a means of coping with self-image changes and depression.

PELVIC CANCERS IN MEN

Pelvic cancers, including cancer of the prostate, bladder, testis, penis, colon, and rectum, account for 46% of all malignancies in men.

In the United States, approximately 1 out of 11 men will develop prostate cancer during his lifetime; it has been estimated that 100,000 new cases of prostate cancer are diagnosed each year (Rous, 1988). The risk for prostate cancer increases with age; roughly 80% of cases are diagnosed in men over 65 (National Cancer Institute, 1989). Fortunately, however, the 5-year survival rate for all stages of prostate cancer is 72% (Silverberg et al., 1990). Treatment for prostate cancer can involve surgery, radiation, chemotherapy, and hormone therapy (National Cancer Institute, 1989).

If surgery is indicated, then a radical (or total) prostatectomy will be performed. In this procedure, the prostate gland, vas deferens, seminal vesicles, and prostatic urethra are removed. Unfortunately, the sympathetic and parasympathetic nerves that surround the prostate (which are responsible for the increased arterial inflow of blood to the penis) are usually destroyed in the process. Although some urological surgeons (e.g., Walsh & Mostwin, 1984) claim good success in sparing these nerves (thereby preserving erectile functioning), many surgeons have not had this success; others argue that this "nerve sparing," as it is called, may leave some cancer cells behind (see Rous, 1988). Thus, many men undergoing a radical prostatectomy will not be able to achieve an erection after surgery; however, they will be able to experience sexual desire, pleasurable genital sensation, and orgasm (Schover, 1987). Thus, a primary therapeutic task is to encourage the man and his partner to expand their sexual repertoire to include noncoital activities. Of course, the couple may also want to consider medical interventions such as a penile prosthesis, use of a vacuum device, or vasoactive therapy (see Chapter 8).

Treatment of advanced prostate cancer may also involve the use of radiation and endocrine therapy. Radiotherapy is believed to impair erectile functioning in approximately 50% of all patients because of permanent vascular stenosis (Rous, 1988). Endocrine therapy, which may involve bilateral orchiectomy (i.e., removal of both testicles), estrogen administration, or both, is also associated with reduced sexual desire (because of lowered testosterone) and a high prevalance of erectile difficulties. However, because endocrine therapy is used primarily in the event of extensive regional spread or metastatic disease, it is difficult to know whether the erectile difficulties are treatment side effects, or effects of the malaise, weight loss, anemia, and pain that these patients experience (Andersen, 1985).

Bladder cancer is three times more common in men than in women, and accounts for 7% of all male cancers. The incidence of bladder cancer increases with age, with the mean age for men being 68 years (Shipley, Schwartz, Zinman, & Soto, 1986). The most common treatment for invasive bladder cancer in the United States is radical cystectomy (i.e., removal of the bladder, prostate, upper urethra, and seminal vesicles), often preceded by radiation therapy. This procedure requires the creation of a urinary ostomy.

Several studies have suggested that 85% or more of men are unable to achieve erections sufficient for intercourse following radical cystectomy. For example, Schover, Evans, and von Eschenbach (1986) reported that 91% of their patients ($n = 112$) experienced some degree of erectile dysfunction after their surgery. Despite this, 50% remained sexually active; these men reported normal levels of sexual desire and orgasmic capacity with noncoital stimulation. It should be noted that orgasms are "dry" (i.e., without ejaculation) because the prostate and seminal vesicles are removed. Interestingly, Schover et al. (1986) reported that the potential for continued sexual activity postsurgery could be predicted from the man's sexual history. More specifically, men who had provided and received noncoital stimulation prior to surgery were most likely to resume sexual activity after surgery. Also noteworthy was their observation that participation of the wife in sexuality-related educational and follow-up sessions was related to enhanced sexual adjustment.[8]

Cancer of the testis is relatively rare, and accounts for only 1% of all male cancers; thus, only 3 out of 1,000 men will develop testicular cancer in their lives (National Cancer Institute, 1986). Unlike most cancers, however, testicular cancer occurs primarily in young men. The good news is that testicular cancer has become the most treatable of all cancers. For all stages and types of testicular cancer combined, the overall 5-year survival rate is 88% (Silverberg et al., 1990).

Treatment for testicular cancer may involve surgery, radiation, and chemotherapy. Unilateral orchiectomy (i.e., removal of one testicle) does not impair sexual functioning or fertility in most men. However, when a bilateral orchiectomy (i.e., removal of both testicles) is required, both inhibited sexual desire and infertility are likely outcomes. In addition, erectile dysfunction and orgasmic difficulties may develop. Radiation does interfere with sperm production, but this interference is usually temporary. Unfortunately, the infertility resulting from chemotherapy is more permanent, although this too may reverse after 2 to 3 years (National Cancer Institute, 1986).

Cancer of the penis is extremely rare, accounting for fewer than 0.5% of all male cancers in the United States. Surgery is the primary treatment for penile cancer. Partial amputation of the penis (i.e., partial penectomy) results in removal of the glans penis and part of the shaft; following partial penectomy, a man is still capable of vaginal intercourse, including erection, orgasm, and ejaculation. However, when a total penectomy (i.e., removal of the glans penis and the entire penile shaft) is necessary, intercourse is not possible; however, erotic sensations and orgasmic potential remain, and ejaculation is still possible (Schover & Fife, 1985). The man will need to relearn what is pleasurable, as his erotic zones will be different.

Of course, despite the preservation of the capacity for erotic sensation, the psychological impact of penectomy can be devastating. The disfigurement that occurs almost inevitably leads to a vastly different body image, lowered self-esteem, embarrassment, and dysphoria. The primary therapeutic goal following surgery will be to provide emotional support, to provide accurate information, and to help the man to re-establish the affection that existed prior to surgery. Rushing to re-establish sexual satisfaction prior to resolving the profound psychological distress can be countertherapeutic.

Colorectal cancer accounts for 15% of all male cancers. As with women, the majority of men with colorectal cancer can be treated successfully by performing an abdominoperineal resection of the rectum (Cohen et al., 1986). Unfortunately, this procedure requires removal of the rectum and the formation of an artificial anal opening in the colon (i.e., a colostomy). In addition to the changed appearance, there may also be changed sexual functioning. Recent data obtained in a small study of 26 patients reveal that roughly one-third of patients undergoing abdominoperineal resection of the rectum will experience complete erectile dysfunction after surgery; another one-third will experience partial difficulties; and one-fifth will lose ejaculatory capability (Danzi, Ferulano, Abate, & Califano, 1983). Erectile dysfunction is believed to be secondary to the damage done to the parasympathetic nerves of the prostatic plexus. Because these nerves can sometimes regenerate, it has been suggested that patients be advised to wait at least 6 months following surgery before deciding upon a penile prosthesis (Schover & Fife, 1985).

GENERAL ISSUES IN COPING WITH CANCER

In her two excellent patient booklets on sexuality and cancer, Dr. Leslie Schover (1988a, 1988b) identifies 10 challenges that most cancer patients will confront, regardless of the site of their cancer. These challenges are likely to arise during the course of therapy, and will require therapeutic attention; they include the following:

1. Coping with changes in appearance
2. Combating negative thoughts
3. Coping with the outward effects of chemotherapy
4. Overcoming depression
5. Rebuilding self-esteem
6. Maintaining good communication
7. Overcoming anxiety
8. Resuming sexual activity with one's partner
9. Making intercourse more comfortable
10. Rekindling sexual desire

It is noteworthy that the resumption of sexual activity is not the highest priority. It is important for both the partner and the therapist not to rush a return to the bedroom; the coping process requires patience and time. Also, as mentioned previously, patients should be encouraged, within the scope of their value systems, to expand their sexual repertoire beyond intercourse—there are many ways to give and receive pleasure, and to be intimate. Moreover, perhaps as much as during any other time in their lives, couples can cope with this adversity by maintaining (and developing anew) the sense of interpersonal affection and trust that is afforded by sexual intimacy.

Specific Effects of Diabetes

Diabetes mellitus is the seventh leading cause of death in the United States, and was responsible for over 37,000 deaths in 1986. It is estimated that approximately 6 million Americans have diabetes (National Diabetes Advisory Board, 1988; Wing, Epstein, Nowalk, & Lamparski, 1986).

Diabetes mellitus results when the pancreas either totally stops producing insulin, or does not produce adequate amounts of the hormone (Pohl, Gonder-Frederick, & Cox, 1984). Inadequate insulin leads to poor absorption of glucose and, as a result, hyperglycemia (i.e., high levels of glucose in the blood). The primary reason why diabetes is so troublesome is that chronic hyperglycemia (over the course of many years) damages virtually every organ of the body. The effects of chronic hyperglycemia include diabetic blindness, nephropathy (i.e., kidney disease), myocardial infarction, stroke, and gangrene of the feet; these chronic effects result from diabetes-related microangiopathy (i.e., disease of the small blood vessels), macroangiopathy (i.e., disease of the large blood vessels), and neuropathy (i.e., disease of the nerves).

There are two forms of diabetes. Type I diabetes, also known as juvenile-onset diabetes and insulin-dependent diabetes, arises early in life and requires a self-managed treatment involving a controlled diet, moderate exercise, and daily injections of exogenous insulin. Type II diabetes, also known as adult-onset diabetes or non-insulin-dependent diabetes, typically arises in middle age in people who are overweight. Type II diabetes may be treated by (1) diet and exercise alone; (2) diet, exercise, and oral hypoglycemic agents; or (3) diet, exercise, and insulin injections. Although you are likely to encounter both Type I and Type II diabetics in clinical practice, Type II diabetes is approximately 20 times more common than Type I diabetes. However, both types of diabetes place an individual at increased risk for microangiopathy and neuropathy—two factors that have been associated with sexual dysfunction.

DIABETES IN WOMEN

Research with female diabetics has been somewhat sparse. In our review of the literature, we located seven studies (Ellenberg, 1977; Jensen, 1981; Kolodny, 1973; Newman & Bertelson, 1986; Schreiner-Engel et al., 1985; Schreiner-Engel, Schiavi, Vietorisz & Smith, 1987; Tyrer et al. 1983). These studies are mixed in their findings, and all are flawed by an exclusive reliance upon self-report.

In one of the first published studies of sexual functioning in diabetic women, Kolodny (1971) reported a significant difference in orgasmic dysfunction between diabetic and nondiabetic women. Of the 35% of diabetic subjects who were completely nonorgasmic during the preceding year, 91% reported impaired sexual response following the onset of their diabetes. Sexual dysfunction in diabetic women was correlated with the duration of diabetes, but there was no relationship with age, insulin dose, or diabetic complications (e.g., neuropathy, retinopathy, nephropathy, or vaginitis).

Ellenberg (1977) could not replicate Kolodny's findings in an uncontrolled study. His study attempted to investigate the hypothesized neuropathic etiology of sexual dysfunction; however, Ellenberg found that 81% of the neuropathic and 79% of the non-neuropathic women retained both desire and orgasmic ability. These figures are similar to those reported by Kinsey et al. (1953) in thier large-scale survey of all women (see also Pietropinto & Arora, 1989).

Jensen (1981, 1986) found only a minor difference in the self-reported rate of sexual dysfunction between diabetic (27.5%) and nondiabetic females (25%). Reduced desire was the most common dysfunction reported for both diabetic and control women. The highest rate of sexual dysfunction among diabetic women (i.e., 47%) has been reported by Newman and Bertelson (1986). In this study, no association was found between neuropathy and sexual difficulties.

The one relatively consistent finding across studies is that diabetic women seem to report difficulties with sexual arousal, particularly vaginal lubrication (i.e., Jensen, 1981, 1986; Schreiner-Engel et al., 1987; Tyrer et al., 1983).

In an interesting study, Schreiner-Engel et al. (1987) compared Type I and Type II diabetics. Diabetic type was highly associated with sexual responsiveness and marital satisfaction; that is, Type I diabetes was found to have little or no effect on women, whereas Type II diabetes had a negative impact on sexual desire, satisfaction, and activity; orgasmic capacity; lubrication; and relations with partners. Schreiner-Engel (1988) suggested that the intrusion of a restricted regimen on Type II diabetics may undermine a woman's self-image and produce distress, dysfunction, and marital discord.

Prather (1988) reviewed this literature and concluded that exact estimates of the prevalence, as well as well-documented etiological pathways, remain elusive—a conclusion that we share. Indeed, a major problem in all of these studies is their method of measurement; that is, these studies have relied upon self-report, a methodology that can be flawed by numerous response biases. For example, subjects may perceive that one "should" be sexually active or arousable, and therefore may inflate their estimates; conversely, subjects may feel embarrassed about their sexuality and underestimate their true response (Myers & Morokoff, 1986). Furthermore, fear of the possible effects of diabetes and other expectancies may bias subjective reporting. Other methodological problems (e.g., the definition of sexual arousal and dysfunction have varied from study to study) limit the confidence that we can have in the studies described above.

To begin to remedy this deficiency, Albert and Wincze (1990) have recently completed a psychophysiological investigation of sexual response in Type I female diabetics. In this study, five Type I diabetic females were compared to five matched nondiabetic (i.e., control) women on their subjective and physiological response to erotic videotapes. Although all women in both groups reported feeling sexually aroused and described physiological sensations of arousal, the diabetic women showed significantly less physiological arousal as measured by vaginal photoplythesmography. During the erotic stimulus presentation, four out of five of the diabetic women showed almost no vaginal pulse amplitude response, while all five of the controls showed significant increases relative to baseline and neutral conditions. Although these data were obtained from a small group of subjects, they suggest that Type I diabetics may be prone to sexual arousal difficulties.

DIABETES IN MEN

To our knowledge, very little research has been conducted on desire disorders in male diabetics. In his longitudinal study, Jensen (1981, 1986) found that 24–27% of his male subjects reported reduced sexual desire. The mechanism by which low desire occurs in diabetics has not been studied; thus, our conclusion in Chapter 2 (namely, that there appear to be many pathways to low sexual desire) seems appropriate.

Erectile dysfunction appears to be the most common sexuality-related complication of diabetes in males (Meisler et al., 1989; see Case 5 in Chapter 10). Estimates of the prevalence of erectile dysfunction have ranged from 28% to 75% of all diabetic men (see Zemel, 1988). As noted by Bancroft (1989), there tends to be an increasing prevalence of erectile dysfunction with increased duration of diabetes. Thus, the wide range of prevalence estimates may reflect differences in subject characteristics, particularly age and duration of diabetes, across research samples.

Considerable research attention has been devoted to determining the mechanisms by which diabetes might cause erectile difficulties. These mechanisms include endocrine, neurological, vascular, and psychosocial pathways. One hypothesis is that diabetes affects erectile functioning through deficits in hormone production. To investigate this hypothesis, Schoffling, Federlin, Ditschuneit, and Pfeiffer (1963) measured urinary excretion of gonadotropins, ketosteroids, and corticoids in diabetic men with erectile dysfunction, nondysfunctional diabetics, and "normal" controls. Their results revealed a higher incidence of hypogonadism in the dysfunctional diabetic group. Using improved methodologies, however, more recent studies (e.g., Buvat et al., 1985; Cooper, 1972; Ellenberg, 1971; Faerman et al., 1972; Kolodny et al., 1974; Lester, Grant, & Woodroffe, 1980) have challenged Schoffling et al.'s findings. These studies have found no differences between dysfunctional and nondysfunctional diabetic men on measures of gonadotropins or testosterone. Current thinking (e.g., Bancroft, 1989) suggests that hormonal deficiencies do *not* appear to be responsible for the erectile dysfunction seen in male diabetics.

An alternative hypothesis is that peripheral neuropathy may be a significant factor in the etiology of diabetic erectile difficulties (Ellenberg, 1980). Histological studies have provided supportive evidence. For example, Faerman, Glocer, Fox, Jadzinsky, and Rapaport (1974) performed postmortem histological examinations of the nerve fibers of the penile tissue in five diabetics who, prior to their death, had complained of erectile dysfunction. Faerman and his colleagues found morphological changes of the nerve fibers in four of the patients, lending support for the role of structural neuropathy in diabetic erectile dysfunction. In contrast to these findings, however, Melman, Henry, Felten, and O'Connor (1980) examined samples of erectile tissue from 16 patients undergoing penile implant surgery and found that the penile nerve supplies remained intact. They did find reduced concentrations of penile norepinephrine, however, suggesting that a neurotransmitter deficit, rather than damage to the nerve fibers per se, may be a factor in neuropathy-related erectile dysfunction.

Studies using clinical measures have also provided support for the neurological mechanism. The clinical measures used have included observations of neuropathic symptoms and signs (e.g., numbness, parasthesia, and diminished reflexes), as well as sophisticated measures of nerve conduction velocity, cystometrography, evoked responses, and bulbocavernosus reflex (BCR—see Chapter 3) latency. In addition, a number of simple yet sensitive tests of heart rate and blood pressure responses—thought to reflect autonomic function in other systems—have also been used, including the Valsalva maneuver, beat-to-beat variation in heart rate, and blood pressure responses to sustained muscle exercise. Investigations using these clinical measures have also provided empirical support for the neuropathic mechanism. For example, as discussed in Chapter 3, Ellenberg (1971) compared 45 dysfunctional diabetics with 30 diabetic controls. Eighty-four percent of the dysfunctional patients evidenced some symptoms of peripheral neuropathy (e.g., pain, paresthesia, absent deep reflexes), as compared to only 20% of the control patients. Ellenberg concluded that many cases of erectile dysfunction in diabetics are caused by neurogenic factors. In a subsequent study of 175 diabetic men, Kolodny et al. (1974) found that neuropathy was the only factor to discriminate significantly between functional and dysfunctional groups. Recently, Sarica and Karacan (1987) tested neurological function in 24 diabetic men and 14 normal controls complaining of erectile dysfunction. The results indicated that 66% of the diabetic patients exhibited significantly slowed (or, in some cases, absent) BCRs, supporting further the importance of the neuropathic factor. Several recent studies by McCulloch and his colleagues (McCulloch, Campbell, Wu, Prescott, & Clarke, 1980; McCulloch, Young, Prescott, Campbell, & Clarke, 1984) have also demonstrated a consistent relationship between neuropathy and erectile dysfunction. In sum, the available evidence indicates that a peripheral neurological mechanism is probably responsible for many cases of diabetic erectile dysfunction.

Recently, Nofzinger and Schmidt (1990) have proposed that deficits in the central (rather than the peripheral) nervous system might help to explain the increased prevalence of diabetic erectile dysfunction. They studied the sleep architecture of 10 dysfunctional diabetics and related these sleep measures to nocturnal penile tumescence (NPT—see Chapter 6) results. These 10 patients were also compared to two other sexually dysfunctional groups: (1) 10 patients whose dysfunction resulted from pelvic trauma or surgery, and (2) 9 patients whose dysfunction was described as "primarily psychogenic." The results indicated that rapid eye movement (REM) density was lower in the diabetic subjects, and that this sleep abnormality was correlated with impaired NPT findings. On the basis of these results, Nofzinger and Schmidt proposed that central autonomic dysfunction may be a contributing factor in the erectile difficulties of diabetic men. Although intriguing, these findings need to be replicated.

Because erections result from vascular changes, malfunctions in either the blood inflow (i.e., arterial) or outflow (i.e., venous) systems can impair erectile function. The vascular mechanism for diabetic erectile difficulties has also received considerable research attention. In a comprehensive, prospective study, McCulloch et al. (1984) found that erectile dysfunction was highly predictive of subsequent retinal microangiopathy. Jetvich, Edson, Jarman, and Herrera (1982) used Doppler examination to study vascular function in 47 impotent diabetic men and found that 96% of these patients exhibited some vascular occlusion, with 65% also evidencing neuropathy (as measured by BCR reflex latency and/or cystometrography). Lehman and Jacobs (1983) reported that 68% of their sample of 31 impotent diabetics evidenced vascular occlusion and 26% had signs of neurological abnormalities. Despite the discrepancy between these studies, there exists a compelling similarity: Jetvich et al. (1982) reported that there were 29 patients with penile arterial obstruction but with no penile neuropathy; notably, however, there was no patient with nerve damage who did not also have some form of vascular occlusion. Similarly, Lehman and Jacobs (1983) stated that, of 21 patients with vascular abnormalities, 15 had no neurological pathology; however, of seven patients with neuropathy, only one did not also show signs of vascular occlusion. The authors concluded that neurological changes may be secondary to angiopathy, a hypothesis consistent with the vascular mechanism of the pathogenesis of diabetic neuropathy (Johnson, Doll, Cromey, & Cromey, 1986). Thus, as a whole, the literature provides strong support for a vascular (specifically, an arterial) factor in diabetic erectile dysfunction.[9]

Many sex therapists have speculated that the psychological stress associated with having a chronic disease such as diabetes may increase patients' vulnerability to erectile difficulties. Indeed, studies by Karacan et al. (1978) and Lehman and Jacobs (1983) suggest that roughly 20% of impotent diabetic men have symptomatology consistent with a primarily psychogenic origin. Similarly, El-Bayoumi, El-Sherbini, and Mostafa (1984) indicated that roughly 38% of erectile dysfunctions in a sample of 75 diabetic men could be attributed primarily to psychological causes. As mentioned earlier with regard to women, Jensen (1981, 1985, 1986) has published several papers documenting the natural history of sexual dysfunction in diabetics. Jensen's studies evaluated large groups of patients in great detail. Standard tests of neurological functioning were conducted, and additional health information was obtained from medical records. Although vascular function was not assessed directly, it was inferred on the basis of degree of retinopathy. In addition, a wide range of psychosocial data was collected through the use of a comprehensive interview and self-report questionnaire. In the most recent follow-up, Jensen (1986) reported that, of the organic factors, only peripheral neuropathy correlated with erectile dysfunction. With regard to psychological factors, a couple's acceptance of diabetes was predictive of sexual function, *independent* of neuropathy. It appears that patients and their partners who were able to cope effectively with the stress of the disease were less likely to develop sexual difficulties, regardless of the presence of organic pathology. Although these findings need to be replicated before great confidence can be placed in them, they do highlight the importance of a careful assessment of disease-related acceptance and appraisal. Indeed, several measures of diabetic-related stress appraisal are available (e.g., the Disease Acceptance Scale—see Schover & Jensen, 1988; and the Appraisal of Diabetes Scale—see Carey et al., 1991).

In summary, then, research on the mechanisms by which diabetes causes erectile dysfunction has been abundant. This research has suggested that hormonal abnormalities are not the most likely cause of erectile dysfunction in male diabetics. In contrast, there is good evidence that neurological, vascular, and psychosocial mechanisms are all capable of impairing erectile functioning. What this implies for clinical practice, then, is that a multidisciplinary approach is essential. When evaluating a diabetic male, it is critical to work with a physician who can screen competently for organic contributors.

What does this body of research imply for the management of erectile dysfunction in diabetic men? We think that a conservative (i.e., least invasive) approach is indicated. By this we mean that we recommend a trial of sex therapy (see Chapter 7) prior to initiating medical treatments (Chapter 8). In some cases, a favorable response to sex therapy will occur. Even when no improvement in erectile functioning occurs, men and their partners will still be helped to improve their communication and to adjust to their chronic illness.

Finally, difficulties related to orgasm in male diabetics has also been reported. Most common appears to be reductions in semen volume or "dry orgasms" (Ellenberg, 1971; Fairburn et al., 1982; Jensen, 1986). This difficulty, referred to in Chapter 4 as "retrograde ejaculation," appears to be a consequence of the failure of the reflex closing of the internal bladder sphincter; the latter occurs as a result of autonomic neuropathy (see Greene & Kelalis, 1968).

Concluding Comments

From our brief review, it is apparent that conditions such as diabetes, cancer, substance abuse, and fear of STDs can all set the stage for sexual difficulties. Although space limitations prevent us from thoroughly cataloguing all of the psychological conditions and physical disorders that may increase a person's risk for sexual dysfunction, we can strongly encourage you to further your knowledge of those conditions that occur most often in your practice.

Notes

[1] The U.S. Public Health Service and the Centers for Disease Control estimate that between 1.0 and 1.5 million persons in the United States are currently HIV-positive (i.e., infected with the virus responsible for AIDS; Centers for Disease Control, 1988). Worldwide estimates suggest that there may be over 10 million people currently infected (Crooks & Baur, 1990), and as many as 100 million people worldwide are likely to become infected in the next few years (Davison & Neale, 1990).

[2] The reader who is interested in a more general understanding of AIDS and STDs is referred to the excellent books *The Science of AIDS* (1989), and *Sexually Transmitted Diseases* (Zinner, 1985).

[3] This publication *(AIDS: 100 Questions and Answers)* is available, free of charge, from the New York State Department of Health (telephone number: 800-541-AIDS).

[4] Although other conditions (e.g., end-stage renal disease, cardiovascular disease, multiple sclerosis) can also affect sexual adjustment, we do not discuss these conditions because of space limitations. Readers interested in more information than is provided here are referred to Schover and Jensen (1988) and Kolodny, Masters, and Johnson (1979).

[5] Information provided in this section includes revised material from a previously published periodical article (Carey, 1990).

[6] A small number of men, fewer than 1,000 per year, also develop breast cancer.

[7] As an aside, we have also found self-help support groups to be very valuable for many women. Among the most widely available is Reach to Recovery, a program of the American Cancer Society. For information on this program, call any local office of the American Cancer Society.

[8] This observation is consistent with experiences with penile prosthesis recipients (Krauss et al., 1989; Meisler et al., 1988): Partner participation in presurgical assessments, education, counseling, and decision making is associated with postsurgical satisfaction and adjustment.

[9] The importance of the venous system in the maintenance of erection must also be emphasized. Relaxation of the smooth muscle of the corpus cavernosum produces an inflow of blood and dilatation of the penile vascular spaces, causing outward pressure, which compresses the penile veins. The venous mechanism thus acts as a valve, trapping the blood in the penis in order to attain and maintain the erection. Although impairment in venous function (i.e., "venous leakage") has been reported to cause erectile difficulties, the extent to which diabetes affects the venous system directly is not fully understood.

10

Case Illustrations

All six of the cases presented in this chapter were seen by us and were selected to illustrate commonly encountered client and therapist problems. Whenever possible, exact quotations have been used to provide you with a better understanding of each case. Case presentations include demographic information, problem description, etiology, assessment procedure, therapy, and/or disposition.

Although the names and certain identifying factors have been changed in order to protect the confidentiality of our clients, the pertinent clinical information is represented accurately.

Case 1: Mr. Adams (Male Erectile Disorder)

Description

Mr. Adams was a 45-year-old divorced male who first presented to a medical clinic with complaints of erectile dysfunction. Mr. Adams had been divorced for 7 years and began experiencing erectile problems approximately 5 years ago. He described his problem as emerging gradually; also, he denied experiencing erections during sleep,[1] during masturbation, or while viewing erotic materials.

Mr. Adams reported that he wasn't even attempting to date women because he knew he couldn't "perform." An example of Mr. Adams's attitude toward women and sexual relations is illustrated in the following interchange:

THERAPIST: Mr. Adams, is there any woman you know whom you are fond of and can be close to without attempting intercourse?

CLIENT: Phew! Are you kidding? I would never put myself in that position. I would be too embarrassed. Every woman wants real sex, and I don't know any woman that doesn't.

THERAPIST: When is the last time you had attempted relations with a woman?

CLIENT: About 6 or 7 weeks ago I met a real dog. She was awful, and even with her, nothing. Can you imagine that?[2]

THERAPIST: Mr. Adams, if this woman was not attractive to you, why would you even expect to become aroused?

CLIENT: If you're a man and you're with a woman, you get hard. It always worked that way before and now it don't. Look, do you have a pill you can give me? It's not in my head, you know.

Mr. Adams was not compelled by logical argument and was totally committed to a medical solution for his problem. He was argumentive and angry; moreover, he viewed the interview as only a means to get what he wanted (a "potency" pill or an implant), and not as a means of learning about his problem.

Assessment

A comprehensive medical assessment was undertaken. Mr. Adams's medical history revealed that he had experienced two myocardial infarctions 10 and 12 years ago; he also had a 10-year history of hypertension, a 10-year history of duodenal ulcer, and a 20-year history of alcohol abuse. He had stopped drinking 5 years ago and had been on the same medications for hypertension and ulcers for 10 years.

The erectile dysfunction workup included the following: penile blood pressure, cavernosography, sacral evoked response, hormone evaluation, daytime erotic arousal study (using the penile strain gauge), and nocturnal penile tumescence (NPT) monitoring. The results were as follow:

1. Penile–brachial index: .97 (within normal limits)
2. Cavernosogram: Normal venous blood flow (i.e., no leakage)
3. Sacral evoked response: Normal latency (i.e., no neuropathy)
4. Hormones: Testosterone and prolactin within normal limits
5. Daytime erotic arousal: No response
6. NPT monitoring: Full normal erection response

When Mr. Adams was provided with these results, he insisted that the data were wrong and that he did not get erections at night. He was asked once again about his masturbation and intercourse experience. This time he reported that his last successful intercourse had been 1 year ago and that recently he had been able to masturbate to full erection and ejaculation. He discounted these erections, however, insisting they were not as good as they should have been. It seemed clear that he was focusing on his negative rather than on his positive experiences.

Etiology

The onset of Mr. Adams's erectile difficulties seemed to coincide with his abstinence from alcohol. It is common for recovering alcoholics to be much more aware of and vigilant of their surroundings and their own behavior (see the "Substance Abuse" section of Chapter 9). This hypervigilant period continued with Mr. Adams's rigid views of masculine sexuality and focused his attention onto his sexual performance. A classic case of "performance anxiety" (Masters & Johnson, 1970) resulted. This was maintained by his avoidance of favorable conditions for sexual relations and his all-or-none thinking pattern. "All-or-none" thinking is illustrated by an individual's inability to appreciate gradations in the occurrence of a specific factor, behavior, or trait. For Mr. Adams, this meant that he was only able to define sex for himself as equal to having a hard penis and engaging in intercourse. He could not accept gradations of pleasuring sexual activity.

Mr. Adams's age and undetected medical factors could have weakened his erectile response further.

Therapy

It was clear that Mr. Adams's attitude and behavior were self-defeating and led him to failure experiences. The ideal therapy would have helped him to restructure such maladaptive cognitions, and helped him to create positive erotic experiences without threat or worry of failure. Sensate focus should have been helpful in such a case once the appropriate attitude was achieved, and a loving, nonthreatening partner was located. Unfortunately, Mr. Adams was resistant to accepting any explanation other than a medical one. He was not willing to explore any other options other than an implant, and requested a referral to a urologist.

Mr. Adams's attitude and his reaction to the assessment are not uncommon. Some men with this attitude can be engaged in therapy, but every step must be stated and repeated in very concrete language. Even when the therapist feels that things are perfectly clear, there is still room for error! It is not uncommon for a client to return on the next session (after very specific instructions) and announce, "I did what you said, Doc, and it didn't work." Careful questioning then may reveal that the client did exactly the opposite of what was instructed.

Clients like Mr. Adams can be very frustrating and often terminate therapy prematurely. If the therapist is able to gain the client's confidence and not to be viewed as the "nut doctor," then persistence over a long period of time can reverse the erectile problem, and can prove to be a very rewarding experience for both the client and the therapist.

Case 2: Mr. Simon and Ms. Smith
(Female Hypoactive Sexual Desire Disorder)

Description

In common parlance, Mr. Simon and Ms. Smith would be described as "yuppies" (i.e., young, upwardly mobile professionals); that is, both were in their late 20s, were college-educated, and were from upper-middle-class families. Although they shared this label and other superficial characteristics, this was where their similarity ended.

Ms. Smith was from an emotionally controlled family in which disagreements among family members were quietly negotiated. Responsibilities were left up to individuals with very little guidance and prodding. Both parents were professional academicians. In contrast, Mr. Simon came from an emotionally out-of-control family in which disagreements among family members were settled by whoever could yell the loudest and longest. Family fights were frequent; if any children stepped out of line they were told so, and in no uncertain terms. Mr. Simon's family owned a very successful family business, which Mr. Simon was being trained to manage.

Needless to say, Mr. Simon and Ms. Smith were different in many ways. They were, of course, well aware of these differences and had "worked through" the major problem areas. They were now seeking help for their sexual behavior, which they saw as the last stumbling block before marriage. They first entered therapy approximately 8 months before their wedding date. The presenting complaint was Ms. Smith's lack of desire and lack of orgasm during intercourse.

Assessment

As recommended in Chapter 6, separate interviews were conducted with each partner. It was learned that each partner was committed to the relationship and wanted to go through with the planned marriage. Furthermore, each had had prior satisfying sexual relations with other partners. Although they had initially enjoyed sexual relations with each other, at the time they entered therapy sexual relations had become very strained. Ms. Smith could achieve orgasm through manual stimulation, but rejected this as unsatisfactory because it "wasn't the real thing"; furthermore, she felt that she "couldn't have a true orgasm so [she] had to do it that way."

Ms. Smith was not complaining of any pain and had had a recent medical evaluation. No medical conditions could explain her sexual difficulties. Also, she was not taking any prescription medications; nor was she using "recreational" drugs or alcohol, which might affect her sexual response.

The assessment revealed that both partners were focusing on sexual performance. They were emphasizing the importance of intravaginal orgasm to the point where its absence was being looked upon as symbolic of Ms. Smith's lack of commitment to the relationship.

Etiology

It appeared that the origin of the sexual problem was Ms. Smith's reaction to Mr. Simon's stylistic approach to conflict. He would criticize her during and immediately after sex; this made her very angry and insecure, especially since the criticism focused on nuances of her sexual expression. Although he felt he was being constructive, open, and helpful, she was clearly upset with his direct approach; she interpreted his comments as negative criticism. Mr. Simon's comparative statements about the sexual normality of his past sexual partners did not help. Ms. Smith kept her anger to herself and was unwilling to confront Mr. Simon because of his argumentative style. Her lack of desire was not a lifelong problem; rather, it appeared to be acquired during her current relationship with her fiancé.

Therapy

The couple's interaction and communication style was hypothesized to be the source of desire and orgasmic problems; nevertheless, Ms. Smith was reluctant at first to express her negative feelings directly. Therapy began with a sensate focus strategy outside of sessions and communication training within sessions. It became readily apparent, however, that the nonsexual problems—which the couple thought they had settled—were still sources of considerable conflict. Conflict was related to feelings about each other's family, about commitment to the relationship, and about roles and responsibilities within their relationship. Furthermore, issues about religion, child rearing, or even what name Ms. Smith would use after marriage (hyphenated, her maiden name, or his name) were never discussed. Sex therapy lasted only two sessions; at that point, the couple conceded that conflict over other issues was interfering with their sexual adjustment. Therapy then refocused more on marital issues and enhancing communication.[3]

The focus on communication and other couple conflict issues continued approximately 5 months (15 sessions). During this time, the couple was instructed to avoid having sex whenever either partner was upset or angry with the other. Once the partners were communicating more effectively and feeling much better about each other, the sessions then shifted to discussions of sexual matters. More explicit instructions were given about performance, and the couple was encouraged to focus on nonintercourse pleasuring, but no ban was placed on intercourse. A very important element of therapy at this time was challenging Ms. Smith's negative feelings about orgasm outside of intercourse. Equally important was changing Mr. Simon's style of providing a running commentary and criticism during and immediately after sexual relations. (Apparently Mr. Simon was a big sports fan and couldn't resist the opportunity to provide play-by-play and color commentary.)

Four additional months of therapy (eight sessions), which focused on sexual matters, resulted in significant change in their sexual satisfaction. Desire increased for both partners, and neither felt that it was important for intravaginal orgasm to occur. Interestingly, Ms. Smith did experience at least two orgasms intravaginally during the last month prior to termination of therapy. Although she was very pleased by this development, she was encouraged to enjoy it but not to expect or require it. That is, she was discouraged from "striving" for coital orgasms, but encouraged to enjoy them when they occurred.

Case 3: Mr. and Mrs. Neale (Vaginismus)

Description

Mr. and Mrs. Neale had been married 4 years but had not consummated their marriage. About once every 3 weeks Mr. Neale rubbed up against Mrs. Neale to the point of ejaculation while touching her breasts. Mrs. Neale was not enthusiastic about this activity and would never allow or participate in genital touching. "I hate to touch him on the penis."

Mrs. Neale was a very bright woman who held a graduate degree in business. She was from a lower-middle-class home and described her upbringing as "very peculiar." Her father would very often lounge around the house only in his underpants, and she had memories of him caressing her in the vagina when she was very young. Mrs. Neale had participated in therapy several times to help her deal with feelings of rage. She felt that her last therapist, who was a female, "came on to her," and this upset her very much; she left therapy in a panic. In spite of this experience, she questioned whether or not she could trust a male therapist.

Mr. Neale was from a very loving middle-class family and was a health professional. He might best be described as a "nice guy" and was very tolerant and somewhat unassertive. He had had some sexual experiences before marriage, but did not have a very strong sex drive. He put most of his energies into his profession; he claimed that he was mainly concerned about his wife's rage (e.g., throwing dishes), and was not overly concerned about the lack of sexual intercourse.

Assessment

Mr. and Mrs. Neale entered therapy because they were considering having a baby. It was very clear that there were many issues to be dealt with, and separate interviews provided a glimpse into the extent of the disturbance. Mrs. Neale had very angry feelings toward men. She also had uncontrolled periods of rage, during which she would damage her house and strike her husband. She also hinted that there were issues of sexual abuse when she was a child, and "questioned" whether or not she had any attraction toward men at all. She had previously been diagnosed as having Borderline Personality Disorder and had been prescribed Xanax.

Etiology

The etiology of Mrs. Neale's vaginismus did not become clear until well into therapy. She had been sexually abused by her father and had also observed a very unloving relationship between her mother and father. Her mother was very overprotective. In conditioning terms, men (and heterosexual relations) had negative associations, whereas women (and physical closeness to women) had positive associations.

Therapy

It was very clear that Mrs. Neale needed individual therapy before couples therapy would be worthwhile. One important process issue was whether or not she could learn to trust a male therapist. This issue was discussed with

Mrs. Neale, and she agreed to try several individual sessions. In a very nonthreatening manner, the issue of childhood sexual abuse was addressed. She reported that she had never dealt with this issue previously, and was reassured that the therapist was comfortable and experienced in dealing with these sexual issues.

Mrs. Neale gained trust in the therapist; slowly and tearfully, she talked about her father's sexual encounters with her. She was encouraged to read books about the effects and experiences of sexual abuse by women authors (e.g., Bass & Davis, 1988) and was referred to a survivors' group. She became very involved in the reading and in talking to other women about abuse. She was also referred to a psychiatrist for consideration of medication to manage shifts in her moods. She was prescribed an antidepressant medication; this seemed to help her somewhat.

Discussion about sexual matters addressed Mrs. Neale's attractions to both males and females, as well as gender dysphoria. Discussions and readings helped her clear up misunderstandings about gender dysphoria, and therapy focused on helping her accept homosexual attractions.

Once Mrs. Neale had accepted that part of her sexual makeup was composed of attraction to women, she then became more comfortable with herself and with her married relationship. She no longer felt "weird"; importantly, she no longer looked upon attraction to men and sex with her husband as a test of normality. She could relax and accept (in principle) sex with her husband in non-performance-oriented terms. It was important for Mrs. Neale to understand that the presence of attractions toward women did not mean that she had to act on them. To act on an attraction for another person (male or female) was discussed as a moral choice within one's value system; that is, being attracted to another person did not require that she act out on that attraction.

In addition, she was able to understand the association between her anger toward men and her anger toward her abusive father. Both of these changes in her understanding of her background led to greater comfort in moving forward to participate in couples therapy focused on the vaginismus problem.

Therapy then proceeded with communication training, sensual pleasuring, and practice in gradual comfort with penile insertion. Progress was relatively rapid, and successful intercourse was achieved within 3 months of conjoint therapy.

Individual therapy lasted approximately 1½ years. This preliminary therapy was necessary before couples therapy could proceed. Mrs. Neale was not able to discuss any of her feelings about women or concerns about gender dysphoria in front of her husband. Conjoint therapy would most likely have been sabotaged or at least stalled if the individual issues had not been addressed first. This case demonstrates the need to conduct individual interviews as part of the initial assessment. Without the separate interviews, the important issues of sexual abuse and attraction to women would not have been addressed.

Case 4: Mr. and Mrs. Brown (Male Hypoactive Sexual Desire Disorder)

Description

Mr. and Mrs. Brown were in their early 30s, had middle-class backgrounds, and were college-educated; they had been married for 4 years when they entered therapy. The presenting complaint was this: Mr. Brown never initiated sexual contact and rarely appeared interested in sex. Sexual intercourse had occurred only once during the past 7 months. He never experienced erectile dysfunction. He professed love for his wife, and denied interest in any other women.

Mrs. Brown expressed a similarly positive picture of her marriage during her separate interview. She loved her husband very much, was interested in and enjoyed sex, had no interests in other men, and could not identify any problems in their relationship other than her husband's lack of sexual interest. She felt that his lack of sexual interest was the likely result of his strict religious background.

Assessment

Separate assessment interviews were conducted; in addition, Mr. Brown went to a urologist who specialized in male sexual disorders. The interview with Mrs. Brown reaffirmed her love and attraction to Mr. Brown, but she was concerned that Mr. Brown no longer found her attractive.

Please note that it is usually helpful to ask each partner what he or she believes may be the cause of the problem. It is common for female partners of males experiencing problems to blame either themselves, another woman, or another man. It is important to know each person's implicit hypotheses or attributions, because each person may actually be operating on the assumption that they are true when, most often, the hypotheses are unsubstantiated.

Mrs. Brown added that whenever she tried to act sexy, such as wearing erotic undergarments, Mr. Brown would laugh and discourage her. Currently, she said that she just shut down and didn't bother thinking of sex any more. She was worried about this because she wanted to become pregnant.

The medical assessment of Mr. Brown revealed no medical factors that could explain his low desire. During the interview, Mr. Brown reaffirmed his attraction to and love for his wife; he denied any outside pressures or problems that might be contributing to stress or distraction. He denied homosexual interests, denied any interest in another woman, and denied any substance abuse.

Etiology

The interview with Mr. Brown revealed some factors that might be possible contributors to his lack of sexual initiation and low arousal. Although Mr. Brown's religious upbringing did not affect his overall interest in sex, it did seem to dichotomize in his mind sex with "good girls" versus "bad girls." He had experienced very arousing sexual experiences with a number of women before marriage. In his words, if the women were very "slutty" and sexually demanding, he became highly aroused. On the other hand, if a woman was "proper" and deserving of respect, he found it very difficult to become aroused. His wife was very attractive but very wholesome; this wholesome image seemed to contribute to a restrained approach to sex on his part.

Other possible contributing factors emerged. Mrs. Brown used to initiate sex, but during the past 2 years she had left the responsibility up to Mr. Brown. Also, he viewed her as always available for sex, and this may have taken away any element of risk in their sexual relationship. Furthermore, Mr. Brown never used sexual fantasies to enhance his arousal and did not expose himself to erotic materials. Finally, Mr. Brown said that he would approach his wife for sex only if he felt fully aroused. It did not occur to him that arousal would evolve as a by-product of sexual activity.

Therapy

All of these possible etiological factors were discussed with Mr. and Mrs. Brown. The Browns were encouraged to try sensate focus, with Mr. Brown taking the initiative. He was reminded that he did *not* have to be sexually aroused to start. He had a great deal of trouble initiating any kind of physical activity; in fact, after failing to initiate during home practice, he disclosed in therapy that he had *never* initiated contact with any female. By not initiating, he never took the chance of being rejected. He also had difficulty in expressing his emotions and found it unmanly to do so. These issues were discussed at length, with a focus on his cognitions, and he was encouraged to continue with his initiation of the sensate focus sessions.

Mrs. Brown was encouraged to be expressive of her sexual feelings in dress and in action, whereas Mr. Brown was encouraged to work on accepting her sexuality. Cognitive restructuring with Mr. Brown focused on his long-standing beliefs regarding women and sexual expression, especially as these related to Mrs. Brown's sexual behavior.

Mr. Brown was also encouraged to practice bringing erotic thoughts into his life. He was given assignments to read erotic passages and to enjoy sexual material he viewed on TV rather than turning away from it.

Fifteen therapy sessions were held over 10 months, and the couple experienced a very positive change in their sexual relationship. Mr. Brown became much more emotionally expressive and felt comfortable initiating sexual contacts. At the end of therapy, the couple was participating in sexual intercourse approximately once a week, and both partners were satisfied with this rate. Both took equal responsiblility for initiating sex.

Case 5: Mr. and Mrs. Fogarty (Adjustment to Chronic Illness)

Description

Mr. and Mrs. Fogarty had been married for 25 years and had two sons aged 18 and 21 years; both sons lived at home. Mr. Fogarty was 50 and worked as a supervisor in a jewelry factory; Mrs. Fogarty was 47 and worked as a secretary.

Mr. Fogarty reported a decline in his erection response over the past 10 years. For the past 3 years, there had been no erections noted during sexual activity, nor had there been any NPT responses noted. Mr. Fogarty's reaction to his erectile difficulties was to withdraw totally from any affection or sexual activity. Mrs. Fogarty was angry and hurt by Mr. Fogarty's withdrawal, but she had difficulty confronting him on this issue, and the couple rarely discussed this.

Mr. Fogarty had been diagnosed as having diabetes 12 years prior to therapy, and he had become insulin-dependent about 5 years prior to therapy. He was referred by his diabetologist to a urologist for treatment of his erectile difficulties.

Mr. and Mrs. Fogarty had different personalities. Mrs. Fogarty was a somewhat unassertive, flexible, and very accepting person, whereas Mr. Fogarty was very rigid, highly critical, and suspicious man who saw the world as either black or white. Needless to say, their personalities clashed, and even a hint of criticism would lead Mr. Fogarty to pouting and long periods of withdrawal.

The two sons were described by Mr. and Mrs. Fogarty as "freeloading bums" who were reluctant to work. Their presence in the home was a continual source of tension and led to long, bitter battles. Although both Mr. and Mrs. Fogarty viewed their sons similarly, their methods of dealing with their sons' problems were very different. Thus, no solution to this problematic situation was ever reached.

Assessment

Urological assessment found that Mr. Fogarty showed insufficient NPT responding; it was assumed that the dysfunction was related to his diabetes. Mr. Fogarty objected strongly to the idea of a penile implant and stated that he was horrified by the thought of anything "artificial"; he stated that he would even object to getting contact lenses if he needed them! He dismissed the idea of a vacuum pump device (e.g., the Erec-Aide) on similar grounds, but was amenable to trying injection of vasoactive agents (i.e., papaverine). After his 5-month follow-up visit to the urologist, the urologist wrote the following letter to the diabetologist:

Dear Dr. Denton:

Mr. Fogarty returned to my office this week, 5 months after we started him on his papaverine program. Although we had some initial success with this regimen, Mr. Fogarty has discovered that an erect penis is not the only requirement for adequate sexual relations. At this time, although the papaverine worked well, he and his wife are having great difficulties in their relationship, particularly as related to their sexual satisfaction. Both of them were recently in my office, and the hostility was quite evident. Mr. Fogarty feels that although he gets an erection with papaverine, it is not really satisfactory; that is to say, the erection alone was not all he was hoping for. I have referred him to [a sex therapist] as I believe counseling would be of great benefit for them.

Sincerely yours,

Dr. Ulrich

Psychological assessment confirmed the interpersonal differences and interpersonal hostility noticed by the urologist. Mr. Fogarty had used the papaverine injections on about six occasions and, although he always achieved satisfactory erections, he admitted that he was having sex to "prove something"; he admitted that he was not aroused or interested in sex. In fact, on some occasions he was angry just prior to sex and felt resentful at having been pressured into having sexual relations.

Mr. Fogarty had been an extremely insecure person all of his life, and this led to his defensive style. He was prone to making quick judgments about people based on very little information. Communication between Mr. and Mrs. Fogarty was characterized by second-guessing; use of extremes and character assassination (e.g, "You are *always* a *jerk* when you talk to the boys"); and an inability to stick to the subject under discussion.

In addition to the communication problems, Mr. and Mrs. Fogarty both had very poor sexual knowledge and believed a number of sexual myths.

Mr. Fogarty believed, for example, that sexual intercourse was the only true sex and that a man's loss of erection made him less masculine. The revelation of this belief shed light on his insistence in achieving an erection by "natural" means to restore his masculinity and balance in his relationship.

Etiology

This case is presented to underscore the necessity of including careful psychological assessment, even in cases when it is known that organicity is the basis of the sexual dysfunction. The client was insistent on obtaining an erection to solve his problems; as Schover (1989) has so aptly pointed out, the more a man insists on a medical solution to his sexual problems, the more he is probably in need of psychological intervention!

Mr. Fogarty's rigid attitude linking masculinity with an erect penis and his basic insecurity exacerbated his (organically based) erectile difficulties. The ineffective communication style between Mr. and Mrs. Fogarty led to a great deal of marital strife; in turn, this strife fed into Mr. Fogarty's insecurities and withdrawal from sex. ("Why should I even try when sex just leads to punishment and criticism of my masculinity?").

Mrs. Fogarty was not critical of her husband's masculinity, nor did she place great importance on intercourse. Her concerns involved her husband's love for her and a desire for a relationship in which affection could be exchanged openly.

Therapy

Therapy focused on three goals: attitude change, communication training, and behavioral change. Following the assessment, an etiological formulation was provided to enhance understanding and indicate a rationale for therapy. The couple committed to the therapy process. Therapy began by focusing on faulty attitudes related to sex and gender. Specific readings were given to facilitate and augment the therapy sessions, including *Male Sexual Awareness* by Barry McCarthy (1988), and a couples communication brochure. Through the readings and discussions of sex roles and the meaning of sexual behavior, the partners came to shift their attitudes about their own sexuality and each other's sexual motivation. After a few sessions that focused on attitude change, communication skills training began. During these sessions, problems were reviewed with a focus on process issues within communication. To facilitate actual behavioral changes, the couple was encouraged to set aside specific periods of time during the week for high-quality, uninterrupted communication sessions. This proved to be a valuable therapeutic procedure and led to constructive problem solving and improved feelings toward each other. A key element seemed to be that each partner saw the other as trying to enhance the relationship.

Once a more trusting and amicable relationship was established and faulty attitudes had been challenged, then frank discussions of sexual issues ensued. Sensate focus exercises were introduced to promote behavioral change and the appropriate use of papaverine injections was discussed. Twelve 1-hour therapy sessions led to significant positive changes in the couple's relationship and sexual behavior.

The very rigid and stereotypical views of sexual behavior and gender roles expressed by Mr. Fogarty are commonly encountered in sex therapy. Although Mr. Fogarty was not college-educated, college education alone does not, unfortunately, always override these attitudes. For example, a recent male client from an Ivy League school expressed the following concerns about his girlfriend:

CLIENT: I am angry at my girlfriend. I had ordered her not to go to that new dance club while I was out of town, but she disobeyed me and went anyway.

THERAPIST: You use the words "ordered" and "disobeyed"; do you really mean to convey your wishes that strongly? Isn't that offensive?

CLIENT: As the man, I expect that my girlfriend will obey me. I admit it is a double standard, but that is the way I think. It is OK for me to go to the club, because I can take care of myself and I know what it's like there.

This highly educated young man had attitudes very similar to Mr. Fogarty's. He also saw intercourse as the only true sex and felt that if he couldn't perform intercourse, then he was less masculine. Interestingly, he suffered from erectile dysfunction and was avoiding all sexual contacts when he entered therapy.

Case 6: Mr. and Mrs. Bradley
(Premature Ejaculation)

Description

Mr. and Mrs. Bradley were in their late 20s and had been married 3½ years when they entered therapy. They had no children and lived in an upstairs apartment above Mrs. Bradley's parents. Both were high-school-educated and were in white-collar, lower-level management positions.

Mr. Bradley came from a very dysfunctional family. His father was a compulsive gambler and had spent time in jail; his brother was a drug addict.

His mother was described as very seductive and would often walk around the house naked. Doors were never closed for privacy, and his parents would have intercourse in clear view of whoever might walk by their door. Mr. Bradley's mother was also "very critical and always complaining," and set a very negative tone in the family.

Mrs. Bradley on, the other hand, was raised in a very loving and well-integrated family. Family members were very open with their feelings but sensitive to each other's needs. Mrs. Bradley was comfortable and confident with her sexuality and was able to express her emotions openly. In contrast, Mr. Bradley was a loner who held his feelings inside and who had very unpleasant associations with sex. Although Mrs. Bradley's criticism of Mr. Bradley was much less destructive than his mother's criticism, he nevertheless would respond with withdrawal whenever he was criticized.

The presenting problems were premature ejaculation and lack of desire on Mr. Bradley's part. Mr. Bradley would usually ejaculate within 30 seconds of penetration, and following ejaculation he would withdraw and become angry at his "failure." As this scenario repeated itself over time, Mrs. Bradley became hurt, angry, and critical. In turn, Mr. Bradley withdrew emotionally and showed little interest in sexual activity. He also began expressing doubts about his erectile capacity; this led to Mrs. Bradley's becoming more critical and angry, because she felt she was being rejected.

Assessment

Separate interviews were held with each partner. Mr. Bradley reported in his interview that he had had a brief sexual encounter outside of his marriage. He had no difficulty in obtaining a full erection with this other partner; however, he did experience premature ejaculation. Mr. Bradley also reported firm nocturnal erections. When asked about low sexual desire, Mr. Bradley described the "bind" he was in with his wife. He gave as an example the persistent criticism and questioning he received from his wife if he appeared interested in an attractive woman on television. To avoid conflict, he developed the strategy of showing no interest in sensuous or erotic stimuli; she interpreted this as his lack of desire.

Mrs. Bradley reported feeling very angry when Mr. Bradley first experienced premature ejaculation and, later, lack of desire. Mrs. Bradley was angry because of the following misunderstanding: She assumed that her husband's premature ejaculation was a reflection of his lack of interest in her; she believed that his ejaculatory difficulties "could be controlled if he only tried harder." She felt rejected by him, and her attempts to put more pressure on him only served to encourage more avoidance on his part.

Use of separate interviews allowed frank discussions that might otherwise have been inhibited with the partner's presence. Through these interviews, the following information was obtained:

- Mr. Bradley did have strong sexual desire.
- Mr. Bradley was afraid of disappointing his wife, whom he cared a great deal about.
- Mr. Bradley associated his wife's sexual demands with his mother's inappropriate seductive behavior.
- Mrs. Bradley misunderstood Mr. Bradley's sexual problem; as a result, she was contributing to a "vicious circle" by pressuring him to control his ejaculation.
- Mr. Bradley had a personal style of withdrawing from confrontation.

Etiology

Mr. Bradley entered the marriage as an insecure man who had negative attitudes about sexuality. Once he experienced premature ejaculation, and came under criticism for this from his wife, his feelings of insecurity surfaced. He coped by using sexual withdrawal. In response, his wife's demands for sex increased (in order to work on the problem), and Mr. Bradley's negative attitudes abut sex were thus exacerbated. A vicious cycle was set in motion as emotional withdrawal and demanding anger interacted with each other. This cycle was difficult to reverse because of misunderstandings and poor communication.

Therapy

Often in cases of premature ejaculation, the treatment of choice is the "squeeze technique" (Masters & Johnson, 1970). Although this procedure is purported to be highly effective in the short term, there are no long-term follow-up studies. Thus its effectiveness over time is unknown. In addition, inherent in this procedure is a covert message that it is essential for the male to control his ejaculation in order to enjoy sex and please his partner. This message runs counter to the goal of reducing a performance orientation and focusing on mutual pleasure. So, although the goal of ejaculation control may be reached through the use of the squeeze technique, a couple utilizing this technique may derive from it a message emphasizing the importance of performance. This may be countertherapeutic in the long run.

An alternative approach is to address the attitudes that a couple has concerning the need to control ejaculation. Often, as in the case of Mr. and Mrs. Bradley, there are misunderstandings about a partner's motivation, misunderstandings about contributing factors, and ignorance about normal sexual behavior. Educating a couple about these matters can often lead to significant therapeutic changes in the partners' attitudes toward each other; such information can also reduce performance anxiety.

In addition to restructuring attitudes surrounding ejaculatory control, we also encourage couples to continue with intercourse and sexual play *after* ejaculation. The male is specifically told to enjoy his orgasm rather than interpret it as an unsatisfactory response—even if it is quick! Also, he is encouraged to continue thrusting after orgasm (see Note 4 on p. 123); for most males, the erection will remain firm for a brief period before the refractory period is complete. (In fact, as mentioned in Chapter 4, some men do not always experience detumescence following orgasm, and may be able to experience a second orgasm; see Dunn & Trost, 1989.)

Overall, this strategy will decrease the emphasis on performance-oriented control and increase the emphasis on enjoyment of orgasm and mutual pleasuring. Continuing to address attitudes and encouraging postejaculatory thrusting may remove the performance pressure and allow a couple to focus on enjoyment of pleasure during sex. In our experience, this strategy also leads to better control, although we advise against leading clients to expect this during the therapy discussions.

The strategy was applied successfully to Mr. and Mrs. Bradley. Mrs. Bradley was understanding and responsive to the therapeutic discussions. She immediately understood the deleterious effects of her blame. She also felt relieved that her husband's negative sexual attitude predated their relationship, and was not a reflection of either his love for her or her sexual desirability.

Within six sessions, the couple reported increased enjoyment of their sexual encounters. Mr. Bradley was now initiating sex and showed more affection; no longer did he have to worry about criticism, and he was able to focus on pleasure. Whether ejaculation occurred within 10 seconds or after 5 minutes of thrusting (which he reported did occur on at least one occasion) was no longer so important.

Notes

[1] Please note: The therapist should not ask, "Do you experience erections at night or when you are sleeping?" This phrasing may lead to a misunderstanding on the client's part, since he may think that the therapist is asking whether he gets erections with his partner at night or when sleeping with his partner. A better way to inquire about the occurrence of the NPT response is to ask, "Do you find that on some occasions when you wake up in the morning, or when you wake up in the

middle of the night to go to the bathroom, your penis is hard?" We have found that this wording rarely leads to confusion; in contrast, there is often misunderstanding with the first phrasing. The term "piss hard-on" also seems to be understood by a large segment of the male population, despite its physiological inaccuracy.

[2] A clear example of where therapist and client value systems might differ. Note the pejorative way in which this client described another human being.

[3] It was clear from the assessment that this couple had many unsettled nonsexual issues that had to be addressed prior to focusing on sexual concerns. Ms. Smith was very resistant and angry at the suggestion that nonsexual issues were interfering with sexual relations. She had accepted the notion that something was sexually wrong with her and it had to be fixed. Although it was out of sequence to focus on sexual issues first, this strategy brought to light very quickly the futility of doing so. The couple then appreciated the need to re-evaluate the nonsexual issues.

11

Continued Professional Development and Practice

This chapter is designed to address two questions that you might have at this point: First, how do I obtain further training in sex therapy? And, second, how do I go about starting a sex therapy practice?

Further Training and Continued Development

There are many ways to develop further your knowledge of sexual health and dysfunction, and to hone your clinical skills. Below we provide specific suggestions both for the student-in-training (at the postbaccalaureate level) and for the practicing professional (who has already received the terminal degree in his or her discipline). These suggestions are certainly not exhaustive, and we encourage you to be creative as you seek out further training.

Students-in-Training

1. *Find a mentor*. For those of you who are still students-in-training, our first piece of advice is to identify a senior-level professional in your discipline with an interest in human sexuality, and to ask that person to serve as your mentor. A mentor can help you to develop efficiently and effectively by providing ongoing research and clinical supervision, by informing you of recent developments in the field (well before these are available in print), and by serving as a role model for your development.

2. *Take didactic courses*. Regardless of whether or not you can locate a mentor, you should take didactic courses related to human sexuality. It is

important to emphasize that these courses should not be limited to your academic discipline; that is, if you are a student in a department of psychology, be sure to explore options in other university departments (e.g., social work, human development, and nursing), as well as in the medical school (e.g., departments of psychiatry, urology, gynecology, and family medicine). Also, be sure to consider courses in the basic sciences, such as anatomy, endocrinology, and physiology. A well-rounded, biopsychosocial background in human sexuality will serve you well.

3. *Obtain clinical training and experience.* If your training program has supervised clinical practica or clerkships that afford experience with the sexual dysfunctions, take them! You might also consider externships and internships that offer specialty tracks in sexuality.

4. *Get involved in research.* Finally, if you are at a major research university or a large medical center, you can look for opportunities to become involved in sexuality research. Even well-known and internationally recognized scientists welcome volunteer assistants and enjoy nurturing junior colleagues. If you get involved with a research team, you will probably have the chance to present findings at national or international meetings and conventions.

Established Professionals

For those of you who are practicing professionals, there are several formal and informal avenues to continued development.

1. *Read the "classics."* The least restrictive approach to self-initiated development involves independent reading. Although a number of excellent overview books are available, the book we recommend most highly is John Bancroft's (1989) *Human Sexuality and Its Problems* (2nd ed.; Edinburgh: Churchill Livingstone). A number of other excellent overview books are available. Of those we are familar with, the following are recommended:

Hawton, K. (1985). *Sex therapy: A practical guide.* Northvale, NJ: Jason Aronson.
Kaplan, H. S. (1987). *The illustrated manual of sex therapy* (2nd ed.). New York: Brunner/Mazel.
Leiblum, S. R., & Rosen, R. C. (Eds.). (1989). *Principles and practice of sex therapy* (2nd ed.): *Update for the 1990s* New York: Guilford. Press
LoPiccolo, J., & LoPiccolo, L. (Eds.). (1978). *Handbook of sex therapy.* New York: Plenum.
Masters, W. H., & Johnson, V. E. (1970). *Human sexual inadequacy.* Boston: Little, Brown.

Once you have acquired a good overview of the field, you may want to read some specialty books. Each of the following books goes into greater depth in specific areas.

Leiblum, S. R., & Rosen, R. C. (Eds.). (1988). *Sexual desire disorders.* New York: Guilford Press.
Rosen, R. C., & Beck, J. G. (1988). *Patterns of sexual arousal: Psychophysiological processes and clinical applications.* New York: Guilford Press.
Schover, L. R., & Jensen, S. B. (1988). *Sexuality and chronic illness: A comprehensive approach.* New York: Guilford Press.

2. *Stay abreast of current developments by reading professional journals.* In additional to reading the "classic" professional books, we encourage you to stay current by subscribing to and reading (this is the harder part!) some or all of the following journals:

Archives of Sexual Behavior—published by Plenum Publishing Corporation, 233 Spring Street, New York, NY 10013.
Journal of Psychology and Human Sexuality—published by Haworth Press, 28 East 22nd Street, New York, NY 10010-6194.
Journal of Sex Education and Therapy—published by American Association of Sex Educators, Counselors, and Therapists (see below), 435 North Michigan Avenue, Suite 1717, Chicago, IL 60611.
Journal of Sex Research—published by Society for the Scientific Study of Sexuality (see below), P.O. Box 29795, Philadelphia, PA 19117.
Journal of Sex and Marital Therapy—published by Brunner/Mazel, Inc., 19 Union Square West, New York, NY 10003.
Journal of Social Work and Human Sexuality—published by Haworth Press, 28 East 22nd Street, New York, NY 10010-6194.
Medical Aspects of Human Sexuality—published by Hospital Publications, Inc., 360 Lexington Avenue, New York, NY 10017.
Sexuality and Disability—published by Human Sciences Press, 72 Fifth Avenue, New York, NY 10011.

3. *Join professional organizations devoted to research of human sexuality.* Finally, it is a good idea to join at least one of the many professional organizations devoted to the dissemination of recent information about sexuality. Among the most well-known organizations are the following:

American Association of Sex Educators, Counselors, and Therapists (AASECT) is an educational association that provides a certification program, holds annual meetings, and publishes the *Journal of Sex Education and Therapy.* For information write to AASECT, 435 North Michigan Avenue, Suite 1717, Chicago, IL 60611.
Society for the Scientific Study of Sexuality (SSSS) is an international organization dedicated to the advancement of knowledge about sexuality. SSSS brings together an

interdisciplinary group of professionals who believe in the importance of both the production of high-quality research and the clinical, educational, and social applications of research related to all aspects of sexuality. SSSS holds an annual meeting and publishes the *Journal of Sex Research*. Membership information can be obtained by writing to The SSSS at P.O. Box 29795, Philadelphia, PA 19117.

International Academy of Sex Researchers (IASR) is the most exclusive professional organization. IASR is a scientific society whose objective is the promotion of high standards of research and scholarship in the field of sexual behavior by fostering communication and cooperation among scholars engaged in such research. Membership is contingent upon scientific productivity in the field. IASR holds an annual meeting (which alternates between the United States and other countries) and publishes the journal *Archives of Sexual Behavior*. Membership information can be obtained by writing to Kenneth J. Zucker, Child and Family Studies Centre, Clarke Institute of Psychiatry, 250 College Street, Toronto, Ontario M5T 1R8, Canada.

Society for Sex Therapy and Research (SSTAR) is a professional organization formed to enhance communication between clinicians and clinical investigators interested in the treatment of human sexual disorders. SSTAR began as an informal coalition of sex therapists primarily associated with medical schools in the northeastern United States, but has subsequently expanded its membership and society goals. SSTAR holds an annual meeting and publishes a newsletter for its members. Membership information can be obtained by writing to Lawrence F. Kuhn, MD, 621 S. New Ballas Road, Suite 4018, St. Louis, MO 63141.

Holding memberships in these societies will make it easier for you to attend conventions and enroll in workshops. In addition, through their publications you will find it easier to follow current developments in the field.

4. *Seek formal postdoctoral training.* If your life situation will allow you to make less money, and to live in another city for a year or two, you might seek more formalized training experiences. For example, you might consider supervised externships and postdoctoral training opportunities. Such opportunities are increasingly available in major cities. Below we list several postdoctoral opportunities that have been available in recent years. We do not endorse these training opportunities, but simply list them for your convenience. Many other opportunities are available, and can be located through professional publications such as the American Psychological Association's *Monitor*.

Mini-Residency in Sex Therapy. Available through the Department of Psychiatry, The Mount Sinai Medical Center, One Gustave L. Levy Place, New York, NY 10029-6574.

Institute for Advanced Study of Human Sexuality. For information, write 1523 Franklin Street, San Francisco, CA 94109.

Kinsey Summer Institutes at Indiana University. For information, write Kinsey Institute for Research in Sex, Gender, and Reproduction, Morrison Hall, Third Floor, Indiana University, Bloomington, IN 47405.

Postdoctoral Fellowship in Human Sexuality. For information, write Center for Human Sexuality, Case Western Reserve University School of Medicine/University Hospitals of Cleveland, c/o Stanley E. Althof, PhD, 11400 Euclid Avenue, Suite 200, Cleveland, OH 44106.

Program in Human Sexuality. For information, write Department of Family Practice and Community Health, 2630 University Avenue, S.E., Minneapolis, MN 55414.

Starting a Sex Therapy Practice

The purpose of this section is to provide some guidelines for setting up a successful private practice that focuses on the assessment and treatment of sexual dysfunctions. Although we touch upon aspects of professional practice that may be classified as entrepreneurial or business sense, our primary goal is to discuss the components of professional practice that are unique to the speciality area of the sexual dysfunctions. Our belief is that the nitty-gritty of business, such as whether to rent or buy your office, how to hire support personnel, and what office equipment to select, can be addressed better in other sources (e.g., S. J. Kaplan, 1984). Therefore, we turn our attention to the following issues: certification and licensure, client recruitment, insurance reimbursement, and ethics.

Certification and Licensure: What's in a Name?

Certification is legislation that protects and defines the role and duties of a therapist; licensing legislation protects professional titles. To our knowledge, however, there are no *states* that grant a specific licensure or certification for "sex therapist." Those professionals who call themselves sex therapists and who claim to be licensed or certified by a state board of professional regulations are usually licensed in a core discipline, such as psychology, social work, medicine, or nursing. As a result of the absence of state licensure or certification, it is possible for anyone to present himself or herself as a sex therapist without any credentials, training, or expertise.

AASECT (see above) does offer a certification program. To be eligible, a professional needs to have a master's degree plus 3 years of professional experience in the field, or a doctorate with 2 years of experience. In addition, the therapist must also have completed 150 hours of sex therapy supervised by an AASECT-certified therapist. Although a reasonable program, the

AASECT certification procedure is not regulated on a state level, is not required for practice, and is not recognized by most consumers. Not surprisingly, then, there are many excellent sex therapists who do not take the trouble to obtain this certification.

In addition to the matter of licensure and/or certification, there is the related matter of what one should call oneself professionally (e.g., how to list oneself in the telephone directory). This is not a trivial matter. Consider, for example, the following experience. One of us (John P. Wincze) was recently called upon as an "expert" witness to give testimony in a criminal case regarding a sexual offense. The opposing attorney did his homework, and attempted to disallow Wincze's testimony on the grounds that he was "merely a sex therapist" and not a professional expert. When it was demonstrated that the witness was a "licensed PhD clinical psychologist," who happened to have expertise in human sexuality, the testimony was allowed. Although this may have been an isolated incident, an informal survey of colleagues from across the country has convinced us that, professionally, one gains more credibility by titling oneself in terms of primary professional training (be it in psychology, social work, medicine, nursing, etc).

Client Recruitment

One's title may affect client recruitment, although we know of no research that has addressed this issue. For example, regarding telephone directory listings, our impression is that these listings result in few if any direct referrals. It seems that telephone listings are most useful to current clients and colleagues who have forgotten our number! Instead, there seem to be two excellent sources of client referrals: other professionals (especially physicians) and clients. Indeed, the best advertising may be a satisfied client. Because there is not much one can do, for ethical reasons, to enhance client-based referrals, we recommend the "other professionals" route.

Several strategies seem to be effective to alerting other professionals to your expertise, the clinical services, you offer, and so on. A method that appears very useful is to give free talks to professional organizations, such as local attorneys or physicians. Of course, it is important that you gear your talk (vocabulary and content) to your audience, and that you be well prepared. A second method would be to provide in-service training to local practitioners, trainees, and clinics. In this way you become known as the person who is comfortable and skilled in dealing with sexual dysfunctions. Third, once you are experienced, and only after you are very adept at handling difficult questions, you might try carefully selected interviews with the local news media (print and electronic). This can be slippery and dangerous ground, though, so beware! Finally, we have found that publishing research findings generates a surprisingly large number of referrals from outside our local areas. So if you have an opportunity to do research, or to collaborate with other colleagues on research, you may find that this provides some dividends in terms of clients. Moreover, involvement in research is stimulating and challenging in its own right.

It is also important to establish links with other professionals so that you will be able to provide the highest-quality care. In our view, the clinical practices that serve clients best are those multidisciplinary services that aim to incorporate the latest biopsychosocial and technical advances in assessment and treatment. These practices tend to be associated with teaching hospitals and university clinics. If you are not a part of such a setting, you will have to pull together a collaborative effort with other professionals in order to offer your clients comprehensive treatment.

To establish such a team, you should try to develop a working collaboration with professionals having several medical specialties: urologists, gynecologists, and endocrinologists. The urologist should be familar with the comprehensive assessment, diagnosis, and treatment of male sexual complaints. (Preferably, the urologist will be sensitive to psychosocial contributions to sexual dysfunctions, and not just interested in penile implant surgery!) A gynecologist is invaluable for the assessment of female disorders. Like urologists, gynecologists vary widely in their knowledge of and sensitivity to sexual problems. It is a positive sign if the gynecologist and urologist with whom you work recognize that the restoration of intercourse is not the only goal in helping clients with sexual problems. Finally, the last "core" physician is the endocrinologist, who will be needed to complete hormonal evaluations and to monitor hormone therapy when this is indicated. Also, because endocrinologists tend to know a lot about diabetes, and diabetes is a common precipitating cause of sexual dysfunction in men and women, it is very helpful to have a colleague in this area.

In addition to this "core" group, you will occasionally need to consult with a cardiologist (regarding the effects of hypertension, antihypertensive medications, and the effects of various forms of cardiac illness), a neurologist (regarding the influence of seizure disorders and other neurological problems upon sexual function), and an infectious disease specialist (regarding AIDS and other sexually transmitted diseases). Finally, because there is always the need for general medical screening, it is good to know an internist or family practitioner to whom you can refer. Also, such "medical generalists" often need psychosocial colleagues to whom to refer their patients as well, so they can be a good source of referrals.

We believe that it is feasible to be in private practice and to treat sexual problems. However, if this is your situation, we strongly encourage you to establish the kind of referral network or comprehensive team described above. To work without such collaboration and consultation, in our view, teeters dangerously close to the kind of professional "know-it-all-ism" that might lead to malpractice. Besides, it's professionally lonely!

Insurance Reimbursement

Health care insurance, especially so-called[1] "mental" health care insurance, is a nightmare—not just for sex therapy, but for all psychotherapies. Every practitioner has his or her horror stories to tell, and we are no different. Given the plethora of coverages, companies, and plans, it is difficult to provide a global statement. However, in our experience, most insurance companies do reimburse for treatment of sexual dysfunctions.

Ethics and Sex Therapy

We have previously described the absence of state-regulated licensure and/or certification. Perhaps it is true that part of the reason why such formal recognition is absent is that there is skepticism associated with the "sex therapist" label. The general public, and elected officials who represent them, may still be affected by the bad press associated with sex therapists during the 1960s and early 1970s. In a superb text published by the Walk-In Counseling Center of Minneapolis, Schoener, Milgrom, Gonsiorek, Luepker, and Conroe (1990) point out that the human potential movement of the 1960s resulted in considerable experimentation with types and practices of psychotherapy. Specifically, there were articles published in professional journals and presentations made at professional meetings that advocated the use of bizarre and unethical practices such as nude marathon sessions with clients; touching, hugging, and kissing of clients; and sexual intercourse with clients. Although the advocates of these unethical approaches were in the minority, to be sure, the popular press magnified their message. Thus, a widespread impression of sex therapists as "flaky perverts" was created. Unfortunately, these impressions are still with us, and they are in the minds of clients who enter therapy.

Because of this history, those who practice sex therapy today have to be impeccable professionals. Not only should we abide by the ethical standards of our professions, but we must also avoid even the appearance of impropriety. Although we do not have the space to elaborate upon all ethical violations that are to be avoided, we wish to mention the most important.

You must absolutely avoid sexual intimacies with clients, and observe appropriate professional boundaries in your work. Because therapy inevitably places clients in a vulnerable position and creates a psychological dependence upon the therapist, a power differential exists that creates a potential for sexual victimization. In addition to the usual factors that contribute to patient vulnerability, the explicit discussion of intimate sexual material increases the potential for transference and countertransference to occur. Moreover, many persons who seek treatment for sexual dysfunctions have had a history of sexual abuse; these persons appear to be at increased risk of being revictimized by therapists (Leslie R. Schover, personal communication, December 30, 1990). For these reasons, you must be especially sensitive to client welfare. You should establish professional policies that insure against crossing the sacred boundaries that have been established.

Most professionals quickly dismiss this matter as not applying to them. However, surveys suggest that the prevalence of sexual abuse of patients by professionals (i.e., physicians, psychologists, social workers, and pastoral counselors) ranges from 3% to 18% (e.g., Holroyd & Brodsky, 1977)! That is, 3–18% of those surveyed have admitted to having sexual contact with their clients on at least one occasion. Schoener et al. (1990) remind us that the single most frequent basis for a malpractice suit against psychologists is sexual malpractice. Similarly, in a 1985 survey of social workers, the leading cause of legal claims was sexual contact with clients (Besharov, 1985). Furthermore, indirect evidence for the continuing problem comes from the state legislatures: At least four states (i.e., Colorado, Minnesota, North Dakota, and Wisconsin) have passed laws making any therapist or physician who has sexual contact with a patient subject to criminal felony charges. These charges apply regardless of whether the contact occurred inside or outside of the examining office or consulting room, and for up to 2 years after a patient has left the physician's or therapist's care. It is our understanding that some states are considering the forbidding of such contact in perpetuity.

Concluding Comments

In this book we have tried to present a first course in the assessment and treatment of sexual dysfunctions. In conjunction with supervised experience, we hope that this book will help you to feel comfortable about and prepared to address the sexual difficulties of your clients. Moreover, we have broached many topics that we hope have stimulated your thinking and will encourage further study.

In the course of providing sex assessment and therapy, we have been impressed by the grateful responses of our clients. Many report that they are expressing their sexual concerns and secrets for the first time. This opportunity to discuss sexual matters openly and without shame can be therapeutic for many clients. Even more gratifying are those moments when, through the straightforward therapeutic approach described in this book, we can help our clients to re-establish sexual functioning and satisfaction. In closing, we wish you many such moments.

Note

[1] We say "so-called" because the separation of health care into "somatic" and "mental" categories simply repeats the age-old mind–body problem.

References

Abarbanel, A. (1978). Diagnosis and treatment of coital discomfort. In J. LoPiccolo & L. LoPiccolo (Eds.), *Handbook of sex therapy* (pp. 241–259). New York: Plenum.

Adams, A. E., Haynes, S. N., & Brayer, M. A. (1985). Cognitive distraction in female sexual arousal. *Psychophysiology, 22,* 689–696.

Albert, A., & Wincze, J. P. (1990). *Sexual arousal in diabetic females: A psychophysiological investigation.* Unpublished manuscript, Brown University.

Althof, S., Turner, L., Levine, S., Risen, C., Kursh, E., Bodner, D., & Reonick, M. (1987). Intracavernosal injection in the treatment of impotence: A prospective study of sexual, psychological, and marital functioning. *Journal of Sex and Marital Therapy, 13,* 155–167.

American Medical Association. (1988). *House of Delegates resolution regarding AIDS.* Chicago: Author.

American Psychiatric Association. (1980). *Diagnostic and statistical manual of mental disorders* (3rd ed.). Washington, DC: Author.

American Psychiatric Association. (1987). *Diagnostic and statistical manual of mental disorders* (3rd ed., revised). Washington, DC: Author.

American Psychological Association. (1987). *Casebook on ethical principles of psychologists.* Washington, DC: Author.

Anastasi, A. (1988). *Psychological testing* (6th ed.). New York: Macmillan.

Andersen, B. L. (1985). Sexual functioning morbidity among cancer survivors: Current status and future research directions. *Cancer, 55,* 1835–1842.

Andersen, B. L. (1987). Sexual functioning complications in women with gynecologic cancer: Outcomes and directions for prevention. *Cancer, 60,* 2123–2128.

Andersen, B. L., Anderson, B., & deProsse, C. (1989a). Controlled prospective longitudinal study of women with cancer: I. Sexual functioning outcomes. *Journal of Consulting and Clinical Psychology, 57,* 683–691.

Andersen, B. L., Anderson, B., & deProsse, C. (1989b). Controlled prospective longitudinal study of women with cancer: II. Psychological outcomes. *Journal of Consulting and Clinical Psychology, 57,* 692–697.

Andersen, B. L., & Hacker, N. F. (1983). Treatment for gynecologic cancer: A review of the effects on female sexuality. *Health Psychology, 2,* 203–221.

Ard, B. N. Jr. (1977). Sex in lasting marriages: A longitudinal study. *Journal of Sex Research, 13,* 274–285.

Assalian, P. (1988). Clomipramine in the treatment of premature ejaculation. *Journal of Sex Research, 24,* 213–215.

Athanasiou, R., Shaver, P., & Tavris, C. (1970, July). Sex. *Psychology Today,* pp. 39–51.

Babaian, R. J. (1982). Radical cystectomy: Female. In D. E. Johnson & M. A. Boileau (Eds.), *Genitourinary tumors: Fundamental principles and surgical techniques* (pp. 477–484). New York: Grune & Stratton.

Baldwin, J. D., & Baldwin, J. I. (1988). Factors affecting AIDS-related sexual risk-taking behavior among college students. *Journal of Sex Research, 25,* 181–196.

Balko, A., Malhotra, C., Wincze, J., Susset, J., Bansal, S., Carney, W., & Hopkins, R. (1986). Deep penile vein arterialization for arterial and venous impotence. *Archives of Surgery, 121,* 774–777.

Bancroft, J. (1984). Hormones and human sexual behavior. *Journal of Sex and Marital Therapy, 10,* 3–21.

Bancroft, J. (1988). Sexual desire and the brain. *Sexual and Marital Therapy, 3,* 11–27.

Bancroft, J. (1989). *Human sexuality and its problems* (2nd ed.). Edinburgh: Churchill Livingstone.

Bancroft, J., & Coles, L. (1976). Three years' experience in a sexual problems clinic. *British Medical Journal, i,* 1575–1577.

Bancroft, J., & Wu, F. (1983). Changes in erectile responsiveness during androgen replacement therapy. *Archives of Sexual Behavior, 12,* 59–66.

Bansal, S. (1988). Sexual dysfunction in hypertensive men: A critical review of the literature. *Hypertension, 12,* 1–10.

Bansal, S., Wincze, J. P., Nirenberg, T., Liepman, M. J., & Engle-Friedman, M. (1990). *Sex-steroid levels in chronic alcoholic males: Relationship to age and liver functions.* Unpublished manuscript, Brown University.

Barlow, D. H. (1986). Causes of sexual dysfunction: The role of anxiety and cognitive interference. *Journal of Consulting and Clinical Psychology, 54,* 140–148.

Barlow, D. H. (1988). *Anxiety and its disorders: The nature and treatment of anxiety and panic.* New York: Guilford Press.

Barlow, D. H., Hayes, S. C., & Nelson, R. O. (1984). *The scientist–practitioner: Research and accountability in clinical and educational settings.* Elmsford, NY: Pergamon Press.

Barlow, D. H., Sakheim, D., & Beck, J. G. (1983). Anxiety increases sexual arousal. *Journal of Abnormal Psychology, 92,* 49–54.

Barnes, J. (1981). Non-consummation of marriage. *Irish Medical Journal, 74,* 19–21.

Barnes, J. (1986a). Primary vaginismus (Part 1): Social and clinical features. *Irish Medical Journal, 79,* 59–62.

Barnes, J. (1986b). Primary vaginismus (Part 2): Aetiological factors. *Irish Medical Journal, 79,* 62–65.

Bass, E., & Davis, L. (1988). *The courage to heal: A guide for women survivors of child sexual abuse.* New York: Harper & Row.

Bazar, J. (1989, December). Family problems alike in U.S., Soviet Union. *American Psychological Association Monitor,* p. 34.

Beck, A. T. (1976). *Cognitive therapy and the emotional disorders.* New York: International Universities Press.

Beck, A. T. (1988). *Love is never enough.* New York: Harper & Row.

Beck, J. G., Barlow, D. H., & Sakheim, D. (1983). The effects of attentional focus and partner arousal on sexual responding in functional and dysfunctional men. *Behaviour Research and Therapy, 21,* 1–8.

Becker, J. V. (1989). Impact of sexual abuse on sexual functioning. In S.R. Leiblum & R.C. Rosen (Eds.), *Principles and practice of sex therapy* (2nd ed.): *Update for the 1990s* (pp. 298–318). New York: Guilford Press.

Beggs, V. E., Calhoun, K. S., & Wolchik, S. A. (1987). Sexual anxiety and female sexual arousal: A comparison of arousal during sexual anxiety stimuli and sexual pleasure stimuli. *Archives of Sexual Behavior, 16,* 311–319.

Bennett, A. H. (Ed.). (1982). *Management of male impotence.* Baltimore: Williams & Wilkins.

Bennett, A. H. (1988). Venous arterialization for erectile impotence. *Urologic Clinics of North America, 15*, 111–113.

Besharov, D. J. (1985). *The vulnerable social worker: Liability for serving children and families.* Silver Springs, MD: National Association of Social Workers.

Brindley, G. (1983). Cavernosal alpha-blockade: A new technique for investigating and treating erectile impotence. *British Journal of Psychiatry, 143*, 332.

Buffum, J. (1982). Pharmacosexology: The effects of drugs on sexual function—A review. *Journal of Psychoactive Drugs, 14*, 5–44.

Buffum, J. (1986). Pharmacosexology update: Prescription drugs and sexual function. *Journal of Psychoactive Drugs, 18*, 97–106.

Burish, T. G., Meyerowitz, B. E., Carey, M. P., & Morrow, G. R. (1987). The stressful effects of cancer in adults. In A. Baum & J. E. Singer (Eds.), *Handbook of psychology and health: Vol 5. Stress* (pp. 137–173). Hillsdale, NJ: Erlbaum.

Burnap, D. W., & Golden, J. S. (1967). Sexual problems in medical practice. *Journal of Medical Education, 42*, 673–680.

Buvat, J., Lemaire, A., Buvat-Herbaut, M., Fourlinnie, J. C., Racadot, A., & Fossati, P. (1985). Hyperprolactinemia and sexual function in men. *Hormone Research, 22*, 196–203.

Byer, C. O., & Shainberg, L. W. (1991). *Dimensions of human sexuality* (3rd ed.). Dubuque, IA: William C. Brown.

Cacioppo, J. T., & Tassinary, L. G. (1990). Inferring psychological significance from physiological signals. *American Psychologist, 45*, 16–28.

Caird, W., & Wincze, J. P. (1977). *Sex therapy: A behavioral approach.* New York: Harper & Row.

Carey, M. P. (1990). Sexual adjustment among cancer survivors: Research findings and therapeutic suggestions. *The Cancer Journal, 3*, 310–314.

Carey, M. P., Flasher, L. V., Maisto, S. A., & Turkat, I. D. (1984). The a priori approach to psychological assessment. *Professional Psychology: Research and Practice, 15*, 515–527.

Carey, M. P., Jorgensen, R. S., Weinstock, R. S., Sprafkin, R. P., Lantinga, L. J., Carnrike, C. L. M., Jr., Baker, M. T., & Meisler, A. W. (1991). Reliability and validity of the Appraisal of Diabetes Scale. *Journal of Behavioral Medicine, 14*, 43–51.

Catalan, J., Bradley, M., Gallwey, J., & Hawton, K. (1981). Sexual dysfunction and psychiatric morbidity in patients attending a clinic for sexually transmitted diseases. *British Journal of Psychiatry, 138*, 292–296.

Centers for Disease Control. (1988). Quarterly report to the Domestic Policy Council on the prevalence and rate of spread of HIV and AIDS—United States. *Morbidity and Mortality Weekly Report, 36*, 1–191.

Chambless, D. L., Stern, T., Sultan, F. E., Williams, A. J., Goldstein, A. J., Lineberger, M. H., Lifshitz, J. L., & Kelly, L. (1982). The pubococcygens and female orgasm: A correlational study with normal subjects. *Archives of Sexual Behavior, 11*, 479–490.

Chambless, D. L., Sultan, F. E., Stern, T. E., O'Neill, C., Garrison, S., & Jackson, A. (1984). Effect of pubococcygeal exercise on coital orgasm in women. *Journal of Consulting and Clinical Psychology, 52*, 114–118.

Clark, J., Smith, E., & Davidson, J. (1984). Enhancement of sexual motivation in male rats by yohimbine. *Science, 225*, 847–848.

Cocores, J. A., Miller, N. S., Pottash, A. C., & Gold, M. S. (1988). Sexual dysfunction in abusers of cocaine and alcohol. *American Journal of Drug and Alcohol Abuse, 14*, 169–173.

Cohen, A. M., Kaufman, S. D., & Kadish, S. P. (1986). Cancer of the colon and rectum. In B. Cady (Ed.-in-Chief), *Cancer manual* (7th ed. pp. 212–221). New York: American Cancer Society.

Cole, W. G. (1956). *Sex in Christianity and psychoanalysis*. London: George Allen & Unwin.

Coleman, E. (1987). Sexual compulsivity: Definition, etiology, and treatment considerations. In E. Coleman (Ed.), *Chemical dependency and intimacy dysfunction*. (pp. 189–204). New York: Haworth Press.

Coleman, E. (1990). The obsessive–compulsive model for describing compulsive sexual behavior. *American Journal of Preventive Psychiatry and Neurology, 2,* 9–14.

Connell, R. W., & Kippax, S. (1990). Sexuality in the AIDS crisis: Patterns of pleasure and practice in an Australian sample of gay and bisexual men. *Journal of Sex Research, 27,* 167–198.

Conte, H. R. (1983). Development and use of self-report techniques for assessing sexual functioning: A review and critique. *Archives of Sexual Behavior, 12,* 555–576.

Conte, H. R. (1986). Multivariate assessment of sexual dysfunction. *Journal of Consulting and Clinical Psychology, 5,* 149–157.

Cooper, A. J. (1972). Diagnosis and management of "endocrine impotence." *British Medical Journal, ii,* 34–36.

Corcoran, K., & Fischer, J. (1987). *Measures for clinical practice: A sourcebook*. New York: The Free Press.

Crooks, R., & Baur, K. (1990). *Our sexuality* (4th ed.). New York: Benjamin/Cummings.

Damrav, F. (1963). Premature ejaculation: Use of ethyl amino benzoate to prolong coitus. *Journal of Urology, 89,* 936–939.

Danzi, M., Ferulano, G. P., Abate, S., & Califano, G. (1983). Male sexual function after abdominoperineal resection for rectal cancer. *Diseases of the Colon and Rectum, 26,* 665–668.

Davidson, J. M., Camargo, C. A., Smith, E. R., & Kwan, M. (1983). Maintenance of sexual function in a castrated man treated with ovarian steroids. *Archives of Sexual Behavior, 12,* 263–274.

Davis, C. M., Yarber, W. L., & Davis, S. L. (Eds.). (1988). *Sexuality-related measures: A compendium*. Lake Mills, IA: Graphic.

Davison, G. C., & Neale, J. M. (1990). *Abnormal psychology* (5th ed.). New York: Wiley.

DeBuono, B. A., Zinner, S. H., Daamen, M., & McCormack, W. M. (1990). Sexual behavior of college women in 1975, 1986 and 1989. *New England Journal of Medicine, 332,* 821–825.

Denney, N. W., Field, J. K., & Quadagno, D. (1984). Sex differences in sexual needs and desires. *Archives of Sexual Behavior, 13,* 233–245.

Derogatis, L. R., Fagan, P. J., Schmidt, C. W., Wise, T. N., & Gilden, K. S. (1986). Psychological subtypes of anorgasmia: A marker variable approach. *Journal of Sex and Marital Therapy, 12,* 197–210.

Derogatis, L. R., & Melisaratos, N. (1979). The DSFI: A multidimensional measure of sexual functioning. *Journal of Sex and Marital Therapy, 5,* 244–281.

Derogatis, L. R., & Meyer, J. K. (1979). A psychological profile of the sexual dysfunctions. *Archives of Sexual Behavior, 8,* 201–223.

Derogatis, L. R., Meyer, J. K., & King, K. M. (1981). Psychopathology in individuals with sexual dysfunction. *American Journal of Psychiatry, 138,* 757–763.

Derogatis, L. R., Morrow, G. R., Fetting, J., Penman, D., Piasetsky, S., Schmale, A. M., Henrichs, M., & Carnrike, C. L. M., Jr. (1983). The prevalence of psychiatric disorders among cancer patients. *Journal of the American Medical Association, 249,* 751–757.

Derogatis, L. R., & Spencer, P. M. (1982). *The Brief Symptom Inventory (BSI): Administration, scoring, and procedures manual—I*. Baltimore. Clinical Psychometric Research.

Diokno, A. C., Brown, M. B., & Herzog, A. R. (1990). Sexual function in the elderly. *Archives of Internal Medicine, 150,* 197–200.

Duddle, C. M. (1977). Etiological factors in the unconsummated marriage. *Journal of Psychosomatic Research, 21,* 157–160.

Dunn, M. E., & Trost, J. E. (1989). Male multiple orgasms: A descriptive study. *Archives of Sexual Behavior, 18*, 377–387.

Ebbehoj, J., & Wagner, G. (1979). Insufficient penile erection due to abnormal drainage of cavernous bodies. *Urology, 13*, 507–510.

El-Bayoumi, M., El-Sherbini, O., & Mostafa, M. (1984). Impotence in diabetics: Organic versus psychogenic factors. *Urology, 24*, 459–463.

Ellenberg, M. (1971). Impotence in diabetes: The neurologic factor. *Annals of Internal Medicine, 75*, 213–219.

Ellenberg, M. (1977). Sexual aspects of the female diabetic. *Mount Sinai Journal of Medicine, 44*, 495–500.

Ellenberg, M. (1980). Sexual function in diabetic patients. *Annals of Internal Medicine, 92*, 331–333.

Ellis, A. (1962). *Reason and emotion in psychotherapy.* New York: Lyle Stuart.

Ellis, H. (1906). *Studies in the psychology of sex* (7 vols.). New York: Random House.

Engel, G. L. (1977). The need for a new medical model: A challenge for biomedicine. *Science, 196*, 129–136.

Exner, J. E., Jr. (1986). *The Rorschach: A comprehensive system. Vol 1. Basic foundations* (2nd ed.). New York: Wiley.

Faerman, I., Glocer, L., Fox, D., Jadzinsky, M. N., & Rapaport, M. (1974). Impotence and diabetes: Histological studies of the autonomic nervous fibers of the corpora cavernosa in impotent diabetic males. *Diabetes, 23*, 971–976.

Faerman, I., Vilar, O., Rivarola, M. A., Rosner, J.M., Jadzinsky, M. N., Fox, D., Lloret, A. P., Bernstein-Hahn, L., & Saraceni, D. (1972). Impotence and diabetes: Studies of androgenic function in diabetic impotent males. *Diabetes, 21*, 23–30.

Fahrner, E.-M. (1987). Sexual dysfunction in male alcohol addicts: Prevalence and treatment. *Archives of Sexual Behavior, 16*, 247–257.

Fairburn, C. G., Wu, F. C. W., McCulloch, D. K., Borsay, D. Q., Ewing, D. J., Clarke, B. F., & Bancroft, J. H. J. (1982). The clinical features of diabetic impotence: A preliminary study. *British Journal of Psychiatry, 140*, 447–452.

Fisher, W. A. (1988). The Sexual Opinion Survey. In C. M. Davis, W. L. Yarber, & S. L. Davis (Eds.), *Sexuality-related measures: A compendium* (pp. 34–37). Lake Mills, IA: Graphic.

Fisher, W. A., Byrne, D., White, L. A., & Kelley, K. (1988). Erotophobia–erotophilia as a dimension of personality. *Journal of Sex Research, 25*, 123–151.

Frank, E., Anderson, C., & Kupfer, D. J. (1976). Profiles of couples seeking sex therapy and marital therapy. *American Journal of Psychiatry, 133*, 559–562.

Frank, E., Anderson, C., & Rubinstein, D. (1978). Frequency of sexual dysfunction in "normal" couples. *New England Journal of Medicine, 299*, 111–115.

Freud, S. (1962). *Three essays on the theory of sexuality* (J. Strachey, Trans.). New York: Avon. (Original work published 1905)

Friedrich, E. G. (1987). Vulvar vestibulitis syndrome. *Journal of Reproductive Medicine, 2*, 110–114.

Gagnon, J. H. (1977). *Human sexualities.* Glenview, IL: Scott, Foresman.

Gebhard, P. H., & Johnson, A. B. (1979). *The Kinsey data: Marginal tabulations of the 1938–1963 interviews conducted by the Institute for Sex Research.* Philadelphia: W. B. Saunders.

Geer, J. H. (1987). Psychophysiological assessment of sexual responses in women. In American Cancer Society (Ed.), *Proceedings of the workshop on psychosexual and reproductive issues affecting patients with cancer—1987* (pp. 20–25). New York: American Cancer Society.

Girardi, J. A., Keese, R. M., Traver, L. B., & Cooksey, D. R. (1988). Featured debate: Psychotherapist responsibility in notifying individuals at risk for exposure to HIV. *Journal of Sex Research, 25*, 1–27.

Glatt, A. E., Zinner, S. H., & McCormack, W. M. (1990). The prevalence of dyspareunia. *Obstetrics and Gynecology, 75,* 433–436.

Gloeckner, M. R. (1983). Partner reaction following ostomy surgery. *Journal of Sex and Marital Therapy, 9,* 182–190.

Gottman, J., Notarius, C., Gonso, J., & Markman, H. (1976). *A couples guide to communication.* Champaign, IL: Research Press.

Grant, D., & Anns, M. (1988). Counseling AIDS antibody-positive clients: Reactions and treatments. *American Psychologist, 42,* 72–74.

Greene, L. F., & Kelalis, T. P. (1968). Retrograde ejaculation of semen due to diabetic neuropathy. *Journal of Urology, 98,* 696.

Hathaway, S. R., & McKinley, J. C. (1967). *The Minnesota Multiphasic Personality Inventory manual.* New York: Psychological Corporation.

Hawatmeh, I., Houttuin, E., Gregory, J., & Purcell, M. (1983). Vascular surgery for the treatment of the impotent male. In R.J. Krane, M.B. Siroky, & I. Goldstein (Eds.), *Male sexual dysfunction* (pp. 291–299). Boston: Little, Brown.

Hawton, K. (1982). The behavioural treatment of sexual dysfunction. *British Journal of Psychiatry, 140,* 94–101.

Hawton, K. (1985). *Sex therapy: A practical guide.* Northvale, NJ: Aronson.

Heim, N. (1981). Sexual behavior of castrated sex offenders. *Archives of Sexual Behavior, 10,* 11–19.

Heiman, J. R. (1978). Uses of psychophysiology in the assessment and treatment of sexual dysfunction. In J. LoPiccolo & L. LoPiccolo (Eds.), *Handbook of sex therapy* (pp. 123–135). New York: Plenum.

Heiman, J. R., & LoPiccolo, J. (1988). *Becoming orgasmic: A sexual and personal growth program for women* (rev. ed.). New York: Prentice Hall.

Hite, S. (1976). *The Hite report: A nationwide study of female sexuality.* New York: Dell.

Holroyd, J. C., & Brodsky, A. M. (1977). Psychologists' attitudes and practices regarding erotic and nonerotic physical contact with patients. *American Psychologist, 32,* 843–849.

Hong, L. K. (1984). Survival of the fastest: On the origin of premature ejaculation. *Journal of Sex Research, 20,* 109–122.

Hoon, P. W. (1979). The assessment of sexual arousal in women. *Progress in Behavior Modification, 7,* 1–61.

Hoon, P. W., Wincze, J. P., & Hoon, E. F. (1977). A test of reciprocal inhibition: Are anxiety and sexual arousal in women mutually inhibitory? *Journal of Abnormal Psychology, 86,* 65–74.

Hunt, M. (1974). *Sexual behavior in the 70's.* Chicago: Playboy.

Jensen, B. J., Witcher, D. B., & Upton, L. R. (1987). Readability assessment of questionnaires frequently used in sex and marital therapy. *Journal of Sex and Marital Therapy, 13,* 137–141.

Jensen, S. B. (1981). Diabetic sexual dysfunction: A comparative study of 160 insulin treated diabetic men and women and an age-matched control group. *Archives of Sexual Behavior, 10,* 493–504.

Jensen, S. B. (1984). Sexual function and dysfunction in younger married alcoholics. *Acta Psychiatrica Scandinavica, 69,* 543–549.

Jensen, S. B. (1985). Sexual relationships in couples with a diabetic partner. *Journal of Sex and Marital Therapy, 11,* 259–270.

Jensen, S. B. (1986). Sexual dysfunction in insulin-treated diabetics: A six-year follow-up study of 101 patients. *Archives of Sexual Behavior, 15,* 271–283.

Jetvich, M. J. (1980). Importance of penile arterial pulse sound examination in impotence. *Journal of Urology, 124,* 820–824.

Jetvich, M. J., Edson, M., Jarman, W. D., & Herrera, H. H. (1982). Vascular factor in erectile failure among diabetics. *Urology, 19,* 163–168.

Johnson, P. C., Doll, S. C., Cromey, B. S., & Cromey, M. S. (1986). Pathogenesis of diabetic neuropathy. *Annals of Neurology, 19,* 450–457.

Jones, J. C., & Barlow, D. H. (1987). *Self-reported frequency of sexual urges, fantasies, and masturbatory fantasies in heterosexual males and females.* Paper presented at the annual meeting of the Association for Advancement of Behavior Therapy, New York.

Jones, T. M. (1985). Hormonal considerations in the evaluation and treatment of erectile dysfunction. In R. T. Segraves & H. W. Schoenberg (Eds.), *Diagnosis and treatment of erectile disturbances: A guide for the clinician* (pp. 115–158). New York: Plenum.

Kaplan, H. S. (1974). *The new sex therapy.* New York: Brunner/Mazel.

Kaplan, H. S. (1979). *Disorders of sexual desire.* New York: Brunner/Mazel.

Kaplan, H. S. (1987). *Sexual aversion, sexual phobias, and panic disorder.* New York: Brunner/Mazel.

Kaplan, H. S. (1989). *How to overcome premature ejaculation.* New York: Brunner/Mazel.

Kaplan, M. (1983). A woman's view of DSM-III. *American Psychologist, 38,* 786–792.

Kaplan, S. J. (1984). The private practice of behavior therapy. *Progress in Behavior Modification, 17,* 201–240.

Karacan, I., Salis, P. J., Ware, J. C., Dervent, B., Williams, R. L., Scott, F. B., Attia, S. L., & Beutler, L. E. (1978). Nocturnal penile tumescence and diagnosis in diabetic impotence. *American Journal of Psychiatry, 135,* 191–197.

Katz, R. C., Gipson, M. T., Kearl, A., & Kriskovich, M. (1989). Assessing sexual aversion in college students: The Sexual Aversion Scale. *Journal of Sex and Marital Therapy, 15,* 135–140.

Kilmann, P. R., Mills, K. H., Caid, C., Bella, B., Davidson, E., & Wanlass, R. (1984). The sexual interaction of women with secondary orgasmic dysfunction and their partners. *Archives of Sexual Behavior, 13,* 41–49.

Kinsey, A. C., Pomeroy, W. B., & Martin, C. E. (1948). *Sexual behavior in the human male.* Philadelphia: W. B. Saunders.

Kinsey, A. C., Pomeroy, W. B., Martin, C. E., & Gebhard, P. H. (1953). *Sexual behavior in the human female.* Philadelphia: W. B. Saunders.

Klassen, A. D., & Wilsnack, S. C. (1986). Sexual experiences and drinking among women in a U.S. national survey. *Archives of Sexual Behavior, 15,* 363–392.

Kolodny, R. C. (1971). Sexual dysfunction in diabetic females. *Diabetes, 20,* 557–559.

Kolodny, R. C., Kahn, C. B., Goldstein, H. H., & Barnett, D. M. (1974). Sexual dysfunction in diabetic men. *Diabetes, 23,* 306–309.

Kolodny, R. C., Masters, W. H., & Johnson, V. E. (1979). *Textbook of sexual medicine.* Boston: Little, Brown.

Krane, R. J., Siroky, M. B., & Goldstein, I. (Eds.). (1983). *Male sexual dysfunction.* Boston: Little, Brown.

Krauss, D. J., Lantinga, L. J., Carey, M. P., Meisler, A. W., & Kelly, C. M. (1989). Use of the malleable penile prosthesis in the treatment of erectile dysfunction: A prospective study of postoperative adjustment. *Journal of Urology, 142,* 988–991.

Kyle, G. R. (1989). AIDS and the new sexual order. *Journal of Sex Research, 26,* 276–278.

Lamb, D. H., Clark, C., Drumheller, P., Frizzell, K., & Surrey, L. (1989). Applying *Tarasoff* to AIDS-related psychotherapy issues. *Professional Psychology: Research and Practice, 20,* 37–43.

Lamont, J. A. (1978). Vaginismus. *American Journal of Obstetrics and Gynecology, 131,* 632–636.

Laws, D. R. (Ed.). (1989). *Relapse prevention with sex offenders.* New York: Guilford Press.

Lazarus, A. A. (1988). A multimodal perspective on problems of sexual desire. In S. R. Leiblum & R. C. Rosen (Eds.), *Sexual desire disorders* (pp. 145–167). New York: Guilford Press.

Lehman, T. P., & Jacobs, J. A. (1983). Etiology of diabetic impotence. *Journal of Urology, 129,* 291–294.

Leiblum, S. R., & Rosen, R. C. (Eds.). (1988). *Sexual desire disorders*. New York: Guilford Press.

Lester, E., Grant, A. J., & Woodroffe, F. J. (1980). Impotence in diabetic and nondiabetic outpatients. *British Medical Journal, 281,* 354–355.

Levine, M. P., & Troiden, R. R. (1988). The myth of sexual compulsivity. *Journal of Sex Research, 25,* 347–363.

Levine, S. B. (1984). An essay on the nature of sexual desire. *Journal of Sex and Marital Therapy, 10,* 83–96.

Levine, S. B. (1987). More on the nature of sexual desire. *Journal of Sex and Marital Therapy, 13,* 35–44.

Levine, S. B. (1989). Comprehensive sexual health centers: Is it time? *Journal of Sex and Marital Therapy, 15,* 215–224.

Levine, S. B., & Yost, M. A. (1976). Frequency of sexual dysfunction in a general gynecological clinic: An epidemiological approach. *Archives of Sexual Behavior, 5,* 229–238.

Lewis, R. W. (1988). Venous surgery for impotence. *Urologic Clinics of North America, 15,* 115–121.

Lewis, R. W., & Puyau, F. A. (1986). Procedures for decreasing venous drainage. *Seminars in Urology, 4,* 263–272.

Libman, E., Fichten, C. S., Creti, L., Weinstein, N., Amsel, R., & Brender, W. (1989). Sleeping and waking-state measurement of erectile function in an aging male population. *Psychological Assessment: A Journal of Consulting and Clinical Psychology, 1,* 284–291.

Lief, H. I. (1977). Inhibited sexual desire. *Medical Aspects of Human Sexuality, 7,* 94–95.

Lipsius, S. H. (1987). Prescribing sensate focus without proscribing intercourse. *Journal of Sex and Marital Therapy, 11,* 185–191.

LoPiccolo, J., & Friedman, J. M. (1988). Broad-spectrum treatment of low sexual desire: Integration of cognitive, behavioral, and systemic therapy. In S. R. Leiblum & R. C. Rosen (Eds.), *Sexual desire disorders* (pp. 107–144). New York: Guilford Press.

LoPiccolo, J., & Heiman, J. R. (1978). Sexual assessment and history interview. In J. LoPiccolo & L. LoPiccolo (Eds.), *Handbook of sex therapy* (pp. 103–112). New York: Plenum.

LoPiccolo, J., & Lobitz, W. C. (1972). The role of masturbation in the treatment of orgasmic dysfunction. *Archives of Sexual Behavior, 2,* 163–171.

LoPiccolo, J., & Steger, J. C. (1974). The Sexual Interaction Inventory: A new instrument for assessment of sexual dysfunction. *Archives of Sexual Behavior, 3,* 585–595.

Lording, D. (1978). Impotence: Role of drug and hormonal treatment. *Drugs, 15,* 144.

Lowsley, O. S., & Bray, J. L. (1936). Surgical relief of impotence: Further experience with new operative procedure. *Journal of the American Medical Association, 107,* 2029–2035.

Lue, T. F., Hricak, H., Schmidt, A., & Tanagho, E. A. (1986). Functional evaluation of penile veins by cavernosography and cavernosometry in papaverine induced erections. *Journal of Urology, 135,* 479–482.

Malatesta, V. J., & Adams, H. E. (1984). The sexual dysfunctions. In H. E. Adams & P. B. Sutker (Eds.), *Comprehensive handbook of psychopathology* (pp. 725–775). New York: Plenum.

Malatesta, V. J., Pollack, R. H., Crotty, T. D., & Peacock, L. J. (1982). Acute alcohol intoxication and female orgasmic response. *Journal of Sex Research, 18,* 1–17.

Masters, W. H., Johnson, V. E. (1966). *Human sexual response*. Boston: Little, Brown.

Masters, W. H., & Johnson, V. E. (1970). *Human sexual inadequacy*. Boston: Little, Brown.

Masters, W. H., Johnson, V. E., & Kolodny, R. C. (1988). *Human sexuality* (3rd ed.). Boston: Little, Brown.

McCarthy, B. W. (1985). Uses and misuses of behavioral homework exercises in sex therapy. *Journal of Sex and Marital Therapy, 11,* 185–191.

McCarthy, B. W. (1988). *Male sexual awareness*. New York: Caroll & Graf.

McCarthy, B. W. (1990). Treating sexual dysfunction associated with prior sexual trauma. *Journal of Sex and Marital Therapy, 16,* 142–146.

McCauley, C., & Swann, C. P. (1978). Male–female differences in sexual fantasy. *Journal of Research in Personality, 12,* 76–86.

McCauley, C., & Swann, C.P. (1980). Sex differences in the frequency and functions of fantasies during sexual activity. *Journal of Research in Personality, 14,* 400–411.

McCulloch, D. K., Campbell, I. W., Wu, F. C., Prescott, R. J., & Clarke, B. F. (1980). The prevalence of diabetic impotence. *Diabetologia, 18,* 279–283.

McCulloch, D. K., Young, R. J., Prescott, R. J., Campbell, I. W., & Clarke, B. F. (1984). The natural history of impotence in diabetic men. *Diabetologia, 26,* 437–440.

McDowell, I., & Newell, C. (1987). *Measuring health: A guide to rating scales and questionnaires.* New York: Oxford University Press.

McGovern, K. B., Stewart, R. C., & LoPiccolo, J. (1975). Secondary orgasmic dysfunction: I. Analysis and strategies for treatment. *Archives of Sexual Behavior, 4,* 265–275.

Meichenbaum, D. H. (1977). *Cognitive-behavior modification: An integrative approach.* New York: Plenum.

Meisler, A. W., & Carey, M. P. (1990). A critical reevaluation of nocturnal penile tumescence monitoring in the diagnosis of erectile dysfunction. *Journal of Nervous and Mental Disease, 178,* 78–89.

Meisler, A. W., & Carey, M. P. (1991). Depressed affect and male sexual arousal. *Archives of Sexual Behavior, 20.*

Meisler, A. W., Carey, M. P., Krauss, D. J., & Lantinga, L. J. (1988). Success and failure in penile prosthesis surgery: Two cases highlighting the importance of psychosocial factors. *Journal of Sex and Marital Therapy, 14,* 108–119.

Meisler, A. W., Carey, M. P., Lantinga, L. J., & Krauss, D. J. (1989). Erectile dysfunction in diabetes mellitus: A biopsychosocial approach to etiology and assessment. *Annals of Behavioral Medicine, 11,* 18–27.

Melman, A., Henry, D. P., Felten, D. L., & O'Connor, B. (1980). Effect of diabetes upon sympathetic nerves in impotent patients. *Southern Medical Journal, 73,* 307–309, 317.

Melman, A., & Rossman, B. (1989, June). *Penile vein ligation for corporal incompetence: An evaluation of short and long term results.* Paper presented at the 15th annual meeting of the International Academy of Sex Research, Princeton, NJ.

Mendoza, M., & Silverman, M. (1987). Penile prosthetics: Characteristics of veteran patients and their spouses. *Journal of Sex and Marital Therapy, 13,* 183–192.

Meyer, J. J. (1988). Impotence: Assessment in the private-practice office. *Postgraduate Medicine, 84,* 87–91.

Morales, A., Condra, M., Owen, J., Surridge, D., Fenemore, J., & Harris, C. (1987). Is yohimbine effective in the treatment of organic impotence? Results of a controlled trial. *Journal of Urology, 137,* 1168.

Morales, A., Surridge, D., Marshall, P., & Fenemore, J. (1982). Nonhormonal pharmacological treatment of organic impotence. *Journal of Urology, 128,* 45–47.

Morganstern, K. P. (1988). Behavioral interviewing. In A. S. Bellack & M. Hersen (Eds.), *Behavioral assessment: A practical handbook* (pp. 86–118). Elmsford, NY: Pergamon Press.

Morokoff, P. J. (1978). Determinants of female orgasm. In J. LoPiccolo & L. LoPiccolo (Eds.), *Handbook of sex therapy* (pp. 147–165). New York: Plenum.

Morokoff, P. J., Baum, A., McKinnon, W. R., & Gillilland, R. (1987). Effects of chronic unemployment and acute psychological stress on sexual arousal in men. *Health Psychology, 6,* 545–560.

Morokoff, P. J., & Heiman, J. R. (1980). Effects of erotic stimuli on sexually functional and dysfunctional women: Multiple measures before and after sex therapy. *Behaviour Research and Therapy, 18,* 127–137.

Morrison, C. F. (1989). AIDS: Ethical implications for psychological intervention. *Professional Psychology: Research and Practice, 20*, 166–171.

Moss, H. B., & Procci, W. R. (1982). Sexual dysfunction associated with oral antihypertensive medication: A critical survey of the literature. *General Hospital Psychiatry, 4*, 121–129.

Munjack, D. J., & Kanno, P. H. (1979). Retarded ejaculation: A review. *Archives of Sexual Behavior, 8*, 139–150.

Myers, L. S., & Morokoff, P. J. (1986). Physiological and subjective sexual arousal in pre- and postmenopausal women and postmenopausal women taking replacement therapy. *Psychophysiolology, 23*, 283–292.

Nadig, P., Ware, J., & Blumoff, R. (1986). Noninvasive device to produce and maintain an erection-like state. *Urology, 27*, 126–131.

National Cancer Institute. (1986). *Testicular cancer: Research report*. Washington, DC: U.S. Department of Health and Human Services.

National Cancer Institute. (1989). *Cancer of the prostate: Research report*. Washington, DC: U.S. Department of Health and Human Services.

National Diabetes Advisory Board. (1988). *The national long-range plan to combat diabetes: 1987* (DHHS Publication NIH 88-1587). Washington, DC: U.S. Goverment Printing Office.

Nelson, R. (1988). Nonoperative management of impotence. *Journal of Urology, 139*, 2–5.

Nettelbladt, P., & Uddenberg, N. (1979). Sexual dysfunction and sexual satisfaction in 58 married Swedish men. *Journal of Psychosomatic Medicine, 23*, 141–147.

Newman, A. S., & Bertelson, A. D. (1986). Sexual dysfunction in diabetic women. *Journal of Behavioral Medicine, 9*, 261–270.

New York State Department of Health. (1990). *AIDS: 100 questions and answers*. Albany: Author.

Nofzinger, E. A., & Schmidt, H. S. (1990). An exploration of central dysregulation of erectile function as a contributing cause of diabetic impotence. *Journal of Nervous and Mental Disease, 178*, 90–95.

Nutter, D. E., & Condron, M. K. (1983). Sexual fantasy and activity patterns of females with inhibited sexual desire and versus normal controls. *Journal of Sex and Marital Therapy, 9*, 276–282.

Nutter, D. E., & Condron, M. K. (1985). Sexual fantasy and activity patterns of males with inhibited sexual desire and males with erectile dysfunction versus normal controls. *Journal of Sex and Marital Therapy, 11*, 91–98.

O'Farrell, T. J. (1990). Sexual functioning of male alcoholics. In R. L. Collins, K. E. Leonard, B. A. Miller, & J. S. Searles (Eds.), *Alcohol and the family: Research and clinical perspectives* (pp. 244–271). New York: Guilford Press.

O'Sullivan, K. (1979). Observation on vaginismus in Irish women. *Archives of General Psychiatry, 36*, 824–826.

Osborn, M., Hawton, K., & Gath, D. (1988). Sexual dysfunction among middle aged women in the community. *British Medical Journal, 296*, 959–962.

Papadopoulos, C. (1989). *Sexual aspects of cardiovascular disease*. New York: Praeger.

Parshley, H. M. (1933). Sexual abstinence as a biological question. *Scientific American, 148*, 283–300.

Pedersen, B., Tiefer, L., Ruiz, M., & Melman, A. (1988). Evaluation of patients and partners 1 to 4 years after penile prosthesis surgery. *Journal of Urology, 139*, 956–958.

Person, E. S., Terestman, N., Myers, W. A., Goldberg, E. L., & Salvadori, C. (1989). Gender differences in sexual behaviors and fantasies in a college population. *Journal of Sex and Marital Therapy, 15*, 187–198.

Pietropinto, A., & Arora, A. (1989). Sexual functioning in diabetics. *Medical Aspects of Human Sexuality, 23*, 74–76.

Pinckney, C., & Pinckney, E. R. (1986). *The patient's guide to medical tests* (3rd ed.). New York: Facts on File.

Pohl, S. L., Gonder-Frederick, L., & Cox, D. J. (1984). Diabetes mellitus: An overview. *Annals of Behavioral Medicine, 6,* 3–7.

Poinsard, P. J. (1968). Psychophysiologic (psychosomatic) disorders of the vulvovaginal tract. *Psychosomatics, 7,* 338.

Pope, B. (1979). *The mental health interview: Research and application.* Elmsford, NY: Pergamon Press.

Prather, R. C. (1988). Sexual dysfunction in the diabetic female: A review. *Archives of Sexual Behavior, 17,* 277–284.

Reamy, K. J., & White, S. E. (1985). Dyspareunia in pregnancy. *Journal of Psychosomatic Obstetrics and Gynaecology, 4,* 263–270.

Renshaw, D. C. (1988). Profile of 2376 patients treated at Loyola Sex Clinic between 1972 and 1987. *Sexual and Marital Therapy, 3,* 111–117.

Richwald, G. A., Morisky, D. E., Kyle, G. R., Kristal, A. R., Gerber, M. M., & Friedland, J. M. (1988). Sexual activities in bath houses in Los Angeles County: Implication for AIDS prevention education. *Journal of Sex Research, 25,* 169–180.

Robins, L. N., Helzer, J. E., Weissman, M. M., Orvaschel, H., Gruenberg, E., Burke, J. D., Jr., & Regier, D. A. (1984). Lifetime prevalence of specific psychiatric disorders in three sites. *Archives of General Psychiatry, 41,* 949–958.

Roose, S. P., Glassman, A. H., Walsh, B. T., & Cullen, K. (1982). Reversible loss of nocturnal penile tumescence during depression: A preliminary report. *Neuropsychobiology, 8,* 284–288.

Rosen, R. C., & Beck, J. G. (1988). Patterns of sexual arousal: Psychophysiological processes and clinical applications. New York: Guilford Press.

Rosen, R. C., Kostis, J. B., & Jekelis, A. W. (1988). Beta-blocker effects on sexual function in normal males. *Archives of Sexual Behavior, 17,* 241–255.

Rous, S. N. (1988). *The prostate book: Sound advice on symptoms and treatment.* Mount Vernon, NY: Consumers Union.

Ruzbarsky, V., & Michal, V. (1977). Morphologic changes in the arterial bed of the penis with aging: Relationship to the pathogenesis of importence. *Investigative Urology, 15,* 194–199.

Sacks, E. L., Gerstein, O. G., & Mann, S. G. (1983). Conservative surgery and radiation therapy for breast cancer. *Frontiers of Radiation Therapy and Oncology, 17,* 23–32.

Sakheim, D., Barlow, D. H., Abrahamson, D. J., & Beck, J. G. (1987). Distinguishing between organogenic and psychogenic erectile dysfunction. *Behaviour Research and Therapy, 25,* 379–390.

Sakheim, D., Barlow, D. H., Beck, J. G., & Abrahamson, D. (1984). The effect of an increased awareness of erectile cues on sexual arousal. *Behaviour Research and Therapy, 22,* 151–158.

Salmimies, P., Kockott, G., Pirke, K. M., Vogt, H. J., & Schill, W. B. (1982). Effects of testosterone replacement on sexual behavior in hypogonadal men. *Archives of Sexual Behavior, 11,* 345–353.

Sandberg, G., & Quevillon, R. P. (1987). Dyspareunia: An integrated approach to assessment and diagnosis. *Journal of Family Practice, 24,* 66–69.

Sanger, C. K., & Resnikoff, M. (1981). A comparison of the psychological effects of breast saving procedures with the modified radical mastectomy. *Cancer, 48,* 2341–2346.

Sarica, Y., & Karacan, I. (1987). Bublocavernosus reflex to somatic and visceral nerve stimulation in normal subjects and in diabetics with erectile impotence. *Journal of Urology, 138,* 55–58.

Schain, W. (1987). Sexual and reproductive issues in breast cancer. In American Cancer Society

(Ed.), *Proceedings from the workshop on psychosexual and reproductive issues affecting patients with cancer—1987* (pp. 58–64). New York: American Cancer Society.

Schiavi, R. C., Schreiner-Engel, P., White, D., & Mandeli, J. (1988). Pituitary–gonadal function during sleep in men with hypoactive sexual desire and in normal controls. *Psychosomatic Medicine, 50*, 304–318.

Schoener, G. R. (1990). A look at the literature. In G. R. Schoener, J. H. Milgrom, J. C. Gonsiorek, E. T. Luepker, & R. M. Conroe (Eds.), *Psychotherapists' sexual involvement with clients: Intervention and prevention* (pp. 11–50). Minneapolis: Walk-In Counseling Center.

Schoener, G. R., Milgrom, J. H., Gonsiorek, J. C., Luepker, E. T., & Conroe, R. M. (Eds.). (1990). *Psychotherapists' sexual involvement with clients: Intervention and prevention.* Minneapolis: Walk-In Counseling Center.

Schoffling, K., Federlin, K., Ditschuneit, H., & Pfeiffer, E. F. (1963). Disorders of sexual function in male diabetics. *Diabetes, 12*, 519–527.

Schover, L. R. (1981). Unpublished data. Cited by Schover, L. R., & Jensen, S. B. (1988). *Sexuality and chronic illness: A comprehensive approach* (pp. 59–60, 126, 130–135). New York: Guilford Press.

Schover, L. R. (1987). Sexual problems in men with pelvic or genital malignancies. In American Cancer Society (Ed.), *Proceedings from the workshop on psychosexual and reproductive issues affecting patients with cancer—1987* (pp. 41–46). New York: American Cancer Society.

Schover, L. R. (1988a). *Sexuality and cancer: For the man who has cancer, and his partner.* New York: American Cancer Society.

Schover, L. R. (1988b). *Sexuality and cancer: For the woman who has cancer, and her partner.* New York: American Cancer Society.

Schover, L. R. (1989). Sex therapy for the penile prosthesis recipient. *Urologic Clinics of North America, 16*, 91–98.

Schover, L. R., Evans, R. B., & von Eschenbach, A. C. (1986). Sexual rehabilitation and male radical cystectomy. *Journal of Urology, 136*, 1015–1017.

Schover, L. R., & Fife, M. (1985). Sexual counseling of patients undergoing radical surgery for pelvic or genital cancer. *Journal of Psychosocial Oncology, 3*, 21–41.

Schover, L. R., Friedman, J. M., Weiler, S. J., Heiman, J. R., & LoPiccolo, J. (1982). Multiaxial problem-oriented system for sexual dysfunctions: An alternative to DSM-III. *Archives of General Psychiatry, 39*, 614–619.

Schover, L. R., & Jensen, S. B. (1988). *Sexuality and chronic illness: A comprehensive approach.* New York: Guilford Press.

Schover, L. R., & von Eschenbach, A. C. (1985). Sexual function and female radical cystectomy: A case series. *Journal of Urology, 134*, 465–468.

Schreiner-Engel, P. (1988). Diagnosing and treating the sexual problems of diabetic women. *Clinical Diabetes, 6*, 126–134.

Schreiner-Engel, P., & Schiavi, R. C. (1986). Life psychopathology in individuals with low sexual desire. *Journal of Nervous and Mental Disease, 174*, 646–651.

Schreiner-Engel, P., Schiavi, R. C., Vietorisz, D., Eichel, J. D., & Smith, H. (1985). Diabetes and female sexuality: A comparative study of women in relationships. *Journal of Sex and Marital Therapy, 11*, 165–175.

Schreiner-Engel, P., Schiavi, R. C., Vietorisz, D., & Smith, H. (1987). The differential impact of diabetes type on female sexuality. *Journal of Psychosomatic Research, 31*, 23–33.

The science of AIDS: Readings from the Scientific American magazine. (1989). New York: W. H. Freeman.

Scott, F., Bradley, W., & Timm, G. (1973). Management of erectile impotence: Use of implantable inflatable prosthesis. *Urology, 5*, 479.

Segraves, R. T. (1988). Drugs and desire. In S. R. Leiblum & R. C. Rosen (Eds.), *Sexual desire disorders* (pp. 313–347). New York: Guilford Press.

Segraves, R. T. (1989). Effects of psychotropic drugs on human erection and ejaculation. *Archives of General Psychiatry, 46,* 275–284.

Segraves, R. T., Madsen, R., Carter, C. S., & Davis, J. M. (1985). Erectile dysfunction associated with pharmacological agents. In R. T. Segraves & H. W. Schoenberg (Eds.), *Diagnosis and treatment of erectile disturbances: A guide for clinicians* (pp. 23–63). New York: Plenum.

Segraves, R. T., & Schoenberg, H. W. (Eds.). (1985). *Diagnosis and treatment of erectile disturbances: A guide for clinicians.* New York: Plenum.

Seligman, M. E. P. (1975). *Helplessness: On depression, development, and death.* San Francisco: W. H. Freeman.

Semans, J. H. (1956). Premature ejaculation: A new approach. *Southern Medical Journal, 49,* 353–358.

Shipley, W. U., Schwartz, J. H., Zinman, L. H., & Soto, E. A. (1986). Cancer of the bladder. In B. Cady (Ed.-in-Chief), *Cancer manual* (7th ed., pp. 260–267). New York: American Cancer Society.

Shull, G. R., & Sprenkle, D. H. (1980). Retarded ejaculation: Reconceptualization and implications for treatment. *Journal of Sex and Marital Therapy, 6,* 234–246.

Sherwin, B. B. (1985). Changes in sexual behavior as a function of plasma sex steroid levels in post-menopausal women. *Maturitas, 7,* 225–233.

Sherwin, B. B., & Gelfand, M. M. (1987). The role of androgen in the maintenance of sexual functioning in oophorectomized women. *Psychosomatic Medicine, 49,* 397–409.

Sherwin, B. B., Gelfand, M. M., & Brender, W. (1985). Androgen enhances sexual motivation in females: A prospective, crossover study of sex steroid administration in the surgical menopause. *Psychosomatic Medicine, 47,* 339–351.

Silverberg, E., Boring, C. C., & Squires, T. S. (1990). Cancer statistics, 1990. *CA—A Cancer Journal for Clinicians, 40,* 9–26.

Small, M. P., Carrion, H. M., & Gordon, J. A. (1975). Small–Carrion penile prosthesis: New implant for management of impotence. *Urology, 5,* 479–486.

Spanier, G. B. (1976). Measuring dyadic adjustment: New scales for assessing the quality of marriage and similar dyads. *Journal of Marriage and the Family, 38,* 15–28.

Spector, I. P., & Carey, M. P. (1990). Incidence and prevalence of the sexual dysfunctions: A critical review of the literature. *Archives of Sexual Behavior, 19,* 389–408.

Spiess, W. F. J., Geer, J. H., & O'Donohue, W. T. (1984). Premature ejaculation: Investigation of factors in ejaculatory latency. *Journal of Abnormal Psychology, 93,* 242–245.

Steege, J. F. (1984). Dyspareunia and vaginismus. *Clinical Obstetrics and Gynecology, 27,* 750–759.

Stief, C., & Wetterauer, U. (1988). Erectile responses to intracavernous papaverine and phentolamine: Comparison of single and combined delivery. *Journal of Urology, 140,* 1415–1416.

Stoller, R. J. (1975). *Perversion: The erotic form of hatred.* New York: Pantheon Books.

Strassberg, D. S., Kelly, M. P., Carroll, C., & Kircher, J. C. (1987). The psychophysiological nature of premature ejaculation. *Archives of Sexual Behavior, 16,* 327–336.

Stuart, F. M., Hammond, D. C., & Pett, M. A. (1987). Inhibited sexual desire in women. *Archives of Sexual Behavior, 16,* 91–106.

Stuart, I. R., & Greer, J. G. (Eds.). (1984). *Victims of sexual aggression: Treatment of children, women and men.* New York: Van Nostrand Reinhold.

Sullivan, H. S. (1954). *The psychiatric interview.* New York: Norton.

Susset, J., Tessier, C., Wincze, J., Bansal, S., Malhotra, C., & Schwacha, M. (1989). Effect of yohimbine hydrochloride on erectile impotence: A double-blind study. *Journal of Urology, 141,* 1360–1363.

Szasz, T. (1980). *Sex by prescription.* Garden City, NY: Doubleday/Anchor.

Tan, E. T., Johnson, R. H., Lambie, D. G., Vijayasenan, M. E., & Whiteside, E. A. (1984). Erectile impotence in chronic alcoholics. *Alcoholism: Clinical and Experimental Research, 8,* 297–301.

Tarasoff v. Regents of the University of California. (1974). 118 Cal. Rptr. 129, 529 P.2d 553.

Tarasoff v. Regents of the University of California. (1976). 17 Cal. 3d 425, 551 P.2d 334.

Tiefer, L. (1986). In pursuit of the perfect penis. *American Behavioral Scientist, 29,* 579–599.

Tiefer, L., Pedersen, B., & Melman, A. (1988). Psychosocial follow-up of penile prosthesis implant patients and partner. *Journal of Sex and Marital Therapy, 14,* 184–201.

Tobias, P. (1975). *Project Foundation: An annotated bibliography of scientific studies done since 1900 on sexual abstinence.* (Available from The Institute for the Cultural and Scientific Study of Chastity, P. O. Box 20788, Houston, TX 77225)

Tollison, C. D., & Adams, H. E. (1979). *Sexual disorders: Treatment, theory, and research.* New York: Gardner Press.

Turkat, I. D. (1986). The behavioral interview. In A. R. Ciminero, K. S. Calhoun, & H. E. Adams (Eds.), *Handbook of behavioral assessment* (2nd ed., pp. 109–149). New York: Wiley.

Tyrer, G., Steel, J. M., Ewing, D. J., Bancroft, J., Warner, P., & Clarke, B. F. (1983). Sexual responsiveness in diabetic women. *Diabetologia, 24,* 166–171.

Vessey, M. P., McPherson, K., Roberts, M. M., Neil, A., & Jones, L. (1985). Fertility in relation to the risk of breast cancer. *British Journal of Cancer, 52,* 625–628.

Viosca, K., & Griner, B. (1988). *Use of the Erec-Aide in the management of impotence.* Paper presented at the meeting of the Endocrine Society, New Orleans.

Wagner, G., & Green, R. (Eds.). (1981). *Impotence: Physiological, psychological, surgical diagnosis and treatment.* New York: Plenum.

Wagner, G., & Metz, P. (1981). Arteriosclerosis and erectile failure. In G. Wagner & R. Green (Eds.), *Impotence: Physiological, psychological, surgical diagnosis and treatment* (pp. 63–72). New York: Plenum.

Wakefield, J. C. (1987). Sex bias in the diagnosis of primary orgasmic dysfunction. *American Psychologist, 42,* 464–471.

Waldhauser, M., & Schramek, P. (1988). Efficiency and side effects of prostaglandin El in the treatment of erectile dysfunction. *Journal of Urology, 140,* 525–527.

Walling, M., Andersen, B. L., & Johnson, S. R. (1990). Hormonal replacement therapy for postmenopausal women: A review of sexual outcomes and related gynecologic effects. *Archives of Sexual Behavior, 19,* 119–137.

Wallis, L. A. (1987). Management of dyspareunia in postmenopausal women. *Journal of the American Medical Women's Association, 42,* 82–84.

Walsh, P. C., & Mostwin, J. L. (1984). Radical prostatectomy and cystoprostatectomy with preservation of potency: Results utilizing a new nerve-sparing technique. *British Journal of Urology, 56,* 694–697.

Watters, G., Keogh, E., Earle, C., Carati, C., Wisniewski, Z. S., Alastair, G., Tullach, S., & Lord, D. (1988). Experience in the management of erectile dysfunction using the intracavernosal self-injection of vasoactive drugs. *Journal of Urology, 140,* 1417–1419.

Williams, G., Mulcahy, M. J., Hartnell, G., & Kiely, E. (1988). Diagnosis and treatment of venous leakage: A curable cause of impotence. *British Journal of Urology, 61,* 151–155.

Wilsnack, S. C. (1984). Drinking, sexuality, and sexual dysfunction in women. In S. C. Wilsnack & L. J. Beckman (Eds.), *Alcohol problems in women: Antecedents, consequences, and intervention* (pp. 189–227). New York: Guilford Press.

Wilson, G. T. (1977). Alcohol and human sexual behaviour. *Behaviour Research and Therapy, 15,* 239–252.

Wilson, G. T. (1981). The effects of alcohol on human sexual behavior. *Advances in Substance Abuse, 2,* 1–40.

Wincze, J. P. (1982). Assessment of sexual disorders. *Behavioral Assessment, 4,* 257–271.

Wincze, J. P., Bansal, S., Malhotra, C. M., Balko, A., Susset, J. G., & Malamud, M. A. (1988). A comparison of nocturnal penile tumescence and penile response to erotic stimulation during waking states in comprehensively diagnosed groups of males experiencing erectile difficulties. *Archives of Sexual Behavior, 17,* 333–348.

Wing, R. R., Epstein, L. H., Nowalk, M. P., & Lamparski, D. M. (1986). Behavioral self-regulation in the treatment of patients with diabetes mellitus. *Psychological Bulletin, 99,* 78–89.

Witherington, R. (1988). Suction device therapy in the management of erectile impotence. *Urologic Clinics of North America, 15,* 123–128.

Wolchik, S. A., Beggs, V., Wincze, J. P., Sakheim, D. K., Barlow, D. H., & Mavissakalian, M. (1980). The effects of emotional arousal on subsequent sexual arousal in men. *Journal of Abnormal Psychology, 89,* 595–598.

Wolfe, L. (1978). The question of surrogates in sex therapy. In J. LoPiccolo & L. LoPiccolo (Eds.), *Handbook of sex therapy* (pp. 491–497). New York: Plenum.

Woodruff, J. D., & Parmley, T. H. (1983). Infection of the minor vestibular gland. *Obstetrics and Gynecology, 62,* 609–612.

Zemel, P. (1988). Sexual dysfunction in the diabetic patient with hypertension. *American Journal of Cardiology, 61,* 27H–33H.

Zilbergeld, B. (1978). *Male sexuality: A guide to sexual fulfillment.* New York: Bantam.

Zinner, S. H. (1985). *Sexually transmitted diseases.* New York: Summit Books.

Index